THE MURD1

THE
MURDER
OF REGILLA

A CASE OF DOMESTIC VIOLENCE
IN ANTIQUITY

SARAH B. POMEROY

HARVARD UNIVERSITY PRESS

Cambridge, Massachusetts | London, England

First Harvard University Press paperback edition, 2009

Library of Congress Cataloging-in-Publication Data

Pomeroy, Sarah B.
The murder of Regilla : a case of domestic violence
in antiquity / Sarah B. Pomeroy.
p. cm.
Includes bibliographical references and index.
ISBN 978-0-674-02583-7 (cloth: alk. paper)
ISBN 978-0-674-03489-1 (pbk.)
1. Regilla. 2. Herodes Atticus. 3. Uxoricide—Greece—Athens—History—
Case studies. 4. Wife abuse—Greece—Athens—History—Case studies.
5. Trials (Murder)—Rome—History—Case studies. 6. Upper class women—
Greece—Athens—Biography. 7. Upper class women—Rome—Biography.
8. Civilization, Greco-Roman. I. Title.
HV6542.P66   2007
364.152'3092—dc22   2007002980

To Jesse, Joel, and Simone

CONTENTS

Preface   ix

Genealogical Chart   x–xi

Regilla's and Herodes' Family   xii

Introduction   1

1   Girlhood in Rome   13

2   A Roman Matron in Imperial
    Athens   43

3   Public Life   81

4   Death in Athens and Murder Trial
    in Rome   119

5   Regilla's Final Resting Place   137

Chronological Chart   177

Notes   179

Acknowledgments   229

Art Credits   231

Index   235

PREFACE

THAT THIS IS THE FIRST BOOK about Regilla is doubtless due to the paucity and diversity of the evidence. Yet for every period of ancient history the written evidence typically exploited by modern writers is sparse, and even more so when the subject being studied is women. I am a classicist and an ancient historian. Nevertheless, I have always used every genre of evidence, written and material, not only to compensate for the lack of textual sources on women, but also because the physical context of the world in which they lived is a necessary part of the picture I am painting. M. I. Finley despaired of using archaeological evidence for the writing of history; one of the reasons he cited was that archaeologists tend to classify and describe rather than interpret their data. He also pointed out that the archaeological record is not always consistent with the written one, and that "it is impossible to infer social arrangements or institutions, attitudes or beliefs from material objects alone." To Finley's astute comment I should add that in this study of Regilla it will be seen that both the written word and material evidence may mask the historical reality.

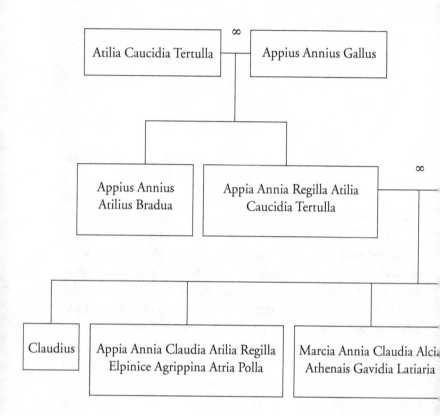

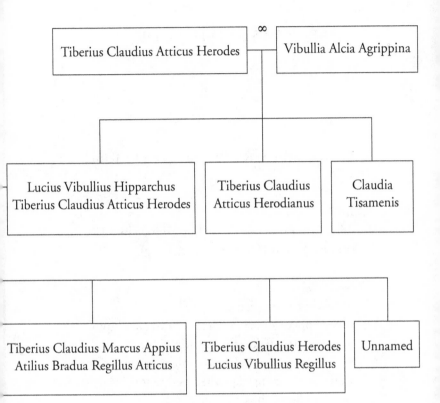

REGILLA'S AND HERODES' FAMILY

Regilla. Appia Annia Regilla Atilia Caucidia Tertulla (ca. 125–160).

Married (138/139) to
Herodes Atticus. Lucius Vibullius Hipparchus Tiberius Claudius Atticus Herodes (101/102–177).

Their children
Claudius (born and died ca. 141).
Elpinice. Appia Annia Claudia Atilia Regilla Elpinice Agrippina Atria Polla (ca. 142–165). One son?
Athenais. Marcia Annia Claudia Alcia Athenais Gavidia Latiaria (born ca. 143/144, died before 161). Married L. Vibullius Hipparchus; one son.
Bradua. Atticus Bradua. Tiberius Claudius Marcus Appius Atilius Bradua Regillus Atticus (born ca. 145).
Regillus. Tiberius Claudius Herodes Lucius Vibullius Regillus (ca. 150–ca. 155).
Unnamed. Eight-month-old fetus died with Regilla (160) or three months after.

THE MURDER OF REGILLA

INTRODUCTION

ROME IN THE SECOND century A.D. was one of the best places to live that the world had ever known, especially for the upper class. Safe from foreign enemies, free of civil disturbance, and ruled by emperors who, if they were not perfect philosopher-kings, came much closer to that ideal than most of their predecessors and successors, the city was the crossroads of the world. As Gibbon wrote:

> In the second century of the Christian era, the empire of Rome comprehended the fairest part of the earth, and the most civilized portion of mankind. The frontiers of that extensive monarchy were guarded by ancient renown and disciplined valor. The gentle but powerful influence of laws and manners had gradually cemented the union of the provinces. Their peaceful inhabitants enjoyed and abused the advantages of wealth and luxury. The image of a free constitution was preserved with decent reverence: the Roman senate appeared to possess the sovereign authority, and devolved on the emperors all the executive powers of government. During a happy period of more than fourscore years, the public administration was conducted by the virtue and abilities of Nerva, Trajan, Hadrian, and the two Antonines.[1]

But perhaps this period was not one of the best for women, even upper-class women.

Let us take Regilla, for example. Why Regilla? Most specialists in ancient history do not even know who she is, though some archaeologists and classicists working in Athens and Rome recall seeing signs bearing her name marking small streets near major monuments. The history of the marriage of a Roman woman and a Greek man at a time when Greece was ruled by Rome offers an opportunity to examine the interplay of ethnicity, gender, and class, and to explore what Gibbon termed "the union of the provinces." It is rare to find a marriage between a woman belonging to the highest stratum of the ruling class and a man, albeit a Roman citizen of consular rank, from a conquered territory. The usual pattern for Greeks and Romans was for a male conqueror to marry a native princess, or, on a lower level of society, for a soldier to marry a provincial woman.

The events narrated here follow the chronology of Regilla's life. This is a tale not only of culture and art, but also of power, sex, violence, and money. The plot inadvertently echoes the structure of a Greek tragedy, with a murderous climax four-fifths of the way through and a catharsis at the end. The focus throughout is on Regilla, a Roman who moved to Greece, and on the fatal consequences of her marriage to Herodes Atticus. Herodes is viewed not so much as the public figure he was, but rather as Regilla's husband and a source for the story of her life and death.

Regilla was born to an elite family in Rome, related to the wife of the emperor. She married the wealthy Sophist Herodes Atticus and the couple moved to Greece. When she was eight months pregnant, she died of a kick in the abdomen. Her husband was brought to trial in Rome on the charge of homicide. He was tried by a senatorial court, but acquitted through the intervention of the emperor. The travesties of grief in which Herodes indulged were tantamount to a confession.

The bare bones of the story are few. We know very little about Regilla, but she was an important woman. Her name appears on major monuments in well-frequented sites. Her life would have been totally different if she had not married a Greek and moved to Greece. Surely her contemporaries at Rome would have taken notice of her and we would have known more about her. Regilla is merely one of many such women who, because of their gender and the quirks of fortune, were destined to be more obscure than their brothers while they lived and consequently to be ignored after death by historians. What we can learn about a woman when the evidence is sparse is a legitimate problem posed by this book. The ancient sources make it possible to know a great deal about the character of Herodes, but it is a challenge for a modern biographer to construct a rounded picture of Regilla. Yet without attempts like the present one, the field of ancient women's history will fail to be developed.

Although numerous biographies of great men were written in antiquity, some of which included a few paragraphs about their mothers or wives, Sappho was the only woman who was the subject of a full-length biography.[2] Nowadays historians are beginning to remedy this situation with biographies of famous women, not only the ever-popular Cleopatra VII, but also Arsinoë II, Livia, Julia (daughter of Augustus), and Julia Domna. These women were either rulers themselves or wives or daughters of men in power. Very few other women have been subjects of modern full-length biographies, certainly few commoners, but Aspasia, a participant in Socratic dialogues and mistress of Pericles, comes to mind, and now there is Regilla. Though she had ties to women who married emperors, Regilla herself was not a member of the imperial family. In her case, gender exerted a more powerful influence than class on the way she lived and died.

Because of the nature of the evidence, Regilla and her marriage must often be viewed through the lens of Herodes, an overpoweringly creative (and destructive) force. What written evidence there is comes to us haphazardly. The chief text for Herodes' biography was written by Philostratus, who died around 249, about seventy-five years after Herodes. Philostratus' account is not impartial, but biased in favor of his subject, who enjoyed the advantage of being a Sophist (i.e., rhetorician and philosopher) and a fellow Greek.[3] Furthermore, Philostratus dedicated his work to Gordian I, who became emperor in 238: Believing that Gordian was a descendant of Regilla and Herodes, Philostratus doubtless minimized the scandalous aspects of the emperor's ancestors.[4] Philostratus was not interested in Romans except insofar as the Sophists interacted with them, and certainly not in women, although he was a member of the circle around the empress Julia Domna.[5] His reports about women are few. To understand Philostratus' viewpoint it is useful to know that in his biographies of other Sophists his references to women are mostly pejorative or demeaning.[6] Although he is generally correct about events in Herodes' career, he can be faulted for giving an expurgated version of Herodes' personality, minimizing what would put his subject in a negative light. For example, although Philostratus reports Herodes' trial for the murder of Regilla, he omits another accusation of murder that is known from the correspondence of Fronto, a Roman orator.[7] This charge is further testimony to Herodes' violent temper and increases the possibility that he was involved in the murder of his wife. In addition to Philostratus, contemporary authors writing in a range of genres, including Fronto, Pausanias, Marcus Aurelius, and Aulus Gellius, give information about Herodes that also illuminates the life of Regilla. Among Greek authors, Plutarch is a good source for family relationships, but he lived slightly earlier, dying within a year of Regilla's birth. In this study, to avoid anachronism, I prefer to cite only authors who lived within a century of Regilla.[8]

More fruitful sources of written evidence are the numerous

inscriptions that accompanied statues and buildings dedicated in Regilla's honor. Monuments in Greece and Italy, mostly clustering around places where they would be seen by important people, constitute a major source of information about Regilla and the world in which she lived. Buildings and statues, however, were erected by people with their own agenda. The dedication of a monument with an accompanying inscription required the construction of a persona being commemorated through an image or an object and a text: for Regilla, more examples of the latter than of the former are extant. The portraits of Regilla have proven more fragile and difficult to reconstruct than the inscribed texts accompanying them. The purpose of the inscription is didactic: to identify the dedicatee and dedicator, to honor the dedicatee, and to instruct the viewer about the person being honored. Dedicators themselves are also commemorated through the choices they have made, the taste they have expressed, and the wealth their monuments reflect. As a dedicator to Regilla, Herodes should be viewed as though he were an author describing a woman, influenced by the artistic styles of the day, by the ideal audience or viewers he had in mind, and by the subject herself. Literary and artistic representations of Regilla constitute the filter through which we can know her, but sometimes these are more of a barrier standing between Regilla and us.[9]

Herodes was not the only donor whose creations and projects are relevant to this study. The city of Corinth and Regilla herself dedicated monuments bearing inscriptions in her honor. The impressive quantity of surviving archaeological material is evidenced by the numerous photographs in this book—far more than in most historical works of similar length on women in classical antiquity.

Monuments and artifacts relevant to Regilla and Herodes in Greece have recently been studied from the viewpoint of archaeology and art history.[10] This material is far better known than the archaeological record in Italy. Now for the first time we can examine Regilla's family estates and Herodes' activities and projects in Italy after Regilla's death as a whole and set them in a historical context.[11] The standard biography of Herodes by P. Graindor[12] predates the most recent excavation of the Palace of Maxentius and the major publication on the subject in the last quarter of the twentieth century.[13] And as Regilla's ancestral estate lies buried under the Palace of Maxentius, this book will also add a new chapter to the long history of the Via Appia, the venerable road where the palace is located.[14]

If based only on the skeletal facts known about her, the story of Regilla's life would not suffice for a book. Since Herodotus and Thucydides, every historian worth reading has imposed his or her own view on the material, adding to it and creating a unique interpretation of the past. Though few historians would deny that even an objective posture must have some subjectivity or viewpoint, my interpretive stance may seem to be more in evidence as I am attempting a reconstruction of the past in the context of a chronological biography of a woman about whom very few facts are known.[15] I will present facts based on my research, sketch possible scenarios to explain the facts, and attempt to establish links between bits of evidence and to knit them together in a comprehensible narrative even when the sources do not tell me exactly what I want to know.

One of the sources for my reconstruction of Regilla's experience is what I know about elite women in the Roman Empire of her time. Lacunae in her background and social context can be filled from what is understood about other elite women in imperial Rome, and, where necessary, a generic picture of upper-class girlhood and adulthood is presented. Thus, for example, Regilla's age at marriage is postulated from what we know about the marriage of other elite young women. Therefore this work is an example of the construction of the biography of a woman in part from prosopographical and archaeological evidence. The first part of Regilla's life conforms to the pattern followed by other upper-class women, but when she moved to Greece, her plot line veered dramatically from the predictable course and from what she may have grown up to expect.

This approach exemplifies Robert Darnton's notion of "incident analysis," in which a single dramatic event such as a murder becomes a means of exploring social relations in the past.[16] In the course of this investigation, as though conducting a trial, the historian evaluates the likely motives of the characters in the plot: perpetrator, victim, prosecutor, judge, and witness.

The protagonists in this book are a woman born in Rome and a man born in Athens who lived together as wife and husband first in Rome, then in Athens. The written sources are in Latin and Greek and the archaeological evidence has been found in Italy and Greece. Thus the question arises: how should the names in this book be spelled? I generally use the Latin spelling of Greek names for consistency, following the patterns established in the *Oxford Classical Dictionary*, where, for example, a relevant rubric is "Herodes Atticus, *see* Claudius Atticus Herodes, Ti."[17] In this book if I simply used Latin names and words and transliterated the Greek, the ethnic difference between the Roman wife and the Greek husband and the mixed names of their joint children would be emphasized, but the reader might find the combination distracting. I have therefore chosen to use Latin spellings in the first four chapters. In chapter 5, however, which discusses monuments in both Greece and Rome, I have retained the Greek spelling of the Greek words and the Latin spelling of the Latin words. This juxtaposition is an objective correlative of the discord within the family of Regilla and Herodes as well as an index of ethnic difference and disunity within the Roman Empire. Both Herodes and Regilla had the experience of being an alien in one half of their lives. He was an outsider in Rome, where his name was misspelled even on a monument for which he had paid; she was an outsider in Greece, where her name was mispronounced.

Like our own, this was a pluralistic society composed of people from different backgrounds. The empire was not homogeneous, not even so far as those who held Roman citizenship were concerned. Despite Gibbon's panegyric, Greek ways were retained in Greece after some 350 years of Roman domination. Although Herodes was a Roman citizen and lived half his life in Rome, he did not follow Roman customs and laws strictly in areas such as exogamy rules, restrictions governing gifts between spouses, and customs concerning erotic relationships with foster children. But the Greek east was also becoming Romanized, and Rome was becoming more cosmopolitan, especially among the elite. This transformation is apparent from the presence of Herodes and the Quintilii from Asia Minor on the venerable Via Appia. As for the private sphere, we must ask: Was the family of Regilla and Herodes more Romanized or less so because the wife was Roman and the husband was Greek? Did their ethnic affiliations and habits change when they moved from Rome to Greece? Were ethnic differences responsible for the clash between Regilla and Herodes that led to her murder?

Almost any question about the social history of imperial Greece is hard to answer because the subject is relatively unexplored.[18] Scholars have long considered the classical period and the archaic period that preceded it the zenith in Greek history and culture. Some writers feel comfortable ending surveys of Greek history with the death of Alexander the Great (323 B.C.), whereas some textbooks make room for a chapter on the three hundred years of Hellenistic history that followed.[19] Under the Romans, Greece became the province of Achaea. Remaining relatively peaceful after the conquest, Achaea does not constitute a major subject in ancient and modern political histories of the Roman Empire. Some of the material remains of Roman Greece are magnificent, but art historians lament the loss of earlier, more modest and tasteful objects that lie beneath the Roman ruins, and archaeologists in the past have often overlooked the study of the Roman strata in their zeal to reach earlier levels.

The period discussed in this book is known as the "Greek Renaissance," when Greek art and literature of the classical period was the preferred model for artists, builders, and intellectuals in both Rome and the Greek east. Herodes was a leading participant in the "Second Sophistic" (A.D. 60–230), a term which evokes memories of the earlier Sophists; likewise some of his monuments, which may be described as "archaizing" or "neoclassical," echo the past. Like some contemporary emperors, in his portraits Herodes chose to have himself shown bearded, resembling a more soigné version of the philosophers and orators of earlier periods of Greek history.[20]

The styles and customs of Greek homosexuality were revived, and no less a figure than the emperor Hadrian set an example. Although he was married, he had a younger male lover. No scholar has seriously raised the question of whether the Greek Renaissance is also characterized by a revival of gender relationships as they were perceived to have been in classical Athens. Since Herodes was a creative force in the art and literature of the period, we must consider the influence it may have had on his private life. One commentator in the second century A.D. observed that the Greek elite were becoming Romanized, though Athens was an outstanding exception to this trend.[21] Herodes was a principal figure in the effort to revive the Athens of Pericles.

This effort was not limited to historicism in art and the recreation or restoration of ancient monuments. There was also an attempt to revive, in some sense, the figures of the past.[22] As Ewan Bowie writes of this period: "The fantasy of the hyper-educated Athenian must have been to walk out into the countryside of Attica and discover that he was in the fifth century.

This is virtually what happened to Herodes Atticus."[23] What this illusion meant for Greek women, or for a transplanted Roman like Regilla, is not clear, but at least we know that Athenians in the fifth century B.C. had no concept of the little settlement on the Tiber that would one day come to rule over them.[24]

At least five scholarly treatises on Athenian courtesans were published in this period. The interest in this topic leads us to wonder whether men like Herodes thought about women as did an orator in the fourth century B.C. who categorized women in relationship to men: mistresses for pleasure; concubines for daily attendance to the body; and wives to produce legitimate children and to be faithful housekeepers.[25] If so, why did he marry a blue-blooded Roman woman? Perhaps it was because with Regilla by his side Herodes' Greek identity as well as its acceptance by the emperor at Rome was demonstrated. Though there are hints of homosexuality in the evidence for Herodes' life, the nature of his conjugal relationship remains more difficult to determine, as indeed for any marriage, past or present. In any case, it would not have been easy for a Roman woman like Regilla to have adapted herself to the seclusion and silence expected of upper-class Athenian women of the classical period.

Herodes Atticus was the wealthiest private person in imperial Achaea and left more long-lasting monuments than anyone else outside the imperial family. More than most women, Regilla has also left her mark on the ancient landscape. By focusing on Regilla, I am venturing into an important, relatively unexplored period in the history of Greece, as well as in the history of women. While we know a fair amount about upper-class women in Rome, their fate outside of Italy has not been closely studied. We cannot know a milieu and a time period without knowing a specific person. We cannot know a person without knowing her or his milieu and time period. Regilla is our vantage point, the means by which we may expand our understanding of the High Empire. Thus this book is not only the history of one woman and her marriage, but a means of examining the time and places in which she lived. In each chapter there is some discussion of Greece and Rome, including Greek and Roman religion, Greek and Roman conjugal and erotic practices, Greek and Roman art and culture, and the use of Greek and Latin.

With the exception of some poetry and philosophical treatises, the words of women in antiquity are not extant. Far fewer women than men were literate; nor did many women enjoy the wealth and leisure necessary to commit their words to papyrus or to be inscribed on more durable materials. Nevertheless, some Greek and Roman authors may preserve reflections of women's voices in their dialogues and other literary works.[26] Though Regilla, like other women of her class, was literate, we do not have her words with the exception of two brief inscriptions at Olympia. What remain as primary evidence are her artistic expressions in the monuments she commissioned.

In my study of the *Consolation* which Plutarch wrote to his wife on the death of their only daughter, I attempted to deduce the character and personality of a woman of the second century A.D. reflected only in the words of her philosopher-husband.[27] The most recently published full-length study on Herodes discusses the living environment of a Sophist,[28] but I wondered again what that of a Sophist's wife might be. The word "Sophist" usually appears in connection with intellectual activity in the classical era in Greece, though some Sophists were active slightly earlier. Socrates was the most famous person to be called a Sophist (though he denied being one). His relationship with powerful Athenian politicians, like his marital relationship, was notoriously poor. Because of the silence and seclusion expected of respectable women, there are very few women among the dramatis personae in texts pertaining to the earlier Sophists, but in the Second Sophistic, Sophists were wealthy influential aristocrats, often in close touch with the imperial house and with Roman women who moved freely in mixed society. Nevertheless, the world of the Second Sophistic was largely male, and this is reflected in most scholarly writing about it.[29] No previous scholar has attempted to deal at length with the Second Sophistic in terms of women.[30]

Much of this book is devoted to a comparison between Greek and Roman private life during the empire. Again, it was work on Plutarch that led me to Regilla. In his *Parallel Lives,* Plutarch sets famous Greek and Roman men beside one another, in pairs, and usually has an epilogue comparing the members of the pair with each other. In some lives, as in those of Lycurgus and of Numa, Plutarch also compares the customs of various ethnic groups, for example, Spartans and Romans. In his *Moralia* he compares Greeks and Romans with regard to many subjects relevant to my current study, including child rearing and marriage patterns.

Although some of Plutarch's ethical writing is prescriptive, much reflects actual behavior and practice.[31] His basic framework is, of course, Greek; but he attempts to understand Roman customs—not always successfully. He seems more familiar with the distant past than with recent events, but that makes his evidence all the more relevant for this study, in which the past is present in Athens. Particularly useful are the passages in Plutarch which are as much a platform for discussing issues of gender and ethnicity as they are portraits of specific persons.

In his comparison of Greek endogamy with Roman exogamy, Plutarch raises the subject of wife abuse.[32] This dire possibility had also been raised in the first Roman law code, the Twelve Tables, in rubrics discussing the consequences for a husband who sold or killed his wife. The life and violent death of Regilla illustrates how brutal that world was, even for an upper-class woman who started life in enviable circumstances.

CHAPTER I

GIRLHOOD IN ROME

WHEN REGILLA WAS BORN in Rome to a wealthy family with the highest social connections, there was no reason to expect that she would attain anything less than great happiness and fortune in life. She married a very rich husband who was an intimate of emperors. But at the age of thirty-five, eight months pregnant, she died from a kick to the womb. Her husband was tried for homicide.

Appia Annia Regilla Atilia Caucidia Tertulla was born around A.D. 125.[1] This long name announced the little girl's place in the social order. Even if we do not know much more about an upper-class Roman woman than her name, we can deduce a fair amount about her from her relationships.[2] Regilla's name was a valuable possession in imperial Rome. She was a member of a family of senatorial and patrician status, with numerous consuls and other high government officials among her remote and recent ancestors.[3] Like Julius Caesar and his imperial heirs, people of this class traced their lineage back to Venus and Anchises, the parents of Aeneas, the legendary founder of Rome.[4]

It was fashionable among the upper class to claim glorious ancestors; some putative lineages were based merely on similarities in name, but some claims of kinship were valid. In any case, even if names are not an unfailing guide to descent, they do convey the parents' notions of family identity. To bear a name like Regilla's was not like being called "Ms. Jones." For example "Appia" brings to mind the Appian Way, one of the oldest and still most traveled roads leading to the city of Rome, constructed by Appius Claudius Caecus in 312 B.C. During Regilla's lifetime, two of her kinswomen were married and related in other ways to reigning emperors. Her father, Appius Annius Gallus, was a member of the venerable family of the Annii Regilli.[5] Through him Regilla was related to Annia Galeria Faustina (Faustina the Elder), wife of the emperor Antoninus Pius and aunt of Marcus Annius Verus, who was adopted by Antoninus and later became emperor Marcus Aurelius. Thus Regilla was also related to Faustina's daughter Annia Galeria Faustina (Faustina the Younger), the wife of Marcus Aurelius.

The atrium of an upper-class home was filled with portrait masks made of wax *(imagines)* and sculpted busts of patrilineal ancestors, and so would Regilla's have been. Strings connected them, guiding family members in tracing their genealogy. Paint ngs of genealogical trees that showed women in their array of family members could be found in the atrium along with the portrait masks.[6] Family tombs inscribed with the names of the dead also might provide instruction. Of course, an aristocratic child would become familiar with family legends and records of historical events involving her predecessors. The ancestors who could be traced were mostly men, but some women, especially those who had lived in the past few hundred years, were included.

Regilla's name also reflects her maternal heritage. She could study the portraits of distinguished members of her mother's family when she visited her mother's relatives.[7] Atilii had been active in Roman government from at least as early as the middle Republic. The name Caucidia may be Etruscan: such lineage was lofty indeed, reminiscent of the early kings of Rome.[8] By the second century A.D., few Romans could legitimately boast about their ancient lineage because civil wars, proscriptions (lists of those condemned to death by the current rulers), bachelorhood, and failure to reproduce, as well as natural attrition, had decimated the old noble families. Nevertheless, there was so much prestige and tradition attached to descent from the earliest noble Romans that the mere appearance of the first three components of Regilla's name elevated her to the highest social class and connected her with the glorious heroes of the past.

The diminutive "Tertulla" means "Little Third Daughter." Since it was part of the name of both her mother, Atilia Caucidia Tertulla, and of her maternal grandmother, Caucidia Tertulla (and appears in the masculine in the name of her uncle, M. Atilius Metilius Bradua Caucidius Tertullus . . . Bassus), it was one of Regilla's given names rather than a nickname to designate her place in her family's birth order. There is no evidence that any of these three women had had two older sisters, which would make each of them the "Little Third." Regilla's name never changed. A married woman in Rome did not take her husband's name, but retained her connection with her parents' families through the names her parents had given her. Girls were officially named on the eighth day after birth, boys on the ninth: their parents had ample time to consider their children's names as well as to see if the infant would survive.[9]

Regilla's name was a feminine form indicating her descent from the Annii Regilli. It means "Little Queen," and that is how she was treated from the moment of her birth. An upper-class baby made her debut before a large audience comprising a midwife and her helpers, female relatives, and a crowd of female slaves. Her father had been alerted. He could summon a male physician if the labor did not progress smoothly. The mother held the baby briefly and examined her before handing her over to a nurse. She did not intend to subordinate her vigor, her social life, and the appearance of her breasts to the feeding claims of a nursling. Her husband was an important person, and she often had to accompany him, a duty which took priority. Besides, though a girl was welcome, her birth was not a major event; her mother did need to become pregnant again and produce boys who were the means of perpetuating the family cult and traditions and who would look after their parents when they grew old. An upper-class mother simply did not have the time to care for children, and no one expected her to do so. Slaves, dedicated to serving the child, were available for that responsibility.

At least a dozen slaves specially trained in baby care will have already been selected to look after her. Most important for the newborn were her wet nurses. These women would be chosen according to the criteria set forth by Soranus, who had recently established himself as the leading gynecologist in Rome during the reign of Hadrian (117–138):

> One should . . . provide several wet nurses for children who are to be nursed safely and successfully. For it is dangerous for the nursling to become accustomed to one nurse who might become ill or die, and then, because of the change of milk, the child sometimes suffers from the strange milk and is distressed, while sometimes it rejects it altogether and succumbs to hunger.[10]

> A wet nurse should not be younger than twenty or older than forty. She should have already given birth two or three times, be healthy, of robust physique, of large bodily frame, and of good color. Her breasts should be medium size, relaxed, soft and not wrinkled, the nipples neither big nor very small . . . She should be self-controlled *(sophron)*, sympathetic, and not have a bad temper, a Greek, and neat.[11]

The Romans believed that the nursing infant would imbibe personal characteristics of the nurse along with her milk. The virtues of self-control, sympathy, a good temper, and neatness were not merely essential in any person to whom a baby was to be entrusted, but desirable in the baby herself. The preeminent virtue sought in women was self-control. For girls and women it connotes especially chastity, and secondarily control over all desires. *Sophrosyne* (self-control, chastity) appears commonly in standard language praising women like Domitia Lucilla, mother of Marcus Aurelius. After Regilla became an adult, inscriptions frequently mentioned her sophrosyne. Xenophon and Plato attributed the virtue to both women and men: men may display this virtue particularly in their use of authority, in practicing obedience, and in orderly behavior.[12]

Of the great variety of slaves available from the Roman Empire, Greeks were considered the best baby-tenders because they were civilized and spoke Greek, the key to the civilization admired by the Romans and the *lingua franca* of the empire in the east that the Romans had inherited from the successors of Alexander the Great. Furthermore, the leading gynecologists, Greeks themselves, had specifically recommended Greek nurses. What happened to the wet nurses' own babies? They were abruptly weaned from their own mother's milk. Perhaps a lactating slave in the household would nurse one along with her own baby. Otherwise a crude cup would suffice to give them their nourishment. At least their mothers had comfortable indoor jobs and were intimate with the family who owned them. The nurses hoped their charges would grow fond of them and treat them well in their old age, even keeping them around to help with their own children. They could hope also that their owners would manumit them as a reward for their service (which did in fact happen, as we know from inscriptions), though they might continue to work for them as freedwomen. Such expectations helped to guarantee good behavior, especially in a situation where the child was too young to complain about mistreatment.[13]

From the moment of her birth Regilla enjoyed the services of a large retinue of specialized slaves.[14] At least one nurse was always with her;[15] skilled seamstresses sewed her baby clothes; attendants heated the water for her bath and brought it to her;

laundresses washed her clothing, diapers, and sheets; hairdressers combed her hair; maids scrubbed her rooms; and boys looked after her pets. Children nowadays may read in the bath and play with bath toys, and those with modern bathrooms may listen to music or watch television while bathing. An upper-class Roman child could direct a slave to read aloud to her, or to play music, or to entertain her with a dramatic skit while she bathed. She could order her nurse to offer her breasts to her playmates and push the nipples into the hard mouths of her dolls and toy animals.[16] Even a young child understood that she owned her slaves' bodies totally. A slave would never be angry with her; at least, slaves did not show anger. A troop of slave children were always on hand to amuse Regilla and to perform the tasks she set for them. As a baby she learned to command her slaves, adults and children alike.

Dressing her dolls taught Regilla the latest fashions in clothes, jewelry, and hairstyles. The women of the imperial family were the leaders in fashion. Their portraits on coins announced the current style to people all over the empire, chignons some years, bangs, upswept hair, or braids at other times. Being in the center of Roman society, Regilla was one of the first to see the new styles. When Regilla played with a doll such as the one shown in Figure 1.1, dressing her in fashionable clothes and role-playing the activities of her mother and other aristocratic women she knew, she imaginatively enacted a grown-up life very different from the one she would actually lead as the wife of Herodes Atticus.[17]

From the Roman perspective, the majority of the inhabitants of the empire were virtually barbarians with the exception of the Greeks, most of whom lived either in Greece itself or in the areas that had been part of the kingdoms of Alexander and his successors. At this time, all upper-class Roman men and women were literate, most of them in both Latin and Greek.[18] Well-to-do homes had their own Greek and Latin libraries and collec-

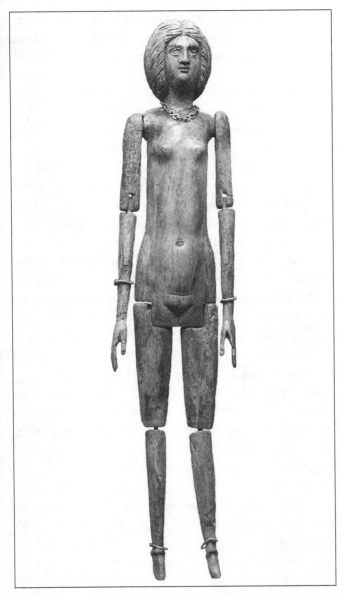

Fig. 1.1.   Doll. This ivory doll was found on the Via Valeria in Tivoli. The features and hairstyle resemble those of Julia Domna, wife of Septimius Severus, and date the doll to the end of the second or the beginning of the third century A.D. The limbs are articulated so that the doll can move.

tions of Greek art. Rome had ruled Greece since the second century B.C., but Greek culture had begun to dominate Roman even before the Roman conquest. Horace had written, "Graecia capta ferum victorem cepit, et artis intulit agresti Latio" (a conquered Greece conquered its savage victor and brought the arts into uncultivated Latium), a witty remark summarizing the political, artistic, and intellectual power relationship between Greece and Rome.[19]

An upper-class child like Regilla learned Greek from the start, listening to her nurses sing lullabies, tell stories, and chatter among themselves. These women were uneducated slaves, chosen for their physical characteristics and personal qualities. They were mostly illiterate; it did not take long for the children they looked after to outstrip them in formal education. The children used ivory letters to learn their alphabets.[20] Quintilian recommended that the Roman child begin with Greek, because Latin was in general use and the child would easily pick it up.[21] Regilla usually spoke Latin to her parents and other members of the family and to her friends, but most of them could speak and read Greek too. As Regilla grew up and her needs changed, her parents would add specialized slaves to her retinue. More men were included. Pedagogues (slaves in charge of children) chaperoned Regilla at home and whenever she went out. Though her wet nurses might continue to work for her as chaperones and general attendants, female pedagogues were rare.[22]

Male slaves were added to guard a wealthy little girl.[23] The empire as a whole was characterized by the *Pax Romana,* but even Rome itself was a dangerous place where thieves lurked, crowds surged, and buildings collapsed. Violent spectacles were not confined to the Colosseum, but could be witnessed in the street. Furthermore, men knew their way around Rome better than women did, and they were more worldly. They knew how children should behave on such occasions as visits to their grandparents or to the imperial family, where Regilla could play with the younger Faustina, who was about five years her junior. An older and younger child could easily sit together on the floor and play with their dolls or engage in games of chance with knucklebones. As in games of dice, points were gained after tossing the bones and seeing which side came up.

Girls' education followed the same curriculum as that of boys. When Regilla was a little older, a Greek tutor would teach her the Greek spoken by the educated upper class, and with him she would read the classics, some dating from a thousand years earlier and written in arcane dialects.[24] The works of contemporary women authors were available as well. At the court of Hadrian, the young Regilla may have seen the empress Sabina's Greek friends, the poets Julia Balbilla, a descendant of Antiochus IV of Commagene, and Claudia Damo Synamate, a landowner from Athens.[25] If these great ladies spoke to her, Regilla would have been able to respond in Greek.

Regilla's brother, Appius Annius Atilius Bradua, was probably about a year younger than she, although their respective ages are not certain, and it is not clear whether there were other siblings who did not survive to adulthood. Judging from the obstetrical histories of Regilla herself and her peers, her mother may have experienced five or six pregnancies, though only two children are recorded. Bradua required an even larger and more select retinue of specialists than his sister, for he was raised to follow his father and a long line of ancestors with a career in government.[26] In the early years, education was based on memorization and repetition. Much information was transmitted orally. Nothing prevented Regilla from listening in on her brother's private lessons in rhetoric and philosophy, though much of boys' rhetorical education took place in schools to which girls were not admitted.

Philosophers thought that daughters and sons should receive similar educations, since they had the same ability to reason, though the ultimate purposes of their education were different.[27] Some of these philosophers were actually present in Rome, and therefore it is possible to assume that their beliefs had some direct impact. For example, the Stoic C. Musonius Rufus (approx. A.D. 30–101/102) mingled with people in the highest social and political circles in Rome. The general view was that women were to be educated so that they would have traditional female virtues, become skilled managers of the household, and be useful to their families.

The Latin orator Fronto lists these virtues in a letter he sent to Domitia Lucilla, mother of Marcus Aurelius, on her birthday: "All women . . . should have celebrated your birthday feast. First, the women who love their husbands and children and exercise self-control *(sophronas);* second, as many as are without affectations and lies; and third, those who are sensible and agreeable and courteous, and not haughty . . . since all the virtues and knowledge suitable to a woman are yours."[28]

Philosophy was an international discourse. Though philosophers wrote mostly in Greek, as we see from Fronto's letter (which was in Greek), their ideas circulated and influenced the Romans. However, some Greek ideas were too strict or impractical or clashed with what was appropriate or thought natural for upper-class Roman women. Plutarch, for example, advocates teaching women mathematics so that they would not engage in dancing, and giving them Plato and Xenophon to read so that they not be interested in witchcraft.[29] Although Roman girls were taught to count on the abacus, they also learned to dance, which was not merely entertaining and amusing, but was part of the musical curriculum and required for some religious observances.[30]

Betrothal and Marriage

The Roman father customarily chose a bridegroom for his daughter, especially when she was young and the marriage was her first. For the elite, the chief reward for raising a daughter came at the time of her marriage, when her father used her as a pawn in his political games.

There was no alternative to marriage for a respectable girl. With the exception of the few who became Vestal Virgins, every upper-class woman Regilla knew had married, often more than once. According to the marriage legislation promulgated by Augustus in 18 b.c., the legal minimum age for marriage for Roman girls was twelve, and motherhood was expected by the age of twenty. Since reproduction was an important goal in marriage, it was usual to wait for menarche to formalize a marriage. Upper-class girls married young, while bridegrooms in the senatorial class were in their mid-twenties.[31] A few women who were members of the imperial family married in their late teens and early twenties, but they were exceptions.[32] Roman marriage was based on the consent of both parties; however, the bride could object to the marriage only in the case of the moral turpitude of the groom, and it was unlikely that a well-chaperoned young girl would know of any allegations against her fiancé.[33] In practice, Regilla could not raise her voice against her father's choice, even if she did know the faults of the bridegroom who had been chosen for her. Regilla's father, Appius Annius Gallus, was alive at the time of his daughter's betrothal, for he was consul in 139.[34] He must have been responsible for the decision to make a marriage alliance with Herodes, or at least to approve it.

While Regilla's parents were looking for a bridegroom, eligible bachelors like Herodes were courting them. Herodes' relationships with the imperial family and Roman society were well established. He had first arrived in Rome around 108 when he was about eight years old. That same year, Regilla's maternal grandfather M. Atilius Metilius Bradua was *consul ordinarius*.[35] Herodes' father Claudius Atticus became a member of the Senate and served as suffect consul. In the imperial period it was normal to have six or more consuls every year, of which the first two were the *ordinarii*, and all the others *suffecti*. The *ordinarii* were replaced at the end of their term (often two months) by the next pair, and so on through the year. Consuls were selected by the emperor.

Being appointed a suffect consul was a great honor, but being *consul ordinarius* was an even greater one. An aspect of the imperial policy was to assimilate upper-class provincials, especially Greek men, and this goal encouraged Herodes' father to bring his son to live for a while in Rome. We do not know whether Herodes' mother and sister accompanied them. Regilla's mother was a member of the same imperial social circle and the same generation as her daughter's future husband. As a youth, Herodes had lived with a family whose daughter Domitia Lucilla was about his age and who became the mother of Marcus Aurelius, to whom Herodes was later appointed a tutor.[36] As a mature woman, Domitia Lucilla was bilingual, for we have seen that Fronto wrote to her in Greek.[37] Her facility in Greek, which may have been remarkable even among a Roman aristocracy who spoke and read Greek, suggests that she could have been very close to Herodes as they were growing up. Herodes then became the tutor of Lucius Verus (who later became emperor with Marcus Aurelius), a further indication of his long-standing relationship with the Antonine emperors and with influential members of the court such as Fronto.[38] Most important, the emperors had met him when they were young and impressionable, and a tutor was exalted as a sort of father figure. Marcus Aurelius was studious himself, and thus more inclined to value a Sophist, especially one who was his old teacher.

The emperor's favor is evident throughout Herodes' career, which included many posts in the city government and official religion at Athens and rapid advancement through the *cursus honorum,* the succession of governmental offices at Rome. About 138/139, while on his way to becoming *consul ordinarius* and having nearly attained the age of forty that the Greeks and Romans considered a man's prime, Herodes married Regilla.[39]

Herodes had recently acquired a huge fortune upon the death of his father Atticus around 138/139. The imperial family may well have indicated to Regilla's father that they were in favor of this match. The marriage was also consistent with their policy of furthering the integration of selected non-Italians into the power structure. Thus Marcus Aurelius chose a *novus homo* (new man, i.e., the first man in his family to be appointed senator) from Antioch as a new husband for his widowed daughter Lucilla, and chose the son of a philosopher from Paphlagonia for his daughter Annia Faustina.[40] As Herodes' wife, Regilla served as the visible emblem of personal imperial beneficence to him. He was a fortunate man. Marriage to Regilla was tantamount to wearing the emperor's favor emblazoned on his chest.

Though at forty Herodes was far older than the average bridegroom at first marriage, he was not unique among men of letters in marrying a very young wife. Nor is there any indication that he had ever been married before. The elder Seneca was about twenty-five years older than his wife Helvia.[41] Pliny the Younger was in his forties when he married Calpurnia, who was probably no more than fifteen, but she was his second or third wife.[42] A bachelor's motives in seeking a bride could be both commonplace and unique. Romantic love in the modern sense was irrelevant to the match. Obviously in addition to gaining economic and social advantages, an important goal in marriage was to create a family. Herodes had long ignored the Augustan legislation encouraging men to marry and reproduce.

Judging from ancient mortality figures, at the time Herodes married, many of his contemporaries had already completed their life cycle, and yet he had not produced an heir for his millions. As Soranus frankly declares, women are married usually for the sake of children and succession and not merely for pleasure.[43] A young wife, of course, had the greatest reproductive potential. Regilla was young. Like other Roman brides, she would dedicate her dolls to Venus at the time of her marriage.[44]

At the age of fourteen she would become a *materfamilias* (respected female head of a *familia*), presiding over a huge household of her own. Soon she would have real babies to look after.

Herodes' other motives must have included a desire to ally himself with an old Roman family. Brides served as links between families. Through his wife, their children-to-be, and his in-laws Herodes might hope to shed the inferiority of a "Graeculus" (little Greekling) and become an insider in Roman society.[45] Regilla's family owned property adjacent to the Appian Way and elsewhere in Italy, but the ample wealth they possessed appeared modest compared with Herodes' fortune, which was not only huge but infamous owing to its origin and a lawsuit concerning the will of his father, who had left a substantial portion of his wealth to the Athenian citizen body.[46] Most Roman parents supplied their daughters with dowries. Regilla's included a parcel of choice real estate. She also had a substantial amount of cash which enabled her to undertake two very expensive building projects in Greece. This cash could have been part of her dowry, but it could also have been inheritance, or a gift from her husband. At any rate, Herodes could not demand a dowry commensurate with his own contribution to the marriage. He was the wealthiest Greek of his day: no bride could supply a dowry on such a lavish scale, especially if she was not an only child. Twenty years after he married Regilla, when he faced his brother-in-law Bradua in a Roman court and his accuser spoke of his own philanthropy to one Italian city, Herodes was able to boast of his benefactions all over the empire.[47]

The general prerequisites for an appropriate match included the good moral character of the bride and groom and of their families. Herodes and his family did not meet this criterion, but their enormous wealth and political connections restored the balance in their favor. Herodes was also a leading member of the educational and literary movement known as the "Second Sophistic." These men were not only powerful in intellectual circles, but some of them also enjoyed a prestigious position at the imperial court and wielded a significant influence in politics, both at Rome and in their native cities in the Greek east. Brilliance, wit, rhetorical skill, and the ability to attract students were necessary assets in the competition among these Sophists; kindness and ethical conduct were not obligatory.

Regilla's family may have considered the marriage a source of funding for their own ambitions and projects. Her father was at the height of his career, serving as consul just before the wedding, and he may not have had time to carry out a thorough investigation of Herodes. A wealthy son-in-law was an asset to Regilla's father, even if it was tactful not to inquire about the sources of the money and the litigation concerning it.

The origins of Herodes' fortune were murky; the hidden source of wealth in this family—which was *nouveau riche* compared to some Roman lineages—suggests illiberal, if not criminal, activities. Philostratus mentions multiple sources of wealth inherited from both the maternal and the paternal line, but he does not state how this wealth was acquired.[48] Usury and banking—which were much despised by Roman aristocrats—come to mind as possible sources.[49] Herodes' father claimed he had discovered a buried treasure, but it is a good guess that he had hidden the treasure himself, either to stop his creditors from seizing it, or to prevent Domitian from appropriating it.[50] In any case, that he was allowed to keep it shows imperial indulgence very soon after the death of Domitian. Herodes' immediate ancestors had held the highest magistracies in Greece under the Antonine emperors.[51] His father was admitted to the senatorial order as a *novus homo*.[52]

Herodes claimed a pedigree that went back to legendary kings, heroes, and mythological figures of Athens including Cecrops, Theseus, Ceryx, and Herse. He asserted that he was also descended from the generals Miltiades and Cimon, who had helped secure the Greek victory over the Persians in the fifth century

B.C. His familiarity with the literature of the classical period and his revival of activities and customs of the remote past added subtle persuasion to this claim. His ancestors, however, can be plausibly traced back only to a Eucles in the second century B.C.[53]

By the Hellenistic period it was not uncommon for Greek families to appropriate illustrious lineages from the heroic and classical ages.[54] Alleging descent from the commander at the battle of Marathon associated Herodes with the most glorious event in Athenian history: the miraculous defeat of the Persians.[55] Even in Plutarch's time, the Athenians celebrated the victory.[56] Tourists in Athens could easily visit the suburb of Marathon and view the trophy, monuments, and tumulus standing above the graves of the fallen heroes. Herodes' own constructions at his estate in Marathon were impressive as well, and included sculptures strategically placed near the tomb of the fallen Athenians where visitors could not fail to see them.

The general Miltiades was also honored at Rome. The Greeks did not use *imagines*, but Herodes tried to compensate with portrait busts, which were more fashionable in the empire anyway. A fine Roman classicizing portrait herm of Miltiades with a bilingual epigram inscribed on the stele below once stood in the Vigna Strozzi at Mt. Coelius in Rome.[57] The fact that the inscription is bilingual and the Latin text is first suggests that Miltiades was as famous among the Romans as he was among the Greeks. The Romans conflated the Persians with their own enemies, the Parthians. By exploiting the legend of Marathon, Herodes enhanced his own image in the eyes of the Romans. He positioned himself in the category of civilized people fighting barbarians. One of Herodes' long poems, in a fragmentary inscription found at Eleusis, alludes to his close relationship with Lucius Verus, the Roman commander against the Parthians (A.D. 162–166).[58]

Herodes' family also forged links with the Romans' favorite

Greeks, the Spartans, through the marriage of his sister Tisamenis to a Spartan[59] and the education of at least one member of his family as a Spartan ephebe (youth or cadet).[60] He was a true man of the Roman Empire, transcending and surmounting ethnic distinctions, and exploiting a broad range of possible identities.

Herodes may have been a great "catch" on the marriage market, but so was Regilla. Her father must have known the marriage could prove dangerous to his daughter. Herodes had spent many years in Rome before marrying Regilla. Though he was highly praised as a rhetorician, he was notorious for resorting to violence rather than persuasion. He had been accused of daring to strike the future emperor Antoninus Pius in 134/135, when he was Regulator *(Corrector)* supervising the free cities in Asia and Antoninus was governor of the province of Asia.[61] At Rome he was also known as contentious.

His quarrels with Fronto, Antoninus Pius, the Quintilii brothers, and intermittently with the Athenians themselves are well documented. In a letter to Marcus Aurelius about Herodes, Fronto mentions "freedmen cruelly beaten . . . and one killed, and a person who must . . . be made out as a murderer."[62] Fronto did not like him at first, denigrating him as a "Greekling" *(Graeculus)*.[63] Though there were other senators in Rome who were born in the eastern part of the empire, Herodes evidently stood out with his Greek costume and use of language mimicking the philosophers and orators of the Greek past.[64] A cursory glance at portraits of Herodes and his contemporaries suggests that he devoted a great deal of time to his appearance, flaunting his Greekness as a means of distinguishing himself from the average senator and consequently provoking Fronto to deride him as a *Graeculus* (see fig. 2.2). At the irresistible urging of the emperor, however, Fronto and Herodes became friendly.[65] Plutarch had characterized Herodes' putative ancestor Cimon as lavish in his benefactions, but also as a voluptuary and undisciplined in his style of life.[66] The ancients believed in the inheritance of acquired characteristics. Some of Cimon's character traits seem to have reappeared in Herodes and his son. Plutarch thought Cimon was overly distraught at his wife's death, and some of Herodes' contemporaries delivered similar verdicts on Herodes' reaction when Regilla died.[67]

The important question is how he treated Regilla and whether she came to like and respect him. From the viewpoint of Regilla, rather than of her father, the unattractive features of this alliance are far more obvious than the advantages. Herodes was old enough to be Regilla's father. He had been a bachelor longer than most men, and his sentimental ties were with men in an age when such liaisons were no longer fashionable even for a Greek philosopher. There are archaeological and textual hints of Herodes' erotic connections with men, and these became clearer as he grew older. Fronto refers to Herodes as his *anterastes* (rival in love) for the younger Marcus Aurelius. This "love" may well have been what we call "platonic," with the rivalry between the two chief tutors of Marcus Aurelius being for his devotion and favor rather than for any more intimate relationship, though in their letters Fronto and Marcus Aurelius use explicitly erotic language.[68] Furthermore, citizens had to love the emperor, but in Herodes' case the sentiment may have been more than *pro forma.*

Some anecdotes in connection with Herodes can be interpreted as misogynistic. In a section of the *Life* of Herodes devoted to misogyny, violence, and Regilla's murder, Philostratus reports a conversation between Herodes and a certain Agathion, a kind of noble savage, who had requested a large bowl of milk that had not been milked by a woman.[69] When the milk was presented, Agathion rejected it, saying, "The milk is not pure, a woman's hand strikes me." Herodes was delighted with Agathion's abilities. This anecdote precedes the mention of the violent confrontation between Herodes and Antoninus Pius. The paragraph immediately following presents the murder charge. In a later section Philostratus also relates that when Herodes met Marcus Aurelius in the presence of Faustina and their daughter, he complained that the emperor was judging him under the influence of a woman and a child.[70]

Wedding

Whether Herodes had had much, if any, sexual contact with women before his wedding is questionable. When he was a young man there may have been encounters with courtesans, prostitutes, and household slaves at symposia that turned into wild parties. In the homes of his less prudish friends, wall paintings displayed the postures of Venus *in flagrante delicto* entwined with Adonis, Mars, and other handsome young lovers, offering uncensored instruction for those who cared to imitate them.[71] Judging, however, from his long bachelorhood and his disdain for women, we assume that Herodes did not gain much sexual experience by courting upper-class divorcées or widows, and that his embrace of Regilla on their wedding night would have been awkward and inconsiderate at the very least.

Regilla, of course, was a virgin bride. She had learned about sexual intercourse from her mother and her nannies. Privacy was not characteristic of the Roman home, for slaves slept at the thresholds of the bedrooms. Often a mere curtain separated the bedrooms from the rest of the household, and she could hear everything that was going on in bed. Because Regilla's family boasted of descent from Aeneas (a son of Venus), Venus, her lovers, and Cupid might well have been represented on their walls, depicted in various amorous positions as in a marriage manual. Indeed, what we would consider "erotic" art was widespread in Roman houses, even in public rooms frequented by children.

On her wedding day, Regilla was so busy that she had little time to think about the night ahead when she would lie in bed in her husband's house. Much of our information about Roman and Greek marriage customs concerns earlier periods, and it is not clear that they were followed in the imperial period. If Roman tradition were followed, her father would have made the wedding sacrifice. The auspices were favorable. The bride dressed before the banquet at her parents' house. She was conspicuous in her flame-colored hair net, veil, and orange shoes identifying her as a bride.[72] She also wore a white dress.[73] After the banquet at her parents' house, choruses of girls and boys escorted her by torchlight to Herodes' house. The streets were lined with onlookers, since this was almost a royal wedding. The girls and boys threw nuts to the crowds as they passed and sang antiphonally to the sound of flutes. Their repertoire included lewd songs emphasizing fertility, the bride's imminent loss of virginity, and details of her sexual initiation, as well as traditional marriage hymns and new ones commissioned for the occasion. A *camillus* (young freeborn boy with both parents living) walked in the procession, bearing a basketful of household utensils symbolic of the bride's role as mistress of her husband's household. Regilla would never perform any manual labor.

This was a mixed marriage fraught with awkwardness and uncertainty. Once Regilla had left her parents' home, which traditions would be followed? The family cult of the Romans involved the Lares and Penates (ancestral household divinities housed in a little wall niche or shrine). According to tradition, Aeneas had rescued the original cult images from the flames of burning Troy and transported them carefully to Italy. Since antiquity the Roman bride brought three copper coins, and gave one to the Lar of the crossroads, another to the ancestral Lar of her husband's home, and the last one to her husband.[74] But Herodes was Greek. His home did not house Lares and Penates. At the home of the Roman bridegroom, the crowd shouted

"Talassio," an ancient word no longer understood, but connected with the first Roman marriages, which resulted from the rape of the Sabine women. Like the legendary first Romans, the husband carried his bride over the threshold and welcomed her with a traditional offering of fire and water, symbols of her role as materfamilias. We have no firsthand reports about the sexual initiation of the Roman bride. The next day she took charge of the domestic religious ceremonies appropriate to her as a materfamilias. But was Regilla to be a materfamilias like her mother, or was she to become a subservient Greek wife?

Roman law prescribed that no two persons more closely related than first cousins were permitted to marry except members of the imperial family by special dispensation from the rule of exogamy. Romans tended to marry people to whom they were not related in any way. In contrast, Greeks favored endogamy to a degree that was outlawed in Rome. In Athens only siblings by the same mother were forbidden to marry, and in Sparta siblings by the same father. Herodes' ancestor Cimon and his half-sister, Elpinice, had had a sexual liaison which may have been a marriage, and his mother, Vibullia Alcia Agrippina, and father, Tiberius Claudius Atticus Herodes, were cousins. Despite the Roman custom and their Roman citizenship, marriage between cousins continued among the elite in Roman Sparta.[75]

Plutarch compared the customary choice of spouses among the Greeks and the Romans from the viewpoint of the bride.[76] He decided that exogamous marriage was preferable for women because if the husband abused his wife, her kinsmen would defend her. In discussing this issue, Plutarch brings the topic of wife abuse to the fore. By maintaining a good relationship with his wife's family, a caring husband avoided turning allies into opponents. For example, Pliny the Younger reports frequently to his wife's kin about her. In his letters, he finds no fault with her; she seems the perfect wife for him. He tells her grandfather that she had a miscarriage.[77] He continues to communicate with his wife's family, who were also interested in potential grandchildren. In judging exogamy preferable, Plutarch was comparing the familial endogamy within a Greek *polis,* and not contemplating such extreme and unusual exogamy as marriage between a Greek man and a Roman woman resulting in her permanent geographical separation from her kinsmen.[78] He was evaluating the normal Greek and Roman marital pattern in which the bride's family gave her to the groom. After Regilla's death, however, the Roman pattern of the wife's being championed by her kinsmen, as described by Plutarch, emerged: Regilla's brother accused Herodes of murdering his sister.

Regilla would have grown up expecting to marry a Roman husband like her father and her brother. Marriage to an outsider was unusual for upper-class Roman women and meant that the couple would eventually leave Rome.[79] Regilla would be permanently separated from her family and friends. While it is true that Herodes was fabulously wealthy, any appropriate husband that her father could have found for her among native Romans would doubtless have been of Regilla's own social and economic class, and such a marriage would not have brought permanent exile and a gruesome dénouement.

Communication

We have every reason to believe that Regilla was bilingual like Herodes, the Greek she eventually married. Herodes was doubtless more comfortable with Greek, and Regilla more at ease speaking, reading, and writing Latin.[80] Inasmuch as Herodes was in charge of Marcus Aurelius's Greek education, he was not merely a native Greek speaker, but an expert in Greek style and literature. By the end of Regilla's life, when she had lived longer in Greece than in Italy, she would have been equally fluent in Greek and Latin. Literacy in Greek was essential for the positions Regilla eventually held such as priestess of Demeter at Olympia and of Tyche at Athens. She is one of the few people for whom a bilingual inscription was later dedicated in Rome.[81]

Although Regilla and Herodes were betrothed and married according to Roman law written in Latin documents, Herodes doubtless preferred to converse with his bride in Greek, where he held the advantage. Furthermore, Fronto and Marcus Aurelius wrote personal letters to him in Greek. This choice suggests that Herodes spoke to Regilla in Greek even in Rome and continued to do so later when they moved to Athens. Regilla was at a disadvantage when conversing in Greek with her husband, who was a native speaker, a rhetorician, and a brilliant and learned man. He not only could use the Atticizing literary style of Greek that characterized the Second Sophistic, and could speak like Critias, a philosopher and much-hated oligarch of the fifth century,[82] but he was also fluent in the *koine* (vulgar) Greek spoken commonly in the empire and even in Rome by Greek immigrants and slaves. In contrast, the oral Greek of upper-class women was usually limited to the colloquial version.[83] There were, however, some exceptions in Regilla's social circle, such as Domitia Lucilla, who was fluent in a cultivated Greek, since Fronto not only wrote to her in Greek but also apologized lest his language skills might not be up to her standard.[84] Even if she spoke Greek to her husband, Regilla probably spoke Latin with her parents, brother, and friends, as well as with her children later when they lived in Greece, so that they would know Latin.

Early Years of Marriage in Rome: Motherhood

Regilla's first child was born in Rome by 141, within a year of her marriage. A birthing room in both Rome and Athens was a very crowded place.[85] The furniture included two beds and a birthing chair. As the head of the household, Herodes dictated which attendants should be on hand and had the greatest say in whether or not a male doctor was present. Even if he had summoned one of the leading physicians in Rome, say Soranus or Galen, they would have monitored the stages of childbirth through the attending midwives, moving into action only if the birth became a difficult one.[86]

Regilla's first child died soon after birth. He evidently died even before a *praenomen* was conferred and is known to us simply as Claudius, the name denoting Herodes' Roman citizenship and borne by all his children. Demographers calculate that in the late Republic and early empire one-third of infants died in their first year and one-half before reaching ten. Of those who survived until ten, one-third lived until sixty and one-seventh to seventy.[87] Death did not respect class distinctions.[88] Even in the upper class the death of infants was common. Among contemporaries of Regilla and Herodes, Gratia and Fronto had six children, of whom only one daughter survived, and of twelve or more children born to Faustina and Marcus Aurelius, only one son and two daughters survived to adulthood.

In the case of Regilla's firstborn, the fragility of the infant's life was increased by the immaturity of the mother. Aristotle had written that it was undesirable for very young women to bear children since their babies were more likely to have the defect of being girls, and the mothers had a more difficult labor and a greater danger of dying in childbirth.[89] He suggested that the optimum age for marriage was eighteen for women and thirty-seven for men. Soranus observed that menarche occurred at around fourteen and that pregnancy before the mother's body was fully developed was dangerous for the embryo.[90] Plutarch approved of Spartan women marrying at a mature age so that their babies would be robust.[91]

At Rome no formal mourning for infants was prescribed. They were not cremated, and their deaths did not cause pollution.[92] In contrast, if an older person died, the house and relatives and anyone who handled the corpse was considered polluted and required purification by means of ancient rituals. Children who died before the age of ten were not to be lamented publicly; nevertheless, individuals might grieve privately.[93] The use of wet nurses may have decreased bonding between mother and newborn.[94] Parents were more likely to mourn the death of an older child. For example, though both men had studied philosophy and should have been implacable in the face of death, Pliny the Younger wrote to a mutual friend, Marcellinus, describing the grief of Minicius Fundanus on the death of his twelve-year-old daughter and suggesting that he write to Fundanus to comfort him.[95]

Two letters are extant concerning the death of Regilla's infant son. Marcus Aurelius wrote to Fronto: "Herodes' son born [today] has died. Herodes is not bearing this with equanimity. I would like you to write a few words to him about this event."[96] Fronto did write a letter of consolation to Herodes, using Greek, which would have been more comforting to the named recipient, if less so to Regilla and more difficult for the writer himself: "For there is no aspect of your age that prevents you from rearing other children. Every loss is difficult if hope is cut off, but easier if some hope remains of recovery."[97] Fronto did not mention Regilla at all and, as we have observed, he wrote in Greek, not Latin. Perhaps Fronto addressed his condolences solely to Herodes because he anticipated publishing his letters and preferred to name a celebrity as recipient, or perhaps he was merely following the emperor's directive, and Marcus Aurelius had not mentioned Regilla. Etiquette, or Fronto's intuition about Greek conjugal relations, may have also played a role. It was expected that the husband would comfort the wife. Thus Plutarch, who was away from home when his only daughter died, sent a letter of consolation to his wife. In addition to comforting her, he exhorts her not to indulge in effusive lamentation.[98] In Greek tradition, one of women's functions in fact was to lament dead kin. Judging by the reflection in the published writings of a thoughtful husband like Plutarch, a mother was potentially capable of expressions of grief that would embarrass a dignified philosopher.

The first baby was not mentioned by Philostratus, although Fronto's correspondence with Marcus Aurelius shows that the death affected Herodes deeply. Philostratus may have failed to mention the death of the infant either because such deaths were frequent, or because he did not care to record Herodes' excessive and unphilosophical reaction. This was apparently one of the few occasions when Herodes had wanted something desperately and could not buy it for all the money in the world. Was Herodes too stricken with grief and too self-indulgent to comfort the baby's mother? He was a famous orator. Did he use his talents to console Regilla?

Fronto did not mention Regilla, not even to point out the probability that she would be able to bear many more children because she was young. After all, a man's age rarely prevents him from becoming a father. Fronto's letter conveys the impression that Herodes alone had lost a child. This may well be a reflection of Herodes' attitude. Regilla was soon pregnant again, and less than two years after the death of her son gave birth to a girl, Elpinice. Her Greek name was a harbinger of the family's future, for after the birth of this child Herodes decided to move his family to Athens. He had fulfilled his ambitions at Rome and completed the *cursus honorum*. Moving to Greece meant that Herodes could get away from Regilla's family and consolidate his power base in the marriage.

Though as a young girl Regilla had visited her family estates near the southern Italian port from which she sailed after two years of marriage, this was probably her first journey to Greece. Regilla's personal slaves as well as an entourage of nurses, wet nurses, and attendants for baby Elpinice accompanied the family on the journey from Rome to Athens.

The Journey to Greece

Upper-class Romans who traveled to Athens usually went overland to Brundisium, passing through Capua. The first leg of the journey was on the Via Appia. After that the Via Appia joined up with the Via Traiana for the rest of the journey to the Adriatic coast. Women like Regilla traveled in a covered carriage with their children and personal slaves, while the rest of the slaves and supplies were transported in more utilitarian wagons. Regilla's carriage was as comfortable as money could buy, but the road was bumpy and the wheels were hard. The family stopped along the way to eat, rest, and sleep in the villas of friends, as well as at the property of Regilla's Annii family in Canusium (modern Canosa) in Apulia, until they reached the port. If the weather was fair, the lap by ship was easier.

From Brundisium, Regilla sailed to the west coast of Greece, probably landing at Epirus where Herodes had connections.[99] Thence the journey was overland to Athens. As a member of a senatorial family, Regilla had learned about the vast and varied Roman Empire, but she had seen little of it. Senators like her father were obliged to remain near Rome except when serving as provincial governors or for other official duties. Young unmarried upper-class Roman men would make the same trip as part of their education at an age when their sisters were already married.[100] Thus the men improved their spoken Greek, mixed with the elites in the provinces, and generally prepared themselves for a career in government: they were to be not only Romans, but citizens and rulers of an empire. Young women, experiencing fewer expeditions outside Italy, were more circumscribed in their ethnic identity. After this trip to Greece, which was her first outside Italy, it is unlikely that Regilla ever returned to Italy. As for Herodes, he had traveled between Greece and Italy before he was married, but he did not continue to do so.

Canusium

When Regilla reached southern Italy and her family estates in Canusium, she found the town was dry and dusty.[101] Wanting to bathe at the end of a long day of travel, she could find barely enough water to wash baby Elpinice. Canusium, once prosperous, had chosen the losing side during the Social Wars of the first century B.C., and thus fell out of favor with Rome, and the city had declined because of the scarcity of water. Trajan and Hadrian, and then Herodes, turned their attention to this problem. Herodes endowed the town with an enormous aqueduct which brought water to the city from twenty miles away.[102] Perhaps he decided to build it during the trip with Regilla. Philostratus credits Herodes with the revitalization of the city.[103] During the reign of Marcus Aurelius, the *municipium* of Canusium was raised to the higher civic status of a *colonia*, evidence of the restoration of imperial favor and prosperity.[104]

Marriage to one of the Annii Regilli provided Herodes with a focus on specific geographical locations in Italy that would help in his efforts to convert himself from an outsider to an insider. Herodes apparently became interested in Canusium in particular because the Annii owned property there.[105] He increased the value of the property of Regilla's kinsmen in Canusium and doubtless also ingratiated himself with them as a consequence. After Regilla's death, Herodes was to return to Italy and once again make improvements to Regilla's property.

Chameleon-like, throughout the first half of his life Herodes reinvented himself by adapting to a broad range of geographical and social contexts. What kind of man was returning to his native Athens? Herodes' political and social connections in Athens had become attenuated because he had spent so much time in Italy. But at least he would feel comfortable at home where his name would be spelled correctly on monuments he had paid for and no sneering Roman would refer to him as a *Graeculus*.[106] Regilla could not know what to expect. Was she to behave like her own mother, or like her mother-in-law and sister-in-law? She had been brought up to fulfill her parents' expectations, to live in her own Roman culture. In Greece, she could try to fit in, to do what was expected of her. But was she fated to be an outsider who had married an outsider?

CHAPTER 2

A ROMAN MATRON IN IMPERIAL ATHENS

THOUGH GREECE WAS more forested in antiquity than it is now, the landscape was rocky and not as green and lush as what Regilla was accustomed to in Latium. Athens could only be a disappointment to her, for she had lived in Rome, which was crammed with marble-clad buildings and with monuments, antiquities, and treasures from all over the empire. Despite the efforts of a few philhellenic emperors and other benefactors from Julius Caesar to Marcus Aurelius, Athens was still much ravaged by war, looting, and the effects of age. Regilla would have been familiar with the style of the buildings erected by the Roman benefactors. For example, Hadrian's Library echoed features of the Temple of Peace in Rome.[1] Pausanias mentions the hundred columns, walls, colonnades of Phrygian marble, gilded roof, statues, paintings, and books housed in the library.[2] No visitor then or now could miss Hadrian's monumental Temple of Olympian Zeus, which had been dedicated in A.D. 131/132. Roman architects attempted both to restore the Athens of the past and to impose order and symmetrical structures on an ancient city that had grown up haphazardly, but in which open space had been deliberately retained for public meetings and commercial and civic activities.

Greek Wife or Materfamilias?

The contrast between Rome and Athens may also be observed in the microcosm of the family. In the Roman familia the wife enjoyed an exalted position as materfamilias, a role well defined by custom. Her statue of Juno stood alongside of the figure representing the Genius of the paterfamilias among their household gods. In the Greek family, however, there was no counterpart to the materfamilias. The Greek wife played whatever role her husband defined for her and could remain an alien, an unhappy stranger in her husband's house. The new bride, like a newly purchased slave, had to be introduced to the gods of her husband's home. In classical Athens her functions were to produce legitimate children and be a faithful housekeeper.[3] In Roman Greece, as the works of Plutarch show, there was a wider range of options for the role of wife, but her status in the family was still determined by the individual inclination of her husband. The fates that Procne lamented in a fifth-century B.C. tragedy could have been those of a wife in Roman Greece:

> I have often regarded the nature of women in this way,
> seeing that we amount to nothing. In childhood in our
> father's house we live the happiest life, I think, of all
> mankind; for folly always rears children in happiness.
> But when we have understanding and have come to
> youthful vigor, we are pushed out and sold, away from
> our paternal gods and from our parents, some to foreign
> husbands, some to barbarians, some to joyless homes,
> and some to homes that are opprobrious. And this . . .
> we must approve and consider to be happiness.[4]

In the same vein, though less severe, some 550 years later Plutarch advised that a wife acquiesce to her husband's moods:

if a wife puts on a glum look when her husband wants
to be playful and affectionate, or if she laughs and jokes
when he is serious, she is a poor wife . . . A wife should
have no feelings of her own, but share her husband's se-
riousness and sport, his anxiety and his laughter.[5]

Though her upbringing had prepared Regilla to become a materfamilias just like her mother and to marry a man who behaved like her father, her experience as a wife once she was in
Greece was closer to the Greek pattern.

The Greek *oikos* (household, family, or estate) included the
members of the family and the property they owned. Slaves
were considered merely part of the property.[6] In contrast, the
Roman familia included the slaves. Furthermore, though in Rome
slaves constituted property while they were slaves, when they
were freed their names showed their connection to their former
owner, and they often were buried in the same columbarium (a
funerary monument with multiple niches for crematory urns).

Regilla's household was extensive. Though the chronology of
all its members is not secure, at its largest the household included her husband and their children, an adopted son, foster
children, her personal slaves who had come with her from Rome,
and Herodes' slaves and freedmen. The staff numbered in the
thousands: they were essential for the maintenance of Regilla's
and Herodes' enormous and elaborate properties in Italy and
Greece and for the personal needs of the familia itself.

Regilla gave birth to at least five children and was carrying a
fetus when she died. In Rome, her female relatives could have
been with her in the birthing room: they would have understood her when she cried out and cursed in Latin, and, when
necessary, they could translate her words to a Greek midwife
or physician. In Greece, there was only a hostile mother-in-law
and an attendant midwife who probably did not understand
much Latin. However, the medical and physical circumstances

of childbirth for an upper-class woman in Greece were similar to what Regilla had experienced in Rome, since the most prestigious and influential gynecologists in Rome came from the Greek part of the empire.

Although male intellectuals wrote with approval about breast-feeding, and Herodes must have read some of their works, Regilla's fertility pattern indicates that she did not nurse her babies.[7] Since her first son had died and her next two children were girls, she needed to produce a male heir, and was frequently pregnant without the long intervals between births that would indicate the contraceptive effect of nursing. The relationship between lactation and contraception was observed.[8] The pace of childbirth slowed after she bore a son who lived. When this son, Bradua, displayed learning disabilities and his father despaired of him, she produced another son, Regillus. After the death of Regillus she became pregnant again, and was in her eighth month when she died. The number of children Regilla produced conforms to the reproductive pattern of married women of her time: the average woman who lived to menopause had borne at least five to six children.[9] Regilla did not live to menopausal age.

Being Roman among the Greeks

The names of the children of Regilla and Herodes not only proclaim their descent from their parents, repeating some of their names, but also reflect their kinship with illustrious lineages in Rome and Athens. Native Greek speakers pronounced their Roman names differently from Latin speakers. Thus, for example, in Italy Regilla was known as "Regílla," her name rhyming with those of other Roman women like Drusilla and Lucilla; now in Greece she was "Régila."

The first daughter was Appia Annia Claudia Atilia Regilla

Elpinice Agrippina Atria Polla.[10] The name of the oldest living child echoes her mother's names and was also influenced by Herodes' lineage, alluding to his descent from Cimon as well as his Spartan connections. Elpinice was born in 142 when the family's move to Greece was imminent. Hence a Greek name was suitable. Most of her names are Roman, but she was known as Elpinice. Herodes claimed descent from the family of Cimon, which had a tradition of favoring Sparta.[11] (Cimon had named his twin sons Lacedaemonius, "Spartan," and Eleius, a reference to Elis, another polis in the Peloponnesus.[12]) Elpinice was named after Cimon's sister, who was perhaps also his wife.[13] No marriage is recorded for Elpinice, who died around 165, perhaps from the plague which ravaged Athens and much of the empire around this time, sparing neither rich nor poor.[14] Her younger sister married first, which was unusual, suggesting that illness prevented her from marrying.

Marcia Annia Claudia Alcia Athenais Gavidia Latiaria was born ca. 143/144 and died before 161.[15] In naming his younger daughter, Herodes followed the precedent set by the Macedonian king Philip II, who called his wife Olympias to celebrate his victory at the Olympic games, and also named his daughters Thessalonice and Europe to mark his conquest of Thessaly and Greece.[16] Herodes was awarded a crown at the Panathenaea (the great religious festival in Athens) in June 139, and thereupon promised to reconstruct the stadium (which had been built in the second half of the fourth century B.C.) before the next celebration four years later.[17] He fulfilled his promise, and the name of Athenais, who was also known as Panathenais, announces his achievement. Philostratus refers to her as Panathenais, but she is called Athenais in inscriptions.[18] Marcia is a feminine form of the common Latin praenomen (first name) Marcus, which was the praenomen of Regilla's grandfather and appears in the names of her younger brother Bradua. In this period such a name was simply a name, not, as earlier, an inherited *gentili-*

cium of a particular Roman *gens,* or family.[19] The full name of Athenais is a hybrid, alluding to both Greek and Roman religion: Athena, of course, is Greek; Latiaris is an epithet of Jupiter, whose cult was on the Alban mount in Rome. Alcia is the name of her paternal grandmother, who outlived her.

Athenais married Lucius Vibullius Rufus. He had been married before and already had at least one son, Lucius Vibullius, whom Herodes later adopted. Alcia, Athenais' paternal grandmother, was a Vibullia. Thus Athenais was married to a relative, though not a close one. Athenais and her husband had one son, Lucius Vibullius Hipparchus, the only recorded grandchild of Regilla and Herodes.[20] In earlier times, parents struggled to perpetuate their lineage through male heirs, but by this time even in the imperial house daughters were also seen as a means to ensure that families did not die out.[21] Athenais thus served Herodes as a way of acquiring a son-in-law and eventual heir whose talents would be more satisfactory than those of his own son, Bradua. The son of Athenais was given a name that had appeared in Herodes' family: Hipparchus. Regilla did not live to see her only grandson. She herself was pregnant when she died about a year before her daughter became pregnant, gave birth, and also died.

Ti. Claudius Marcus Appius Atilius Bradua Regillus Atticus was born around 145, soon after Athenais. Neither Herodes' brother-in-law Bradua nor his son of the same name proved to be pleasing to him. As a child, Bradua could not learn to read, and his father purchased twenty-four boys to whom he gave names beginning with the letters of the alphabet to help his son learn his letters.[22] It was not difficult to assemble a group with names appropriate for the sequence. Because the parentage of slaves was not legally recognized, their names were subject to the whims of their owners and could be changed.

According to an inscription, an Atticus Herodes was an ephebe (citizen-cadet) in Sparta.[23] This could have been either Herodes' father, Atticus, Herodes himself, or his son.[24] Bradua may have been sent to Sparta, much as parents nowadays enroll recalcitrant boys in military academies. The rigorous ephebic training was a Greek tradition without a Roman parallel.[25] It apparently had no long-lasting influence on either Herodes or Bradua, for both were undisciplined and self-indulgent.

It is difficult to compare child rearing in Rome and Greece at this time or to speculate whether Regilla and Herodes had different views on the subject. The best source on both Greek and Roman education is Plutarch's *On the Education of Children*,[26] and what he says about his subjects' childhood in the *Lives*. One may wonder whether Herodes blamed Regilla for the behavior of Bradua, who was such a disappointment to him. Herodes' students and freedmen, jealous of his legitimate family and clamoring for attention and benefactions, may have slandered Bradua.[27] The boy was about fifteen when his mother was murdered, and his reaction to her death and to the accusations by his uncle and namesake Bradua may have caused an irreparable rift with his father. It may have been at this point that Herodes enrolled him as an ephebe in Sparta to get him out of the way. Since Herodes lived longer than most fathers and Bradua was the only surviving child, intergenerational strife was allowed to continue and fester.

Herodes left nothing to his son when he died. Philostratus notes that the Athenians considered this inhumane.[28] Bradua eventually inherited the substantial estate of his mother on the Appian Way; this was after Herodes had launched his building schemes that transformed Regilla's property. Others apparently considered Bradua more competent than his own father did, or perhaps his career as an adult was a natural result of his wealth and status. He was made a patrician by Antoninus Pius,[29] becoming *consul ordinarius* in 185 and Athenian *archon* in 187.[30] He also was awarded a proconsulship in one of the more desirable provinces, the conclusion to an illustrious career.[31] He may have had a reading problem, but it was not much of a disability in a society where even a highly literate man like Pliny the Younger had slaves read aloud to him. Bradua was not a benefactor on such a lavish a scale as his father; his fortune was much smaller. A gift he made to Peiraeus was commemorated, and in 209, in his old age, he was honored as herald of the Athenian Boule (a major magistrate who summoned the Council).[32] Thus within three generations the social status of Herodes' family rose from that of a new man *(novus homo)* to that of consul and then to the rank of patrician. In contrast, Regilla's venerable Roman lineage was far more ancient.

Ti. Claudius Herodes Lucius Vibullius Regillus was born around 150 and died around 155. He is known by his Roman name, Regillus, but his other names reflect his father's lineage rather than his mother's, perhaps a result of the family's longtime residence in Greece.[33] Like the son who died in Rome, Regillus predeceased his mother, but he died after he had reached an age when she must have been relieved that he had survived the hazards of infant and juvenile death. He lived long enough to be portrayed in the family sculptural group depicted on the nymphaeum (fountain) which his mother constructed at Olympia.

The sons of Regilla and Herodes, in preparation for careers in the empire, were known by names that were familiar in Rome, Bradua and Regillus, while the daughters were known by their Greek names. This naming pattern shows how ethnic identity was affected by gender. All the men in Herodes' family, from his grandfather to his two sons, bore the same praenomen, Tiberius. This was the style at the time, but obviously the name could not be used as a means of distinguishing Bradua from Regillus.[34] The formal complete names of Regilla's and Herodes' children refer more to their Roman or Romanized ancestors and connections than to their Greek heritage, an indication that the maternal line was more illustrious than the paternal.[35] The only exception is the youngest son, Regillus, whose names reflect his

Greek lineage more than his Roman, but who is nevertheless known by the masculine form of his mother's name. All of the children, like their mother, were identified in the polyonymous Roman style, which permitted the parents to honor and exploit both lineages. In contrast, the Greek style was originally just a name and a patronymic, with a Roman name added to show Roman citizenship. The influence and authority accruing from class took precedence over gender.[36] The formal name of Herodes himself contained four Latin elements and three Greek. All his children's names included Claudius or Claudia because Herodes' family had received their citizenship during the reign of Claudius or Nero. Living in Athens, Herodes called his daughters by their Greek names, Elpinice and Athenais, as does Philostratus (referring to the younger one as Panathenais).[37] Women usually were a conservative force, maintaining local ethnic, religious, and familial traditions through names given to daughters, while men were equipped with names echoing their father's and an education like their father's that would help them when they went out into the vast world of the empire.[38] In their own marriage and in many aspects of the names they chose for their children, Regilla and Herodes reversed this pattern.

The general precedent for the elaboration of names is to be found among Regilla's ancestors, not Herodes'. That the names of the daughters are as numerous as the names of the sons was the style at this time.[39] These naming patterns are consistent with a sentiment that daughters as well as sons could perpetuate the family line. Plutarch considered that it is natural for mothers to prefer sons, because sons can help them, while fathers prefer daughters, because daughters need their help.[40] This evaluation can help to explain the emotional dynamics in Regilla's and Herodes' family. Of the three children who survived to adulthood, Herodes was closer emotionally to his daughters than to his son. Their Greek names are just one indication of this connection. The Athenian populace was well aware of Herodes' favoritism, as they showed in their reaction to the death of Athenais, and when they learned that Herodes' will excluded his son. Philostratus refers to Bradua as dissolute, perhaps to justify Herodes' rejection of his only surviving natural son in favor of his foster and adopted sons.[41]

Defying mortality statistics, Herodes outlived his wife and all but one of his children. His relationship with his surviving son suggests that Bradua was not emancipated from *patria potestas,* the life-and-death power that the Roman father exercised over his familia. Like most wealthy Roman women, Regilla must have had a marriage *sine manu,* meaning that she remained part of her natal familia, headed first by her father and then by her brother, and that she was not subject to Herodes' *patria potestas.* She lived a great distance from her Roman familia, however, and her life was effectively in Herodes' hands.

Plutarch warns that the initial relationship between a new daughter-in-law and her mother-in-law will be antagonistic, and advises the bride to make an effort to gain the older woman's affection.[42] Evidently Alcia was not won over. After years of being a daughter, wife, and mother, a wealthy Greek widow could enjoy some independence. The mother of a devoted son assumed she would become the mother-in-law of a docile Greek adolescent. Greeks married close relations. Alcia herself had married a cousin. She would have expected her daughter-in-law to be already related to her or, if not, to be a daughter of one of her friends or of an important Greek of her social class. She would have conversed with her easily in Greek. Instead, her daughter-in-law was a wealthy aristocratic Roman, whose script as materfamilias did not include subservience to her mother-in-law. Regilla's presence was a constant reminder that Greece was no longer independent, but was rather a not particularly strategic or rich province of the Roman Empire. Plutarch had observed that mothers favor their sons;[43] certainly Herodes' mother supported her son's preferences. Alcia used her great wealth to commemorate Herodes' foster son Polydeucion in statues with inscriptions calling him "most beloved to [her son] Herodes and to herself [a hero]."[44] In contrast, she was silent concerning Regilla and her children.[45] Three of Alcia's grandchildren predeceased her, while Polydeucion was a more distant connection. All died young enough to evoke pity.

In addition to Regilla and her children, there were young people in the household with whom Herodes enjoyed quasi-familial relationships and who competed with Regilla's children for their father's attention and affection. These included foster sons, an adopted son, and children of his freedman Alcimedon, who played an important part in Herodes' life and was with him for most of the period after he returned permanently to Athens. Herodes' involvement with these children, who were not his biological descendants, doubtless affected his relationship with Regilla and the children she bore to him. According to Roman law, Herodes alone was the adoptive parent, since only men could adopt, and the name of the adoptee reflects the single male parent.[46] An adopted child was legally the same as a biological child and could even succeed an emperor.

Philostratus refers to Achilles, Memnon, and Polydeucion as *trophimoi* (foster sons) equal in Herodes' affections to his natural children.[47] The civic status of trophimoi varied, and not all of Herodes' trophimoi may have had the same status. "Trophimos" was used for children of slaves as well as those of higher social origin on whom a foster parent lavished special care.[48] They were the Greek equivalent of Latin *alumni* (children raised by a person not related to them). There are Greek and Roman precedents for *syntrophoi* (foster siblings) who were taken into families with existing children.[49] These were often orphaned kinsmen, but sometimes they were offspring of lower-status members of the household. Their civic status varied at birth and was subject to change during their lifetime. Among the Greeks and Romans a range of civic statuses existed between slave and free. Sparta may serve as a case in point, particularly since Herodes had special connections to Sparta. After the Peloponnesian War, when Sparta was faced with a population decline, upper-class Spartans reared lower-class children born of helot mothers (helots were slaves belonging to the state). Spartan fathers raised these children along with their own natural offspring long before the practice of incorporating unrelated children into the familia became widespread among the Romans. These children eventually enjoyed a limited form of Spartan citizenship and served in the army.[50] In contrast, there is no name change or anything else to indicate that Herodes ever improved the civic status of his trophimoi. We do not know when they joined his household. More than any other members of his household they seem frozen in time.

In addition to their position in Herodes' household, the names of Achilles and Memnon suggest slave origin. Slaves did not have any lineage of their own, and it was common in this period to give them names drawn from those of gods and heroes.[51] Since Herodes was free to call his slaves by any name, was concerned about the names of his natural children, and characteristically paid attention to detail, we must suppose that he also chose carefully in the cases of his favorites. Memnon was an obvious choice; like the Bronze Age king of Ethiopia for whom he was named, the trophimos was black, and is so depicted in sculpture.[52] (See fig. 2.4.) Achilles and Memnon were an obvious pairing, for they were the names of heroes who fought on opposing sides at Troy where Achilles, who was younger, killed Memnon. Though Achilles' mother was the nymph Thetis and Memnon's mother was the goddess Eos (Dawn), their fathers had been mortal and both heroes died at Troy. Epic poetry ensured their literary immortality. Homer's *Iliad,* the most popular literary work in the Second Sophistic, was a medley of historical fact and heroic fiction, composed some thousand years before the days of Herodes and Regilla.[53] Other popular epics, now lost, told additional tales about the Trojan War. The heroes who fought at Troy were larger than life. Achilles' extravagant mourning for Patroclus and his petulant and ferocious withdrawal from the fray supply major themes of the *Iliad.* As Herodes had advertised his alleged lineage and achievements through the names of his daughters, so did his trophimoi serve as extensions of his personality. Like Achilles, Herodes was famous for his unbridled temper, effusive mourning, and aspirations toward immortality. The Memnon of epic was renowned for his rhetorical skills.[54] All the trophimoi were fond of learning.[55] The trophimos Memnon, with his serious demeanor, represented another aspect of his master. Bronze Age kings presided over huge fluid households whose members had a wide range of statuses and included legitimate and illegitimate children and other dependents. Thus the heroes of the Greek past were an inspiration to Herodes, and he had the means to have them incarnated.

Polydeucion was Herodes' favorite trophimos. Judging from the wealth of evidence, he was the person Herodes loved more than anyone else, including his natural children. More images and commemorative inscriptions from the second century A.D. have been found in honor of Polydeucion than of any other young person not associated with the imperial family.[56] The status of Polydeucion is ambiguous, an artifact of Herodes' tendency to treat people as he wished and not according to established rules of custom and etiquette. An inscription on a herm of Polydeucion found in Kato Souli (Trikorinthos) at Marathon begins: "Polydeucion, whom Herodes loved as a son. Herodes set [this image of him] here, where they used to hunt."[57]

Polydeucion's name is more fully given as Vibullius Polydeucion, indicating that he was somehow related to the Vibullii, and thus was a Roman citizen.[58] Herodes' mother was Vibullia Alcia, and Vibullius appears in the nomenclature of Herodes and of his adopted son Lucius Vibullius Claudius Herodes, as well as in the name of Regilla's and Herodes' grandson Lucius Vibullius Hipparchus. Alcia's behavior at Polydeucion's death supports this view. He may have been freeborn, a nephew, perhaps an orphan, or a freedman of some Vibullius related to Herodes.[59]

We do not know when or how he joined the household. The special way that Herodes treated him and distinguished him from his two other foster sons by elevating him to heroic, or supra-mortal, status suggests that he was freeborn, although other clues point toward a lesser status. For example, in the inscriptions giving his name, the only indication of citizenship is his connection to the Vibulli. Furthermore, the members of the Vibulli and of Regilla's and Herodes' families have multiple names while Polydeucion has only two, or only two are known despite his extensive commemoration (see Genealogical Chart). Finally, there is the name itself. Polydeucion, "Little Polydeuces," is a diminutive of Polydeuces, not a full-fledged name that would be bestowed on a boy who was being groomed to pursue the public career expected of a Vibullius. Polydeucion, Polydeuces, and the Latin Pollux do not appear in Herodes' genealogy and are not attested as personal names in Spartan sources.[60] The name alludes to Spartan mythology. The divinities Castor and Polydeuces, brothers of Helen, were especially dear to the Spartans. Names of divinities tended to be given to slaves because slaves did not have legal, traceable parentage.[61] Philostratus calls Polydeucion by only one name, as he does Achilles and Memnon, and groups the three trophimoi together.

The civic status of Polydeucion is critical in assessing his potential role in Herodes' erotic life. Several social customs governed relationships between older and younger men, though these were not laws and Herodes was free to disregard them. It is relevant to point out that the relationship between the *erastes* (lover) and the *eromenos* (beloved) was originally aristocratic; traditionally, slaves were never eromenoi. Furthermore, trophi-

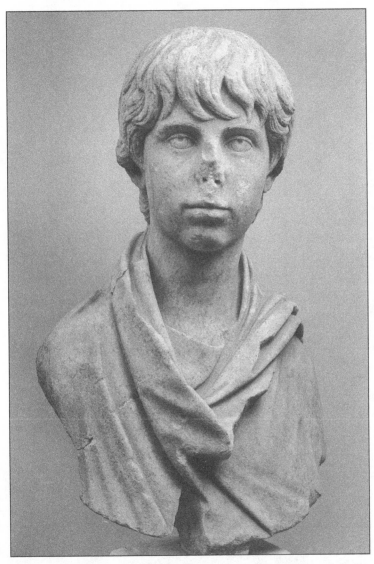

Fig. 2.1.   Portrait bust of Polydeucion. Marble bust from Herodes' villa, found in Cephisia. Polydeucion at about fifteen. This portrait of Polydeucion, emphasizing his boyish features and tousled hair, shares stylistic similarities with the portrait of Herodes in Fig. 2.2. The originals may have been placed side by side in a private portrait gallery at Herodes' estate at Marathon.

Fig. 2.2.   Portrait bust of Herodes. Classicizing marble bust from Herodes' villa, found in Cephisia with bust of Polydeucion, Fig. 2.1. Herodes at about fifty to sixty, looking like a philosopher.

moi were foster children, and there was the same fear of incest in these relationships as in blood relationships. On the other hand, foster children of slave origin were often used for sexual purposes.[62] If Polydeucion was freeborn and a kinsman, an erotic relationship, implicit or explicit, between Herodes and him would have been reprehensible, though it was characteristic of Herodes to indulge his passions and to refuse to be governed by the rules that others followed. Herodes made no attempt to conceal his affection for Polydeucion. An inscription on a herm of Polydeucion discovered at Cephisia announced:

> Hero Polydeucion
> In the past, at these forks in the road
> I turned back to look with you.[63]

Polydeucion was a handsome fellow who charmed not only Herodes, displacing his own sons in his affections, but also Herodes' mother, Alcia.[64] Judging from his portraits, Polydeucion died before the age of twenty.[65] The traditional Greek relationship between the *erastes* and *eromenos* lasted until the younger man grew a beard. Herodes did not need to acknowledge maturity in Polydeucion. He stayed young forever and remained "dear little Polydeucion." Gellius refers to him as a "boy" *(puer)*.[66]

Hadrian's favorite, Antinous, was the archetype of the beloved younger man who died in his youth.[67] Contemporaries variously attributed Antinous' death by drowning in the Nile to voluntary or involuntary sacrifice. Hadrian's amorous relationship with Antinous was no secret. He would go out hunting with him, as Herodes did a little later with his foster sons. The emperor's extravagant mourning and commemoration of the youth made his affection even more public. Whatever the truth about Antinous' death, his early demise and commemoration became a model for Polydeucion's.[68] Whether Polydeucion's early death was an accident or a homicide,[69] by dying "before his time" he retained his youthful bloom.[70] It is possible to assert that the re-

lationship between Herodes and Polydeucion was similar to that
between Hadrian and Antinous. This interpretation is supported
by then evidence of Herodes' excessive mourning for the younger man, the artistic representations, and poems like the ones
mentioned. Though it is difficult to determine the truth about
any erotic experience in the past, and the evidence is not conclu-
sive, it does point in that direction. Herodes was a major figure
in the Second Sophistic, endeavoring to revive the period of the
first Sophists. Philostratus is interested in him as a public figure,
and gives relatively little information on his private life.[71] Nevertheless, a well-known characteristic of the aristocracy of that period was the erotic relationship between an older and younger
man. The relationship had its advocates at the time: a speaker in
Plutarch's *Eroticus*[72] argues for the superiority of the relationship
between two males in much the same way as a speaker in Plato's
Symposium had done in the classical period. Socrates had also set
a precedent just before his death when he dismissed his biological children from his prison cell and addressed Phaedo and
other disciples in the terms of intimacy and affection normally
reserved for kin.[73] But in displacing his biological children in favor of his spiritual progeny, Herodes went counter to the prevailing view of the Romans, including Stoics and others, who
viewed the bonds between parents and children as normal and
natural.

Sculptures portray the foster sons as clearly differentiated.
Memnon, who was older than the other two or perhaps lived
longer, was portrayed with a full beard, a mark of a mature,
learned man.[74] Herodes likewise was bearded like philosophers
and orators of the glorious Greek past.[75] The trophimos Achilles, in contrast to Memnon, had thick tousled hair.[76] The epic
hero Achilles, however, was no simple warrior: his tutor Cheiron
had taught him the arts, and he was skilled at playing the lyre.

The names and appearances of the trophimoi suggest (though
of course cannot prove) that they staged displays of martial

Fig. 2.3.   Achilles. Youth from Cephisia, nude except for a short cape worn for the hunt *(chlamys)* draped across the top of his chest and hanging down his back. The nudity harks back to the heroic nudity of earlier Greek sculpture. A cauliflower ear marks him as an athlete.

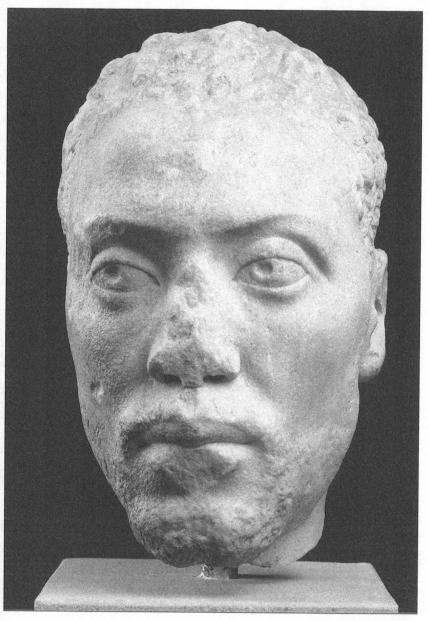

Fig. 2.4.   Memnon. Negroid head in classicizing style, from Herodes' villa at Loukou.

arts, hunting skills, and other entertainments for their master. Herodes and others had already imagined that they were living in the fifth century B.C.[77] Why not the Bronze Age for diversion? A Caucasian fighting an Ethiopian, one contestant from north of the Mediterranean, his opponent from the south, a youth against a mature warrior, was in tune with the taste of the time, when popular gladiatorial combats matched contestants from various corners of the empire armed with exotic weapons from their native lands. When not involved himself, Herodes could enjoy the private pleasure of a voyeur watching the younger men.

The nurturing, affectionate, and sometimes unmistakably erotic relationship between the legendary Achilles and Patroclus, his older and wiser friend, could well have been a model for the relationship between Herodes and his foster sons.[78] Though Patroclus was usually considered older, the warriors were nearly contemporaries. Thus both Herodes and the trophimos Memnon are bearded. The hero Achilles was famous for his skill at hunting;[79] accordingly the trophimos Achilles is portrayed as a hunter. Wild animals ranged naturally over Herodes' country estates, and gamekeepers were employed to make certain that the hunt was always successful. Hunting is also a metaphor for the pursuit of the loved one. Evidence of this usage in the Greek world is plentiful. Thus, for example, in the sixth century B.C. Sappho wrote of her unrequited desire for a girl: "if she flees, soon she will pursue."[80] Hunting was an occasion for erotic pursuit at Sparta.[81] Images of male homoerotic courtship on Athenian pottery beginning in the archaic period often allude to the hunt, with the older bearded lover *(erastes)* presenting a small animal such as a hare to his beloved *(eromenos)*.[82] The recipient is thus effeminized, becoming like a woman who is expected to nurture the young animal and be passive in intercourse, while the donor is active. Furthermore, gifts must be exchanged. What must the younger man give to the older in return? Achilles and Memnon were subordinate to Herodes in social status, and dependent upon him. There can be no doubt that they acquiesced to his desires, whatever they were. Eros, who was known as Cupid to the Romans, is a hunter armed with bow and arrows. In Rome, however, he regularly employs his arrows for heterosexual purposes.

Herodes' attachment to his trophimoi was not a secret, for he himself made it public. It was known in Greece and Italy. Several critics, both Greek and Roman, were sufficiently incensed to deride his relationship with the younger men. The Quintilii brothers sneered at Herodes from their lofty neighboring villa on the Via Appia for doting on his minions and advertising his emotional involvement through statuary.[83] In Greece a visitor had criticized Herodes for histrionics of grief at the death of Polydeucion. His excessive lamentation for a youth who was not even a member of his immediate family was inappropriate for a person of his stature and class. Herodes responded with a speech condemning the *apatheia* (lack of emotion or freedom from passion) of the Stoics.[84]

Apatheia was a common topic of philosophical discussion. Adherents of Aristotelian philosophy advocated *metriopatheia* (moderating the passions), while the Epicureans eschewed activities, involvements, or feelings that would upset them and impair their ideal of peace and calm *(ataraxia)*. In arguing against *apatheia,* Herodes was probably reacting personally, rather than declaiming as an adherent of a philosophical school. In the same way, Herodes' lack of concern at being seen to ignore the Stoic maxim that the love of man and wife was the highest form of love was probably mere self-indulgence rather than a reasoned choice.[85] Stoicism was by far the most popular philosophy of the day. Marcus Aurelius and some other members of the ruling class advocated and practiced Stoicism in the face of personal adversity. Stoics believed that a good person could not experience any real evil. Excessive displays of emotion were not suited to a Sophist or to most philosophers. Seneca believed that philosophical study would ameliorate grief, and in any case grief was considered womanish.[86] Nevertheless, Herodes' personality remained consistent in old age and he indulged in public lamentation at the successive deaths of members of his *familia*.

Herodes' extravagant grief at the death of Polydeucion was famous, if not notorious. Not only did he show his emotions through the cult images of the heroized youth, but also the satirist Lucian mocked him in a dialogue between Herodes and Demonax, an Athenian Cynic.[87] Demonax points out how ridiculous the infatuated Herodes is for making horses, carriages, and dinners available to his dead favorite. A commemorative relief dedicated at the sanctuary of Artemis at Brauron depicts Polydeucion on a couch with a horse in attendance.[88] Lucian was less concerned about Herodes' mourning for Regilla and for his biological children, because there was no reason to criticize him in that area.[89] Others disdained Herodes' attachment to his minions, for the statues were vandalized, despite their location on his private estates. Herodes usually added inscriptions cursing anyone who harmed the statues, but to no avail.[90]

Connubial Arrangements

Herodes probably engaged in erotic connections with men before he married, but Regilla may well have expected him to give up serious extramarital attachments, especially when he became a father. The move to Greece, however, dashed any such hopes. Attitudes in Greece toward homosexuality had always been more lenient than those in Rome, and Herodes freely indulged his inclinations in Greece more than before. Perhaps this was one of the incentives for his return to his native land. Furthermore, he was older, a mature man with a large family of children. Some critics found the idea of a man who was in his fifties cavorting with adolescents and desperately in love with them scandalous, even though the emperor Hadrian had behaved in similar fashion.

We do not have any primary sources written by women on this subject, or any trustworthy sources giving the reactions of Greek or Roman wives to their husband's homosexual involvements.[91] Male authors report that Roman wives generally tolerated their husband's forays in the slave quarters, and that the master took advantage of his freedom to have intercourse with slaves of both sexes. Perhaps Regilla was pleased that her husband had other interests and that he did not seek her company too often. Yet a wife was also demeaned if her husband's public image was ridiculous. Moreover, by making his trophimoi substitutes for his legitimate family, Herodes went far beyond the limits approved by both Greeks and Romans for homosexual and extramarital liaisons.

Herodes' emotional involvement with his trophimoi had repercussions for his wife and her children. Both he and his mother commemorated Polydeucion more than any of Regilla's children. Inasmuch as we are uncertain about the date of Polydeucion's death, we do not know whether Regilla was alive to observe this favoritism.[92] As Bradua grew up, his dead foster brother was idealized, and his talents magnified to a degree unattainable by any mortal. After Regilla and Polydeucion died, Herodes treated them as though they had been equals. His preferences were displayed permanently. He built shrines (heroa) for Regilla and for Polydeucion in Cephisia, and gave them both funeral banquets, thus elevating his foster son to the same heroic status as his wife.[93] He did not heroize any of his natural children, though four of them predeceased him. Herodes disregarded the traditional hierarchy prevailing in the Greek and Roman family that unambiguously situated the wife and legitimate children above freedmen and slaves.

Though Herodes could order his foster sons to impersonate Achilles and Memnon, and though he himself might choose to imitate Achilles' friend and lover, Patroclus, it is difficult to see what role Regilla and her children could have played in this charade. It is fair to say that respectable women in Greek epic were normally confined to child production and household management, though some women stepped out of line, either forced by circumstances or led by their own inclination.[94] Hellenistic history, in contrast, offered more possible role models for respectable upper-class women. Queens such as Phila, who established a charitable foundation for dowerless girls; Arsinöe II, patron of the poet Theocritus; learned Neopythagorean women, and others who endowed their cities with major monuments would have been more comfortable models for Regilla than epic heroines.[95] Hellenistic literature, however, was not fashionable in the Second Sophistic, which preferred to look back to an earlier period, the time of the first Sophists or philosophers.[96] For example, as is obvious from Herodes' purported lineage, alleged ancestors of the classical period were emphasized at the expense of their Hellenistic successors.

Herodes' foster sons were part of Regilla's life the entire time she lived in Greece. The date of Polydeucion's death is controversial, but Achilles and Memnon apparently died in the 160s after Regilla.[97] Commemorative inscriptions and images of the trophimoi have been discovered at sites associated with Herodes' villas and activities.[98] Regilla and her children could not avoid contact with Herodes' extended familia. The ubiquity of their images suggests that the trophimoi themselves were present in all these places. Sculptures commemorating Polydeucion are widespread in public, well-frequented areas of Greece.[99]

Polydeucion was Herodes' heir apparent, so to speak, but it is not likely that Herodes adopted him formally. This is another example of Herodes' disregarding traditional categories and treating people according to his own wishes. On the one hand, that Herodes claimed to love Polydeucion "as a son" would seem to indicate that he was not actually an adopted son. Indeed, why would he adopt from outside the family as long as Regilla was still of child-bearing age? On the other hand, though Polydeucion's lower-class origin would seem to preclude this, if he was adopted by a man of senatorial rank, his status became high. Thus Polydeucion is the first Athenian citizen known to have been elevated to the status of Roman eques (knight, ranked just below senator).[100] Following in Herodes' footsteps, he became an Athenian benefactor, and he displayed his philanthropy and patriotic generosity (evergetism) in a concern for the public baths.[101] Herodes not only raised Polydeucion according to his ideals; he also influenced our view of his foster sons even more definitively than he did our view of his wife.

Herodes married not only in order to have children but also to create a dynasty. Polydeucion probably died in 147 or 148.[102] Bradua Atticus was then a toddler of about two or three and Herodes pinned his hopes on him, only to be disappointed when his own son did not display the gifts of the dead Polydeucion. When he judged his surviving son by Regilla to be inadequate, he sought another heir. Like some of the emperors he knew who had adopted heirs, whether or not they had children of their own, he chose a successor who was mature enough to show his potential as an adult. Furthermore, an adopted child was a dependent, and feelings of gratitude and lack of other kin were likely to make him more obedient than a natural child. Herodes adopted a relative from the Vibulli named Lucius Vibullius, who was thenceforth known as Lucius Vibullius Claudius Herodes.[103] His father was probably Alcia's uncle, the man who married Athenais. Whether Regilla was still alive when Herodes adopted this Vibullius is unclear, since there is no evidence for the date of the inscription recording the adoption.[104]

A Married Couple

The status of Roman women was different from that of Greek women. However, Regilla's future husband, Herodes, who was a

Greek philosopher, surely embraced many of the ideas that had been set forth by other Greek philosophers. Besides, a young bride was malleable. As Xenophon had written in the fourth century B.C. in his *Oeconomicus,* the bridegroom could instruct his wife and mold her to comply with his ideas about women.

Because women married at a much younger age than men, they had fewer years in which to complete their education. For some upper-class women, formal intellectual education continued after marriage. A few came to be regarded as pedants, but not many. Regilla knew some of them or knew about them because they drew attention to themselves, writing poetry, quoting Homer and Vergil, and even debating literary topics with men.[105] But few women would wrangle with a scholar like Herodes: indeed, few men would dare to discuss literature with him. Pliny the Younger[106] and Plutarch were proud that they took on the responsibility of teaching their wives, and in his treatise *Advice to the Bride and Groom,* Plutarch advised a bridegroom to do the same.[107] Certainly Regilla could read the papyrus rolls in the libraries in Herodes' villas, or her slaves could read them aloud to her while she relaxed. But Herodes' interests and writings indicate that his collections were mostly of Greek classics and ancient and current philosophy and rhetoric, dry as dust. Nevertheless, for the sake of completeness he may have purchased copies of novels and of interesting writers like Plutarch. Back in Rome, Regilla's old friends were reading Latin poetry and novels packed with adventure and love. Some authors, especially those who wrote about love, considered that they were writing for a mostly female audience.[108] When Regilla moved to Greece, she could have had the latest literature sent to her from Rome.

Much education could take place in a social context. When Roman women dined with their husbands, they participated in the conversation and watched the entertainments that included concerts and poetry recitations. Whether it was normal for upper-class women to dine with their husbands in Greece at that time and whether Regilla dined with Herodes when he entertained learned guests is less clear. If Herodes was hosting a classical-style symposium, possibly with homosexual activity, certainly she would not have been present. Even in Rome, a husband did not always dine with his wife and children, though quite often he chose to dine with other men while remaining in his own home.[109] Nevertheless, Roman women were not raised to be secluded, and Greek women in Roman Greece joined their husbands and their friends.[110] That Plutarch finds it necessary to advocate that husband and wife dine together (to prevent the wife from indulging in gluttony) suggests that some married couples did not do so. Aulus Gellius, who spent some weeks at the suburban home of Herodes and Regilla in Cephisia, did not mention his hostess. Thus we may assume that he did not meet her, even at meals, or that she did not take part in the conversation, or that for reasons of etiquette he did not write about her, or that she may not have been present in Cephisia when Gellius was her husband's guest.

However, it would not have been customary for Regilla to be formally excluded from all the social and intellectual gatherings of men at her homes. An upper-class wife could listen in and participate in what was still essentially a man's world if she heard anything going on of interest to her. On the other hand, whether she could actually converse freely with men who were not members of the familia if her husband was not present is debatable. In Rome, she could have. In Greece, however, according to Plutarch, a wife could be present with her husband at gatherings with their friends, but should talk only to him or through him.[111] Like a tortoise, she should stay in her house and be quiet. Plutarch does not speak directly of romantic love, but his *Advice to the Bride and Groom* stresses the importance of sexual harmony and mutual respect.[112] Nevertheless, marriage is not a partnership of equals. The wife must accommodate herself to her husband's wishes and moods. Here, in the case of Regilla and Herodes, gender hierarchy conflicted with ethnic hierarchy, for Romans ruled the empire, and Greeks, despite their cultural ascendancy, were a subject people. Though Regilla and Herodes were both private citizens and Roman citizens, their marriage may, in some respects, be compared to a dynastic marriage, joining east and west. As usual, the woman served as the link between the two parties. In Athens the oikos (household, family, or estate) was a microcosm of the polis (city-state). Herodes' fellow citizens perceived him to be aiming at a tyranny in Athens; we have little doubt that he reigned as a tyrant at home.

Homes

Regilla would not have found Herodes' homes in Greece especially foreign. Some characteristics typical of the Roman house, however, were missing: the atrium, a central hallway with an impluvium to catch rainwater, and the *imagines* (wax portrait busts). Instead, an array of marble portrait busts doubtless was displayed in a long hall.[113] Though there are few extant examples, and even fewer that have been well studied, in Roman Greece houses were more open to the public and women less restricted within them than in the classical period.[114] In one house from the early period of Roman Athens, the courtyard was no longer devoted to domestic chores like cooking, but rather to a peristyle with pool and garden.[115] An abundance of water was a feature of Roman improvements in old cities. Hadrian had undertaken the construction of a new aqueduct in Athens to supplement those built in the sixth and fourth centuries B.C., and Antoninus Pius had completed it in 140.[116] The decor was familiar enough, for Roman houses had long displayed Greek sculpture, and versions of Greek myths were painted on their walls and depicted in mosaic. The market in marble was international; Herodes, however, favored local Greek marble, especially the creamy white quarried from nearby Mount Pentelicon.

Preliminary excavations at Herodes' huge estate in Loukou in the Peloponnese do not give much evidence for Regilla and her children.[117] The sculpture and inscriptions there, however, do testify to Herodes' involvement with his trophimoi, for though the villa was luxurious, it was probably a hunting lodge.[118] The representations of women are pretty much limited to imperial and mythological females. The suburban homes at Cephisia and Marathon have proven more fertile for family history, and there is little doubt that Regilla spent time there. The possession of many properties in Greece, with some apparently devoted to masculine pursuits, raises the possibility that Regilla and Herodes spent time apart.

Herodes, with his penchant for conspicuous consumption, did not restrict his homes to his family and familia. For example, in 147 Aulus Gellius and a young Stoic philosopher were visiting the villa at Cephisia at the same time.[119] Gellius, who was recuperating from an illness, describes the property as full of groves, singing birds, and clear water even in the summer and autumn heat. He mentions the long soft paths, the elegant baths, the cool site, and the delightful villa. The author was wealthy himself, though not in the same class as Herodes. He was not a needy philosopher accepting largesse from a wealthy patron and responding with grateful admiration. Gellius was writing literature, not journalism, painting a verbal image of a lovely place.[120] Although a sweet family would have suited the picture, Gellius does not mention seeing a bustling wife and fertile mother or hearing the chirping of a brood of children. Perhaps Regilla was in Cephisia when Gellius was at the villa and he simply did not mention her. But it was also possible for her to leave the city during the summers; for example, she had to

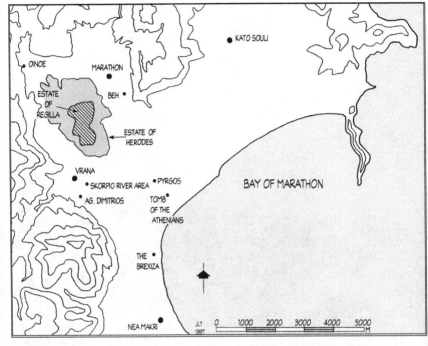

Fig. 2.5.   Ground plan of the estate of Herodes and Regilla at Marathon. The dark gray portion is the part of the estate retained by Herodes. The diagonal lines indicate Regilla's portion.

work as a priestess in Olympia during the hottest part of the year, around the season of Gellius' visit, but this occurred about a decade after his recorded sojourn.

Herodes was born at Marathon and wanted to be buried there. His lineage associated him with this deme (township), famous as the site of a crucial battle in the Persian War (490 B.C.). The local cult of the victorious general Miltiades, whom Herodes claimed as an ancestor, was centered there.[121] Herodes had inherited or built a villa at Marathon before he got married, and lived there with Regilla. His estate was huge, and he shared it with his bride, thus associating her with a glorious moment in

Fig. 2.6.   Wall of Regilla's estate at Marathon. The rugged, rocky terrain is suitable only for pasturing sheep and goats.

Greek history that she may have read about in such authors as Herodotus and Plutarch.

Roman law, including the Lex Cincia, forbade gifts between husband and wife, but it was not uncommon for husbands to give wives property such as farms.[122] Perhaps Regilla purchased the land from Herodes, or traded some property in Italy for her estate at Marathon. Or perhaps no one disputed the transfer. In any case, small gifts were permitted, and considering the size of Herodes' wealth, Regilla's fraction of his estate at Marathon was a trivial gift.

A large and imposing entrance gateway seems to have been part of a three-mile rubble wall surrounding the property.[123] Because the keystone of the gateway has fallen, the direction it faced is not absolutely clear, but archaeologists believe that the enclosed portion of the estate was Regilla's. The way that her property was carved out within the larger estate indicates that it was intended as an impermanent possession that would never be sold off, but would eventually be reunited with the estate on its borders. Regilla's part is surrounded by Herodes' portion in a manner reminiscent of the isolation and encapsulation of women in the women's quarters *(gynaeceum)* in the classical period (fig. 2.5). Her part of the estate was barren and inhospitable (fig. 2.6).[124] Sheep and goats might graze there as they doubtless did at Regilla's family property in Canosa and at their estate on the Via Appia, and still do at the archaeological park of the Caffarella that has replaced it.[125] Such flocks might well be part of a serious effort at pasturalism or might constitute props for an idyll featuring Regilla as a shepherdess. Cultivated rusticity was popular among the jaded elite.

No other example of such a separation of adjacent estates between a husband and wife dating to this period has been found. It was contrary to the marital ideal of community of property and resources proclaimed by philosophers, including Stoics and Plutarch. Thus Plutarch advised that the bride and groom "should pour everything into one fund, mix it all together, and not think of one part as belonging to one and another to the other, but of the whole as their own."[126]

Nevertheless, the entrance gate, known as the "Gate of Eternal Harmony," flaunts the divided ownership of the estates. This is all the more obvious since the property was not part of Regilla's dowry and did not need to be kept separate in case of divorce. On one side of the gate was inscribed: "The place you enter belongs to Herodes." On the other side was written: "The place you enter belongs to Regilla."[127] These inscriptions are pretentious, for they echo those on the Arch of Hadrian at Athens, which is also inscribed on both sides.[128] The side facing the Acropolis states: "This is Athens, the ancient city of Theseus," and the side facing the temple of Olympian Zeus reads: "This is the city of Hadrian and not of Theseus."

The villa has not yet been found, but the gate, walls, inscriptions, statuary, and legends bear witness to Herodes' and Regilla's presence. Strangely enough, there is no evidence at Marathon for their children, but abundant testimony to the trophimoi with whom Herodes used to hunt at the estate.[129] Hunting was a traditional hobby of the elite: in this Herodes behaved like an old-fashioned *kalos k'agathos* (gentleman). Statues of his foster sons in various phases of hunting, and on portrait busts with phalluses on stelae with inscriptions known as herms, were ubiquitous on Herodes' property. They have also been found at Cephisia, Souli, Bei, and Ninoi (presumably from the Marathon estate), at Masi and Varnava in Northern Attica, at Loukou in Cynouria in the Peloponnese, and at Tragounera in Euboea.[130] If the statues and herms had been erected before Regilla died, she could not have avoided looking at them. If they were placed there after Regilla's death, or not on her part of the property until after her death, then she would not have been obliged to encounter effigies of Herodes' boyfriends, at least not on her walks at Marathon.

Fig. 2.7.   Inscription from the Gate of Eternal Harmony.

The site was not so remote and abandoned as it now appears. Even in Plutarch's time, the Athenians still celebrated their victory at Marathon annually,[131] providing an opportunity for mobs of exuberant celebrants to try to trespass on Herodes' property. Farmers and their wives eking out a living in the harsh soil of Marathon could not fail to notice the property of Herodes and Regilla in their midst, for it was huge and ostentatious. Hundreds of slaves worked on the estate, but in emergencies some of the neighbors could also be paid by the day to work there. The neighbors were envious. They knew that the cost of the decorative sculpture alone could maintain the families in the neighborhood for generations. The pet sheep and goats within the enclosure made their mouths water. The sculptures of the trophimoi, appearing arrogant and expensive, were provocative, attractive to vandals, and vulnerable to mutilation. Herodes added curse

Fig. 2.8.   Seated female figure dressed in a thin chiton from the Gate of Eternal Harmony.

tablets to ward off depredations. Judging from the condition of the monuments, Herodes' curses were not effective. The observer nowadays may deduce that people did not obey him, nor did the gods support him.

The Gate of Eternal Harmony with its fragmented sculpture remained as a poignant testimony to a marriage destroyed by disharmony. Tradition at Marathon and Athens preserved a legend about Regilla. The local inhabitants interpreted the trajectory of Regilla's life in terms of a Greek tragedy: a woman whose excessive good fortune leads to hubris and death in a violent catastrophe, murdered by a close relative.

When Regilla died, she was about thirty-five years old. Though many women lived well past their mid-thirties, it was not unusual to die by forty.[132] She missed becoming a grandmother by barely a year. When she died, though she was pregnant, she was old by ancient demographic standards. In the modern western world she would have looked like an old woman. Exposure to the Greek sun while fulfilling her duties at Olympia and elsewhere was not kind to a woman's complexion. Teeth fell out and were not replaced. At least six known pregnancies in barely twenty years under what we would call "third world" conditions were detrimental to Regilla's general health. Unlimited wealth could not make Regilla young again.

A traveler who saw the estate of Regilla and Herodes at Marathon early in May 1676 wrote:

> In the vale, which we entered, near the vestiges of a
> small building, probably a sepulcher, was a headless
> statue of a woman sedent, lying on the ground. This,
> my companions informed me, was once endued [*sic*]
> with life, being an aged lady possessed of a numerous
> flock, which was folded near that spot. Her riches were
> great, and her prosperity uninterrupted. She was elated
> by her good fortune. The winter was gone by, and even

the rude month of March had spared her sheep and goats. She now defied Heaven, as unapprehensive for the future, and as secure from all mishap. But Providence, to correct her impiety and ingratitude, commanded a fierce and penetrating frost to be its avenging minister; and she, her fold, and flocks were hardened into stone. This story, which is current, was also related to me at Athens . . . I was assured that the rocky crags afford at a certain point of view the similitude of sheep and goats within an enclosure or fold.[133]

CHAPTER 3

PUBLIC LIFE

IN ADDITION TO THE members of Regilla's household, other elite women in Athens were available for social gatherings. As was true elsewhere, Athenian society was structured in an economic pyramid, with a few very wealthy families at the top.[1] Like Regilla, the women in these families owned landed estates.[2] Often they shared ownership with men who were relatives, but in some cases they were the sole owners of pieces of real estate and were themselves responsible for charges levied on their property.

The responsibilities of ownership were considerable. The parcels of land were not always contiguous and required the owner or her delegate to travel from one location to another and make special arrangements for each plot. The names of most of the women indicate that they were Roman citizens but, unlike Regilla, they were probably born in Greece to Greek families who had held Roman citizenship no more than a few generations. The men in these families of the provincial elite learned to speak and read Latin so that they might advance in their public careers. They also, like Plutarch, may have visited Rome, but gender was definitely a determinant of assimilation and acculturation.[3]

There were not the same incentives for Greek girls to learn Latin: they were not groomed to make their way in public life beyond local religious venues or panhellenic sanctuaries.[4] Because of the separation of the sexes, they learned more from their mothers than from their fathers. Thus gendered traditions were perpetuated. Though Regilla could speak to the Athenian women easily in Greek, they probably could not converse with her in Latin, and they were less likely than their brothers to have visited Rome. Like Regilla, the Greek women had some education and had read the same Greek classics. They probably had not read any Latin literature; indeed, few of their husbands had. Rather than choosing to do so freely, being obliged to speak Greek, if she wanted to be understood, and to discuss Greek culture with Herodes' female relatives and other women meant that Regilla had to relinquish some of her ethnic identity and prestige as a representative of the highest level of the ruling class.[5]

The use of Latin in a Greek setting by bilingual speakers is associated with Roman imperial power. When Regilla was forced to speak Greek, not only did she join the world of women, but she abandoned the world of the rulers and joined those who were ruled. None of the other women in town was nearly so wealthy as Regilla or so high on the social ladder. Nor were there many permanent residents on her level who had been born in Rome.

In coming to Greece, Regilla was not a pioneer. Roman women had come for brief periods as visitors, as sightseers, and as wives of administrators. Beginning with the civil wars of the first century B.C., Roman wives often traveled with their husbands outside Italy. Celebrities who had come to Greece long before Regilla included Caecilia Metella, who went to Athens to be with Sulla, and Octavia, sister of Augustus, who joined Mark Antony in Athens.[6] During the Perusine Wars of 41–40 B.C., Livia (who later married Augustus) sought refuge in Sparta with Tiberius Claudius Nero and their baby (the future emperor Tiberius).[7]

Under Tiberius, Roman wives were officially permitted to accompany their husbands to the provinces for the term of their governorship, and their presence was often commemorated by the host province with awards of various public honors and sculpture.[8] These sojourns away from Rome generally lasted a year or two, or less. For an upper-class Roman like Julia and the younger Julia (daughter and granddaughter of Augustus), or like Seneca and Ovid who had been involved in political and court life, however, moving to a province permanently and not living in Rome was a fate usually regarded as dire and it was considered a severe punishment, though one might be exiled to a worse place than Athens.

In the decade immediately preceding Regilla's arrival in Greece, Julia Balbilla, a Seleucid princess who was living in Rome and who was a companion of Hadrian's wife Sabina, had come to Greece for an extended visit.[9] Another member of Sabina's court, the Athenian Claudia Damo Synamate, may still have been alive when Regilla came to Athens, as her name appears on an inscription that has been dated to between A.D. 124/125 and 140 or 150.[10] The inscription records a list of women and men who own land and are being assessed for taxes or some other purpose. Twenty-one of the fifty-two landowners listed are women. Damo's assessment is among the lowest, either a true index of the value of her property, or because she was known to enjoy the favor of the imperial court and had brought glory to Athens.

Regilla may have remembered seeing Damo and Julia Balbilla at court when she was growing up in Rome. If they met in Athens, surely Regilla and Damo would have had much to talk about and could easily start a conversation by asking: "Do you know so-and-so?" or "Do you remember when?" Like Balbilla, Damo had written Greek poetry which was inscribed on the northern Colossus of Memnon that had been erected by Amenhotep (Amenophis III, whose rule spanned the end of the fifteenth century and the first quarter of the fourteenth century B.C.) and was a tourist destination for the Romans.[11] Damo's poem is inscribed above Balbilla's on the left leg. This proximity suggests that Balbilla and Damo, like some 5,000 others, had accompanied Hadrian and Sabina on their tour of Egypt in A.D. 130. That the two women were permitted to have their works inscribed on this venerable monument on which there are a total of 107 inscriptions is indicative of their high status.[12] Damo is the only Athenian woman poet whose work is extant. Like Balbilla, she wrote in the archaic Aeolic dialect used by Sappho. Damo mentions the barbitos, an archaic lyre no longer in common use in her day, but perhaps restored for artists interested in reviving early music to the accompaniment of authentic instruments. In this conspicuous location she wrote in elegiac couplets and identifies herself by name as a lyric poet. Her brief poem is about speech and sound. The Colossus was famous for making a sound at daybreak that was thought to be the voice of Memnon. Philostratus uses the word *phthegxasthai* to describe it.[13] This verb is from *phtheggomai* (pronounced "phthengomai"), an onomatopoeic word which sounds like the twang of a string of a lyre. Damo then writes of the sound of her poetry: "Hail, son of Dawn. You spoke to me favorably, Memnon, for the sake of the Muses, to whom I am dear—Damo lover of song. My barbitos has come to my aid and sung always of your power, holy one."[14]

Athens was a major center of culture and tourism, and it was the capital of the league of Greek cities known as the Panhellenion. Regilla would have been able to socialize with visiting Romans and provincials (if she cared to and if Herodes permitted this) in Athens and in other well-frequented sites like Olympia, where Greeks exaggerated, indeed showed off, their Greekness to the Roman conquerors. Hadrian and his successors as well as Herodes himself expended a great deal of effort and money in beautifying Athens, reconstructing features of the classical city, and turning it into an attractive destination for tourists. Indeed, Regilla arrived in an Athens less splendid than the Athens of her death. These improvements were largely due to Herodes' efforts. Like the Antonine emperors, Herodes was extremely energetic, fostering building projects not only in Athens but elsewhere in Greece, traveling to these sites while continuing to teach and entertain guests at his villas. Furthermore, Athens was a university center, a place where philosophers, Sophists, and their students gathered. Some of them visited Herodes at home, but whether Regilla came to know these men is questionable.

Public Activities

In addition to shouldering the paramount duty of child bearing and managing several households like other upper-class Greek and Roman wives, Regilla served as an agent and instrument of her husband's euergetism (benefactions, philanthropy) and conspicuous consumption. Unlike most other women, however, she herself became a generous benefactor and sponsored major architectural projects displaying images of her family and herself.

Though commanding great resources of wealth and owning slaves expert in every aspect of the female toilette, child care, and household management, upper-class women were not expected merely to lead a life of leisure.[15] These women had civic and private obligations, and if they behaved in a responsible fashion, they were busy filling them. Augustus had supported the revival of women-oriented cults of the middle and late Republic, and later emperors, including Hadrian, promoted the restoration of archaic and arcane cults and religious sites that had long been neglected.[16] Scholars and amateur pedants scrutinized their past in an attempt to create an authentic reenactment of earlier rituals. Many fertility cults were based on analogies between the fertility of the human female and the fertility of the earth. Furthermore, for the sake of modesty at the very least, priestesses and other female attendants were required to bathe and dress the images of goddesses. Wealthy women, though they were few, were encouraged to serve as priestesses for the many cults that needed them, for only they had sufficient funds to comply with the requirements of the offices.

At Athens many of the major priesthoods were reserved for women descended from a few families. By this time, because of the dearth of qualified candidates, descent could be traced through the male or female line, but the situation was not desperate enough to recruit outsiders. Regilla's aristocratic Roman lineage, which provided profitable connections for her husband, disqualified her from holding many priestly offices in Greece that would have been appropriate for the wife of a man like Herodes. Some posts were traditionally reserved for descendents of particular Greek clans. For example, a position at Eleusis, a suburb of Athens, would have been convenient, especially for a mother of young children. The Mysteries of Demeter and Kore attracted droves of initiates bringing large revenues to the cult, to Athens itself, and to the priestesses. Regilla was excluded from serving as a priestess at Eleusis because she lacked the requisite Greek lineage, though two of her children, Elpinice and Bradua, are known to have held the office of Hearth Initiate there, both around 150.[17] Though Regilla could not have an important presence in Eleusis during her lifetime, after she died Herodes claimed attention for her and advertised his piety by dedicating her clothing and erecting a monument to her there.

Male members of the senatorial class were likely to hold not only governmental but also sacerdotal posts.[18] Depending upon the wishes of the various emperors, such participation in the public sphere was at least encouraged, if not demanded. As a woman of the senatorial class, Regilla was expected to fill some priestly office even though her circumstances as a Roman woman permanently in Greece were anomalous. Holding religious office usually involved substantial expenditures, but money, of course, was not a problem for Regilla and Herodes, and it served to open some doors. Olympia had a history of being flexible in the face of wealth and political power. Although the Olympic games were closed to non-Greeks, in the fourth century B.C. the Macedonian Philip II, father of Alexander the Great, had been permitted to compete.[19] Nero also was admitted.

Herodes was able to find Regilla a suitable religious post at Olympia by showering the sanctuary with gifts, as he had more locally at Athens by founding a new cult. In return for the honors bestowed on Regilla by various communities, including the Eleans (who controlled Olympia) and the Corinthians, Herodes and Regilla donated expensive and useful monuments at Olympia and Corinth. Many of these structures are so substantial that they have survived fairly well to the present. The citizens of Elis were richly compensated for the honor they had conferred on Regilla. Pausanias mentions that Herodes replaced the old images of Kore and Demeter which had been in the temple with ones made of Pentelic marble, and he may have donated the marble altar too.[20] Inscriptions tie these gifts firmly to Herodes and his family. If Herodes had not married Regilla and produced legitimate children, he would not have had these human counters to play in his role of honored grandee and community benefactor. Religion was the only sphere in which Regilla, like centuries of respectable women in Greece before her, could play a public role, and personal resources allowed her as well to become an honored grandee and community benefactor.

Priestess of Demeter Chamyne

Though a Roman, Regilla was chosen to serve as priestess for at least two major cults in Greece. The Eleans honored her by selecting her to serve as priestess of Demeter Chamyne. The epithet "Chamyne" alludes to Demeter's connection with the earth, the ground, and the underworld, and indicates that the cult was chthonian (under the earth or pertaining to the under-world).[21] Pausanias gives two etymologies.[22] According to his first, the earth opened *(chanein)* for the chariot of Hades and then closed.[23] According to his second hypothesis, Chamynus was the name of a man who had plotted a rebellion against Elis. When he was executed, his property was used to build the sanctuary to Demeter. According to another interpretation, the epithet is derived from *chamai,* referring to the ground or earth.[24] The woman holding this priesthood responsibly was obliged to understand and execute esoteric and antiquated rituals. Doubtless she had a staff of experts who were ready to prompt her if needed. In this capacity she was the only adult woman permitted to view the ancient Olympics, and one of the few ever to look at nude athletes.[25] Athletes were nude for many Olympic events. As a girl in Rome, however, Regilla had seen plenty of naked men who had been condemned or were performing voluntarily in violent spectacles at arenas like the Colosseum.[26]

Regilla sat in a prime location where she could see the most exciting games in classical antiquity, and be seen. The sanctuary of Demeter was at the bottom of a low hill on the north side of the race course. The marble altar of Demeter, where Regilla sat and where she must have also conducted sacrifices, was centrally located across from the judges' viewing stand. She may have climbed up on a footstool and sat on the altar during the competitions (see fig. 3.1). The elevated surface provided a good vantage point and a cold seat; sometimes, she may have preferred a softer, more comfortable conventional chair nearby. Sitting so close to the athletic events was both a privilege and a physical ordeal. The only adult slaves permitted to be present were men, and not women who could help with her personal and hygienic needs.[27] Athletes who competed at festivals were no longer strictly the elite gentlemen of earlier periods. In Roman times they came from all levels of society and included slaves. Though sheltered from the hot summer sun by parasols and fanned by

Fig. 3.1.   Altar of Demeter Chamyne at Olympia. As priestess of Demeter Chamyne, Regilla enjoyed a front-row seat at the most prestigious athletic event in the ancient world. The priestess was the only woman present.

slaves, with the dry dust of the stadium blowing in her face and the stench of perspiration from her own slaves, from the competing men and animals, and from the crowds, Regilla will have longed to bathe as soon as possible. Arrian reports the discomforts described by the Stoic Epictetus, who lived in the generation preceding that of Regilla:

> "But some unpleasant and difficult things happen in life." And don't they happen in Olympia? Don't you grow hot? Aren't you crowded? Don't you bathe poorly? Don't you get soaked when it rains? Don't you have your fill of noise and shouting, and other discomforts?[28]

Thus, as priestess, Regilla would have been acutely aware of the need for cool fresh water and inspired to find a remedy.

Regilla built a nymphaeum (fountain) at Olympia. An inscription engraved on a life-size stone bull (see fig. 3.2) that once stood on the parapet states: "Regilla, priestess of Demeter, dedicated the water and the things connected with the water to Zeus."[29] Zeus was the chief divinity celebrated at Olympia, and in the inscription Regilla links the cult in which she served to his. Bulls were sacrificed to Zeus: the god sometimes appeared in the shape of a bull, for example in the story of the rape of Europa. As a bull, Zeus, like Demeter, was a god of fertility.

In his guidebook to Greece, Pausanias does not mention the nymphaeum. The omission may not have been deliberate. He was a contemporary of Regilla and Herodes, and the monument may not have been completed when he visited Olympia. On the other hand, he generally prefers to discuss monuments dedicated by Greeks rather than Romans and those dating from before the Roman conquest of Greece. Like Plutarch and Herodes himself, Pausanias favored works created when the Greek cities had been independent and the land free from foreign rule. Pausanias often ignores contemporary and recent works, especially when their purpose was not purely religious, and by no means

Fig. 3.2. Statue of bull with inscription. This bull, representing Zeus, stood on top of the nymphaeum constructed by Regilla at Olympia.

does he comment on all the dedications he must have seen at Olympia and elsewhere.[30] Furthermore, Demeter was not the most important divinity at the sanctuary of Zeus in Olympia; the goddess had her own cult centers in Eleusis and elsewhere in the Mediterranean. Since Pausanias wrote a guide that would be used by ancient travelers, the monuments he passed over were doomed to attract less attention. Nevertheless, visitors could scarcely fail to notice the nymphaeum, for it was huge, colorful, ornate, and innovative, and provided a convenient source of healthy water for them. If they wanted to identify the people in the portraits, they would have to pause to read the inscrip-

Fig. 3.3.   Head of Regilla from her statue at her nymphaeum.

Fig. 3.4.   Statue of Regilla from her nymphaeum. Regilla held a sheaf of wheat or a pomegranate, attributes of Demeter as goddess of fertility, in her left hand. This figure became separated from the head shown in fig. 3.3.

tions and study the sculptures. Much of what Pausanias did describe has perished; things made by nature and by human beings which no longer exist and which he passed over (if not described by other writers) have faded from historical memory.

In the case of the nymphaeum, archaeological evidence has survived, most importantly the inscription, which is the crucial piece of evidence that links the construction beyond doubt to Regilla. Pausanias does not ignore women, and gives some information about women's religious practices, commemorative statues erected by or in honor of women, and women who are protagonists in myths.[31] Regilla's nymphaeum did not meet any of these criteria. Lucian does not specifically attribute the nymphaeum to Regilla or to Herodes but he does discuss it in *Peregrinus*.[32] The author may have been reticent about including Regilla in his satire, considering both the sad trajectory of her life and her relationship to the imperial house.

With few exceptions, most modern scholars refer to the nymphaeum as Herodes'.[33] This assumption is based on the knowledge that Herodes was wealthy and is known for other major building projects, many of which involved the ornamental and utilitarian deployment of water. He had completed an aqueduct at Canusium, an elaborate nymphaeum at Loukou, and later he constructed a nymphaeum at Regilla's estate on the Via Appia. Philostratus does credit Herodes specifically with the construction of an aqueduct in honor of Zeus at Olympia, but only the aqueduct.[34]

Regilla was extremely wealthy, too, but she was far from the first woman to pay for public construction projects. Starting in the Hellenistic period, Greek and Roman women erected major secular and religious public structures. Hellenistic queens, with their great wealth, built numerous monuments, and among commoners Phile, who lived in Priene in the first century B.C., was the first woman to construct a reservoir and an aqueduct.[35]

Around 136/137, Julia Balbilla personally supervised the construction of a heroon in honor of her cousin Herculanus, a friend of Plutarch. This was the most noteworthy and expensive funerary monument known to have stood in Roman Sparta. Balbilla was the sister of Philopappus, and the monument to him which is extant in Athens has also been attributed to her.[36] Through Herculanus, Balbilla and Philopappus had kinship ties to Herodes' father and mother.[37] Thus there was a recent and close precedent in their circle for a woman building an impressive and expensive monument.

Scholars who assume that Regilla was not the donor, despite the inscription, and call the monument "the nymphaeum of Herodes Atticus" are like those who claim that poets like Erinna were actually men writing under female pseudonyms.[38] Herodes was not modest and self-effacing. When he himself built a monument like the odeion in honor of his wife, he said so. Restoring authorship to Regilla does not necessarily mean that a domineering husband with as much building experience as Herodes would not have tried to influence the design. Furthermore, though Regilla was responsible for the images of the family, inscriptions credit Herodes with the statues of the imperial house; such a division of public and private between male and female was ubiquitous in antiquity.

The edifices of Regilla and Herodes at Olympia were distinct, but intertwined by function. The aqueduct built by Herodes enhanced the water supply for Regilla's fountain; the latter stood at the end of the aqueduct. Symbolically, the male contribution can be interpreted as active, dynamic, and utilitarian; the female, by contrast, is static, receptive, and lavishly adorned. The juxtaposition of separate spheres for wife and husband echoes the division of their estates at Marathon, marked by the Gate of Eternal Harmony. Herodes and others, including Vibullius Hipparchus (the husband of Athenais), were able to tinker with the nymphaeum after Regilla died, updating the portrait of the emperor and adding family members to the nymphaeum Regilla

Fig. 3.5.   Statue of Elpinice from Regilla's nymphaeum.

Fig. 3.6.   Statue of Athenais from Regilla's nymphaeum.

had constructed between 149 and 153 before she had reached the age of thirty.[39]

Scholars interested in sculpture and design tend to pay scant attention to the practical uses of the nymphaeum as a source of water for the shrine, but a popular sanctuary like Olympia that teemed with visitors, maintenance staff, religious personnel, and sacrificial and working animals required a large and reliable water supply. The demand for water for drinking, bathing, sanitation, cooking, and cleaning, especially during the games which were held every four years during the hottest months of the year, July and August, was enormous.

As a Roman, Regilla was accustomed to an abundance of water, for a characteristic of Roman occupation was the construction of aqueducts, baths, and ornamental fountains. The priestess of Demeter could not but notice that the water supply should be improved. Visitors to Olympia were becoming ill from polluted water.[40] Accordingly, Regilla made a dedication to Hygieia, a goddess of health, in her own name using two words, "Regilla Hygieai" (Regilla to Hygieia).[41] There were other divinities who also were concerned with health, most notably Asclepius, but Regilla chose to honor a female.

The remains of sculpture and of the foundation have permitted archaeologists to understand the nymphaeum in detail. Its general appearance was of the back wall of a theater, with freestanding sculpted figures and others placed in niches. The monument of Philopappus at Athens provided a precedent for the iconographic program at Olympia, for it probably featured representations of Philopappus, his family, and Trajan.[42] At Olympia the images included portraits of three generations of Regilla's and Herodes' family and of the imperial family. The gods too were represented.[43] Inscriptions at the base identified the statues.[44]

The images were arrayed in two stories, the imperial family on the lower story and Regilla's and Herodes' family on the up-

Fig. 3.7.   Statue of Faustina the Elder from Regilla's nymphaeum.

per. Statues of Zeus stood in both central niches. To the left of the viewer facing the statue of Zeus on the lower story were: Antoninus Pius, Annia Galeria Aurelia Faustina (the Elder, see fig. 3.7), Lucius Verus, Domitia Faustina, and T. Aelius Antoninus with Annia Faustina. The last two share a niche and are shown as children. On Zeus's right are: Hadrian, Sabina, Marcus Aurelius, Faustina the Younger, and Lucilla.

Because of Regilla's kinship with both Faustina the Elder and Faustina the Younger, the imperial family was her family. Inscriptions also attest to Regilla's closer relatives. Here, the attention paid to her forebears is additional evidence that she is the donor. Though she had served as a priestess of a Greek goddess at Olympia, she asserted her Roman identity. Another figure of Zeus in the center of the second story is flanked on the viewer's left by Regilla, Appius Annius Gallus (Regilla's father), Atilia Caucidia Tertulla (Regilla's mother, see fig. 3.8),[45] M. Appius Bradua (Regilla's grandfather), and Elpinice. To the right of Zeus stand: Herodes, Atticus (Regilla's father-in-law), Vibullia Alcia (Regilla's mother-in-law, see fig. 3.9), Marcus Atilius Atticus Bradua, and Athenais with Regillus (see fig. 3.6). The last two share a niche; Athenais appears as a young adolescent and Regillus as a child. The name and statue of L. Vibullius Hipparchus (husband of Athenais) was added later when he repaired and made some changes to the nymphaeum.[46]

Dress clearly differentiated the men. The emperors wore a cuirass. Herodes and most of the other men in the family wear a toga, with the exception of Herodes' father and son Regillus who wear Greek dress. The message conveyed by the costume of the three generations is that Herodes is a Roman of Greek background (represented by his father) who has not relinquished his Greekness (perpetuated through his son).[47] Regilla, however, was not distinguished from the women of the imperial house, for all were shown as the large so-called "Herculaneum type," categorized by a style of drapery often worn in sculpture por-

Fig. 3.8. Statue of Atilia Caucidia Tertulla from Regilla's nymphaeum.

Fig. 3.9.   Statue of Vibullia Alcia from Regilla's nymphaeum.

traying dignified mature women.[48] This similarity drew attention to Regilla's kinship with the women in the imperial family.

The head of the figure representing Herodes is not extant. Thus there is no way of determining whether he was portrayed in his usual style, reminiscent of Greek philosophers and orators of the classical period, or whether his portraiture on the nymphaeum was more in the Roman style like those of the rest of the adult men.[49] In any case, the arrangement and choice of the sculptures were a visual expression of Regilla's relationship with both the imperial family and her more immediate family. Any pilgrim who bent down to scoop up water would be paying obeisance, consciously or unconsciously, to the elevated figures sculpted in temple-like niches above. As was the fate of so many pagan monuments, including others associated with Regilla, parts of the nymphaeum were later incorporated into a Christian church.[50]

Priestess of Tyche

The cult of Demeter Chamyne at Olympia was venerable and laden with tradition. In contrast, Regilla also served as the first priestess of Tyche (Fortune), whose cult was new at Athens. Her temple for this cult was erected high on the hill adjacent to the Panathenaic stadium built by Herodes.[51] He had transformed the original stadium on the site from one built in the Greek style for racing to a versatile structure where Roman-type gladiatorial contests and wild animal hunts could also be staged. Tyche, a popular figure in the Hellenistic world, was an appropriate divinity for athletic competitions, since victory was in the hands of Fortune. The stadium was built between 139/140 and 143/144.[52]

Athletic festivals newly established in connection with the Panhellenion as well as traditional competitions such as the

Panathenaia were held at the stadium. These events took place more frequently in Athens than anywhere else in the Greek world and attracted competitors and spectators from other cities.[53] The vast majority of those present were male. Although female athletes had begun to compete in the Greek world in the Roman period at major festivals including the Pythian, Nemean, Isthmian, and others, there is no evidence that they competed at Athens, though girls did compete in musical events there.

In the mid-first century A.D., Hedea, a versatile athlete from Tralles who also held citizenship at Athens and Delphi, won prizes for footracing at Nemea and Sicyon, for driving a war chariot at Isthmia, and for singing and accompanying herself on the cithara in the children's contest at the Augustan games (Sebastea) in Athens.[54] In the Hellenistic period some women owned horses that were victorious at the Panathenaia, but they did not drive the chariots themselves.[55] There is no indication whether women were excluded from attending athletic events at the Athenian stadium as they were in Olympia, or whether they were admitted. In any case, Regilla must have been present. If, as seems likely, ceremonies involving Tyche were held concurrently with all the events in the stadium, this priesthood would have demanded a great deal of Regilla's time and attention.

Since the Tyche cult was inaugurated not long after the opening of the stadium, Regilla would have had to assume the priesthood soon after her arrival in Athens, while she was pregnant with Athenais and was the mother of one toddler.[56] She had to be as energetic as her husband. As the first priestess of the cult, lacking the help of a prior incumbent, she carved out the role herself, prompted no doubt by scholars and specialists in ancient religion and in contemporary imperial cult and cults of Tyche and Fortuna in other places. She would have been familiar with the cult of Fortuna and her priestesses at Rome and with the imperial women who personified this goddess and others on earth. As was true for the priestess of Demeter, the priest-

Fig. 3.10.   Panathenaic stadium, Ardettos hill, and temple of Tyche.

ess of Tyche shared the aura of the goddess. Herodes' aspirations to be related to the gods were permissible in a small provincial city, but had been impossible to satisfy at Rome under the watchful eye of an emperor who reigned as a god.

The temple of Tyche, standing alone on the side of the hill, was Ionic, peripteral (with columns on all four sides), and made of white marble from Mount Pentelicus near Athens. Regilla could reach it by climbing a monumental flight of stairs from the stadium.[57] The temple was sited as if it were in an acropolis 144.8 feet above the stadium floor; thus Regilla had to climb the equivalent of fourteen modern stories. She probably held the priesthood for life, through four pregnancies.[58] Perhaps, especially when she grew older, teams of slaves carried her up on their shoulders in a litter chair, and the procession upward could have constituted part of the spectacle.

The figure of the goddess within was sculpted of ivory.[59] This material brought to mind the statue of Athena Parthenos created by Phidias in the time of Pericles. This statue was one of the most famous monuments on the Acropolis from the classical period; it stood thirty-eight feet tall and was covered with gold and ivory.[60] An association with the venerable Athena lent additional sanctity to the new cult of Tyche. From the perspective of the viewer seated in the stadium below, the temple gleamed large and bright in the Athenian sun like the temple of Athena Nike on the Acropolis,[61] and Regilla's status, both physical and spiritual, was consequently higher than that of the legendary heroes whose statues stood below.

Indeed, Regilla was quasi-divine, though not immortal. She may well have enjoyed playing this role, and would have pleased her husband in doing so. Kinship with this lofty being through marriage elevated Herodes as well: later he would buried be in a tomb on a hill at the opposite side of the stadium from the temple.[62] The stadium held an audience of over 50,000, the same number as the Roman Colosseum.[63] The spectators would be grateful to the donor, and would absorb the not-so-subtle propaganda of the edifice above.

The incumbent priestess was required to pay the huge expenses of the cult, including sacrifices, the salaries of dependent sacerdotal officials, a staff of slaves, and monuments commemorating her term in office. The places where Regilla held priesthoods were well frequented by Greek and Roman tourists and officials, and were centers where luminaries of the Second Sophistic delivered orations and conducted philosophical discussions. Thus she officiated in the presence not only of the local citizens, but also of the elite of the empire who could afford journeys to such centers as Olympia and Athens.

Benefactor at Corinth

Regilla's fame spread: she was commemorated at Corinth as if she were Tyche, though she did not actually hold priestly office there. In other words she was said to be nearly a personification of the goddess. The Council (Boule) of Corinth erected a statue in her honor.[64] The portrait head is not extant. The lower half of the statue indicates that the subject was female, and a trace of a wheel at the right foot associates her with Nemesis-Tyche. The marble base with the dedicatory inscription survives:

> This is a portrait of Regilla. A sculptor carved the figure endowing the stone with all her self-control (sophrosyne). The great Herodes Atticus, outstanding beyond others for attaining the pinnacle of every virtue, gave it. She chose as her husband, acclaimed among all the Greeks, a descendant and flower of Achaea, surpassing all. Regilla, the Council, as if calling you "Tyche" has erected this marble image in front of the sanctuary.

The present tense "calling" (line 7: *eilaskousa*) indicates that Regilla was alive when the portrait statue was dedicated. The worship of Tyche in Corinth had been well established long before Herodes introduced the cult at Athens and appointed his wife as the first priestess.[65] Though a priestess is not necessarily an incarnation of the goddess, the flattering inscription above sees the two as virtually the same. What had Regilla done to inspire the citizens of Corinth to vote her this honor? Doubtless this inscription was a way of showing thanks for a major gift. Several monuments at Corinth are attributed to Regilla or Herodes, though the attributions are not beyond question. The inscriptions do not give exact details about the funding of all the monuments. Moreover, at the relevant sites in Corinth the archaeological record is confusing because the building materials, including inscribed stones, were moved and reused in subsequent construction. In any case, the usual pattern (which we have seen at Olympia) is that a partnership is envisioned between the community and the wealthy benefactor (who may or may not be the same person or group who paid for the monument commemorating the benefaction). It is clear that Corinth

voted the honor and bore some of the expenses of the commemorative inscription and sculpture in order to flatter Regilla and
Herodes. In return Regilla and Herodes themselves paid for a
more expensive item such as a fountain or a temple, and they or
the Boule erected the commemorative inscription.

Rebuilt as a Roman colony by Julius Caesar and his successors, Corinth was a busy port as it once had been before it was
destroyed by the Romans in 146 B.C. Travellers en route to the
east often chose to pass through it. Though no ancient source
names the capital of the province of Achaea, Corinth seems to
have held this position.[66] Among the many influential men who
stopped there were Hadrian, Lucius Verus, Apuleius, and Plutarch.[67] Thus Corinth provided an excellent podium for Regilla
and Herodes to display their piety, their family, and their taste
in monumental sculpture.

Regilla alone may well have been the donor who bore the expenses of the renovation of a fountain complex at Corinth, just
as she was responsible for the construction of the nymphaeum
at Olympia. Nevertheless, and despite evidence to the contrary,
most scholars simply ascribe the nymphaeum at Olympia to
Herodes, and, resting on that assumption, go on to attribute the
nymphaeum at the Peirene springs in Corinth to him as well.[68]
However, archaeologist Betsey Ann Robinson has suggested that
Regilla was the donor of the Peirene fountain.[69] Her arguments
are persuasive, for inscriptions indicate that it was Regilla whom
the Corinthian Boule honored above all at the site. Furthermore, she had the funds to support major acts of beneficence.
Corinth was a Roman city, and thus a prime location for Regilla
to erect a monument that would be seen by people whom she
knew or who knew of her. Her husband was also a benefactor at
both Olympia and Corinth. Furthermore, some artistic and architectural features of the fountains at Olympia and at Corinth
are similar. Both portray Regilla's family and the imperial family.
Without Regilla, the family displayed on the backdrop of the

Fig. 3.11.   Peirene fountain at Corinth.

fountains would not have existed. The imperial family is also part of the sculptural program at both fountains. This courtesy was not only pro forma. Through the sculpture, Regilla recorded an important asset she had brought to her husband and children: her kinship with the imperial house.

The image of Regilla was placed in the tenth niche between the facade and the eastern exedra.[70] Since the female figures appropriate to the chronology and style of the fountain are now headless, it is impossible to identify which, if any, represents Regilla (see fig. 3.12). She may be portrayed in some images of Tyche shown as a mature woman adorned with a crown representing the walled city of Corinth.[71] The portrait statue of Regilla is also thought to have resembled another related sculp-

Fig. 3.12.   Female figure: Regilla's portrait?

ture type of the mature female, the Nemesis of Rhamnous.[72] Attributes that would clearly identify the statues as one goddess or the other are missing; therefore they have also been called "Nemesis-Tyche."[73] (Nemesis "Retribution" is the negative or opposite of Tyche "Fortune," and they were often paired.)

In addition, various other female statues, now headless, are extant.[74] Though most of them were not found at the site, probably these had been part of the fountain of Peirene or the peribolos (enclosed precinct) of Apollo, which is adjacent to it, and represented Regilla and other members of her family. The provenance of the portrait statues may be the result of the devastation wreaked in Corinth as a result of the invasion by the German Heruli people in A.D. 267 and subsequent relocation and reconstruction. Therefore, it is difficult to sort out which sculptures were part of the Peirene fountain complex and which were part of the peribolos, let alone which fragments may have belonged to a portrait of Regilla.[75]

Like some Hellenistic queens and wives of Roman emperors, Regilla could have had a say about her portrayal in sculpture. A principal attribute of Tyche is the overflowing cornucopia, and therefore the cult statue of Tyche at Corinth probably held a cornucopia in her left hand.[76] Similarly in Regilla's portrayal as priestess of Demeter at Olympia she probably held a pomegranate or a sheaf of wheat, attributes of fertility appropriate to the goddess. Both Demeter and Tyche are goddesses of fertility and are associated with wealth, prosperity, and generosity. Regilla's portrayal as a mature, well-nourished woman also refers to her prolific child bearing. The choice of goddesses whom Regilla served is deliberate, and influenced by official ruler cult. Back at Rome, the imperial women were often represented as Ceres, the goddess whom the Romans considered the equivalent of Demeter. The portrait of the emperor's wife as Ceres was common on Roman coins and circulated widely. Thus Regilla became divine, and her husband and their children were intimately associated with imperial women and with divinity.

Fig. 3.13a.   Base of a statue of Regilla, Corinth.

b.   Musical instruments from the base of the statue. This drawing of figures incised on the base of a statue dedicated to Regilla shows her as an educated woman who cultivated the musical arts.

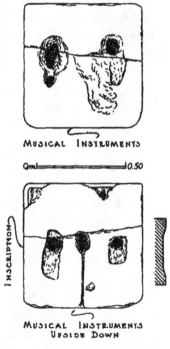

MUSICAL INSTRUMENTS

0m|————————————|0.50

INSCRIPTION

MUSICAL INSTRUMENTS
UPSIDE DOWN

Regilla as Dedicatee

Another statue of Regilla near the six streams of the Peirene fountain was dedicated by the Council of Corinth, and firmly associates her with the site. That the statue base had been used twice before suggests the thrift and inconstant nature typical of a donation by a Boule, but not characteristic of Regilla or Herodes. On the right side of the statue base is a sculpted relief of a garland surrounding three musical instruments (see fig. 3.13).[77] Though the musical instruments had been inscribed on the base for an earlier statue, we may speculate that there were plenty of other bases available to the Boule and that this one was selected as appropriate or flattering to Regilla.[78] Such allusions to culture and education were common in this period in portraits of elite Hellenistic and Roman women and monuments to them.[79] These instruments draw attention to Regilla's accomplishments in the musical arts. Later in Athens Herodes alluded to his late wife's talents by dedicating an odeon (musical theater) to her. Again the inscription in Corinth draws attention to sophrosyne:

> As commanded by the Council of Sisyphus, by the streams of
> the fountains
> you see me, Regilla, the image of sophrosyne.[80]

Thus Regilla was repeatedly honored in Greece for the traditional virtue of Greek women: sophrosyne.

Other Honors

Inscriptions indicate that in Corinth, Regilla was honored for her own munificence. The inscription below in which the Delphic Council honors her in a similar fashion suggests that she was responsible for some benefaction at that sanctuary, though

Fig. 3.14a.   Base for a statue of Regilla at Delphi from the temple of Apollo discovered near the north wall of the cella.

the exedra where it was found has been attributed to Herodes.[81] In Greece, women are usually honored, not as individuals in their own right with their own achievements, but rather as a result of their relationships with important men. Other inscriptions, including some from Athens, Delphi, and Olympia, make it clear that Regilla and her daughter Elpinice enjoyed reflected glory because they were descended from men who served as high officials. Regilla is doubly honored by descent as well as by marriage to a man who had held high offices.[82]

If we evaluate the honors paid to a woman from another viewpoint it seems clear that the male relatives of the honorand are themselves honored because of their relationship with her. For example, an inscription at Delphi from a statue base honored Regilla alone, but lauded her husband too (see fig. 3.14a):

> Appia Regilla,
>
> wife of the benefactor Claudius Herodes
>
> because of her nobility and
>
> 5   self-control (sophrosyne) and her other good reputation,
>
> surpassing in all traditional excellence, because of her self-control
>
> and conjugal affection *(philandrias),* the Council of the Delphians makes this dedication
>
> to Pythian Apollo.[83]

Another inscription that Regilla shared with Elpinice and Herodes manages to honor him as well:

> Appia Annia Atilia
>
> Regilla Caucidia
>
> Tertulla, daughter of

5 the consul Appius Gallus

 . . . wife of . . .[84]

From remote antiquity, religion offered respectable Greek and Roman women an opportunity to be together in public or private without criticism. In both Regilla's religious posts, however, she was isolated from other elite women. As the first priestess of Tyche at Athens, Regilla could not enjoy the advice of an older priestess, and the priestess of Demeter was the only woman present at the Olympic games.[85]

Religion provided an avenue for women to pass down traditions of family participation in particular cults. In Roman Sparta, for example, there are many dedications made by women in honor of other women (often relatives). For the most part the honorands had served as priestesses.[86] In contrast, neither in Greece nor in Rome have any inscriptions been discovered recording that any woman paid tribute to Regilla. Nor have any Latin inscriptions about her been discovered in Greece. Although such a deduction involves an argument *ex silentio,* it ap-

Fig. 3.14b. Base for a statue of Regilla at Delphi from the temple of Apollo.

pears that the absence of such dedications underlines her isolation from her Roman family and from friends. On the other hand, Regilla was honored in Greece in the most important sanctuaries and populous cities, and her wealth allowed her to bestow magnificent gifts at Olympia and Corinth, where she ensured a place in history for herself.

CHAPTER 4

DEATH IN ATHENS
AND MURDER TRIAL IN ROME

IN A.D. 160, when Regilla was eight months pregnant, she died mysteriously. Her brother Bradua learned of her death, and he sued Herodes for murder. Philostratus, consistently a source favorable to Herodes, reports the details of the charge, the trial, the verdict, and the aftermath: "A murder charge was brought against Herodes in this way. When his wife Regilla was eight months pregnant, he ordered his freedman Alcimedon to beat her for trivial reasons. She died in premature childbirth from a blow to her abdomen."[1]

Though Bradua asserted that his sister's husband was ultimately responsible for her violent death, the emperor Marcus Aurelius endorsed a conflicting scenario, exonerating Herodes and placing the sole burden of guilt on Herodes' freedman Alcimedon. No one claimed that she had died of natural causes.

The Suspects

The principal suspects were Herodes and Alcimedon. Two factors influenced the Roman courts to take Bradua's charge seriously. First, in the empire some freedmen with powerful patrons like Herodes or the imperial family wielded an influence unimaginable to anyone familiar only with New World slavery, where the stigma of having been a slave and the mark of color pushed ex-slaves to the margins of free society, and where a freedman who had murdered an upper-class woman would have been summarily lynched. In the public sphere, the emperor's freedmen, for example, could hold positions comparable to those of cabinet ministers in modern states, and some freedmen were counted among the wealthiest inhabitants of the empire.[2] In the private sphere they were equally powerful. Juvenal writes of a husband who decides to divorce a wife who is no longer young, and sends his freedman to inform her peremptorily. The freedman insults the rejected woman and uses imperatives: "Pack your bags and get out. You are annoying to us, and you wipe your nose too often. Hurry up. Another wife with a dry nose is coming."[3] Second, it was not unusual for women to receive letters or to write them. Women normally corresponded with friends and members of the family.[4] Regilla may have discussed her husband's violent temper with her brother and alerted him to marital tensions. Visitors from Rome would also bring back the gossip. What they heard about Herodes was nothing new. Some twenty years earlier in a letter to Marcus Aurelius, Fronto had alluded to murder in connection with Herodes.[5] Herodes' physical violence and tyrannical behavior, including the incident when he hit the future emperor Antoninus Pius, were well known.[6] But according to Roman law, children belonged to the father. If Regilla divorced Herodes she would have been separated from her children, and if she had gone back to Rome she would have been a virtual stranger after being away for twenty years.

Intellectually Herodes was opposed to the repression of emotion. He had fulminated against *apatheia,* the lack of feeling advocated by Stoics. Though much of the evidence for Herodes' emotional indulgence concerns his unsuitable displays of grief, there is also sufficient documentation for his prior violent acts. Philostratus mentions the fight between Herodes and Anto-

ninus Pius just before he reports the more serious charge of killing Regilla.

Wife-beating has doubtless been common in the history of
the western world, but before advocates for women succeeded
in some countries in making such abuse a crime punishable by
the state, it was a private matter and rarely entered the historical
record. Corporal punishment for freeborn children was normal
in antiquity, and wives, especially those married with *manus*
(into the hand [i.e., power] of the husband), in some respects
were legally the same as their children. The husband, however,
was forbidden to kill his wife for any offense without consulting
the woman's kinsmen.[7] Valerius Maximus (a Roman historian of
the first century A.D.), who wrote of moral exemplars, noted
that in early Rome a husband cudgeled his wife to death for
drinking wine. He was not criticized, for it was generally agreed
that drinking was a prelude to the loss of a woman's virtue.[8]
Writing about his mother's tolerance of her husband's behavior,
Augustine observed that the faces of many women were scarred
as a result of being beaten by their husbands.[9] Plutarch suggested that married women needed protectors to whom they
were not married.[10]

Abuse of upper-class women in Rome was unusual. If Regilla
had married a Roman, or at least if she had remained in Rome,
her brother and other kinsmen and friends, and perhaps even
Marcus Aurelius and Faustina, would have monitored her relationship with Herodes. She would have been constantly at-
tended not only by faithful slaves but by the freedmen of the
Annii Regilli who had more power to defend her. Though their
marriage was most likely to have been without *manus*, Regilla's
isolation in Greece gave Herodes a de facto power over her that
he would not have been able to exercise in a marriage without
manus in Rome. Nevertheless, a few infamous precedents for
wife abuse at the highest levels of society are documented in

both Greek and Roman history. Nero comes to mind as the obvious and most recent model for Herodes' tyrannical personality and behavior. In A.D. 65, Nero kicked his pregnant wife Poppaea in the abdomen, and she died as a result.[11] Periander, tyrant of Corinth (ca. 625–585 B.C.), had attacked his pregnant wife Melissa. The abused women had been born into the highest echelons of society: Melissa was the daughter of a tyrant.[12] A remorseful Periander later dedicated the finest clothing of the women of Corinth to her.[13] Herodes dedicated Regilla's clothing at Eleusis. Each husband thus divested himself of the physical reminders of his wife.

Periander, Nero, and Herodes harbored literary pretensions, and ambitious building schemes. All of them wanted to build a canal through the Isthmus of Corinth. Periander was considered one of the Seven Sages of archaic Greece and Herodes a luminary of the Second Sophistic. Like Periander, Herodes built monuments at Corinth. Periander's murder of Melissa alienated his son Lycophron;[14] this emotional dynamic probably developed as well between Herodes and his son Bradua. Nero and Herodes dallied in homosexual and heterosexual relationships, and, like Periander, they indulged their passions. These notorious incidents of wife abuse helped to create a climate in which the charges against Herodes were believable. Philostratus' excuses for Herodes are hardly persuasive, and in fact he states that even during Herodes' lifetime his claims that he had not ordered that such an action be taken against Regilla and his excessive mourning were considered false.[15]

The biographer says that if Herodes himself had been guilty, he would never have dedicated a magnificent theater to her, or have delayed the casting of lots for his second consulship. Nor, if he were polluted by homicide, would he have offended Demeter and Kore by dedicating Regilla's clothing at Eleusis. Only this last point has any validity. Assuming Herodes would not have dared to offend these great goddesses, the reasoning points to Alcimedon as the perpetrator, though it does not relieve Herodes of the charge of complicity in the crime.[16]

The Trial

Regilla's brother Bradua brought a murder charge against Herodes. If his sister had done anything to warrant the unusual punishment that led to her death, her dishonor would have detracted from Bradua's family honor. Since Regilla's father was dead, her brother had become the head of the family and defender of the family honor. According to Plutarch, if a woman's husband mistreated her in an exogamous marriage, her kinsmen would defend her.[17] But Bradua was too late. By the time the news of Regilla's death reached Rome, his sister's body was gone, either cremated or entombed. All the evidence had vanished. The witnesses' lips were sealed.

Private parties were required to press charges, for there was no public prosecutor at Rome. The prosecutor, accused, and victim were all members of the senatorial order.[18] A court of senators was convened. According to Roman mores, Bradua's illustrious lineage was more rare and precious than Herodes' cash. That Herodes agreed with this assessment is evident in his decision to marry Regilla and in the names he chose for his children, favoring their Roman ancestors over their Greek ones. Petulantly and purposefully, however, at his trial Herodes disparaged his accuser. Regilla's brother was a patrician of consular rank, who wore on his sandals an ivory buckle shaped like a half-moon as a symbol of his noble descent. At the trial in Rome Herodes mocked him: "You have your nobility on your toe-joints."[19] Herodes had not forgotten that he was still an outsider in Rome. His grandfather was merely a *novus homo,* not descended from Republican aristocracy like his prosecutor and dead wife. Of course, Herodes was also entitled to wear the sandals of a senator as well as the special toga of a man who had served as consul, but he was not a patrician. On the other hand, he was a rhetorician; that was an advantage. Nevertheless he had not been in Rome for a long time, and the trial was conducted in Latin.[20]

The mere fact that a senatorial court was convened suggests that many at Rome believed the charge. The court comprised Bradua's peers and senators he encountered frequently in Rome. An attack on his sister was an attack on himself, so he delivered an oration about himself and his family. Though Herodes and later Philostratus interpreted this panegyric as an indication that Bradua had no real evidence to corroborate his charge, his recitation of the virtuous traditions of the Annii Regilli served to assure the court that Bradua was not the sort of man who would ask a court to convene for frivolous reasons.[21] The majority of Roman senators were doubtless more favorably disposed to Bradua than to the foreigner Herodes. Bradua is described as "highly esteemed."[22] He was politically active at the time of Regilla's death, serving as consul in 160 along with T. Clodius Vibius Varus. Irascible, alien, and arrogant, Herodes was not well liked at Rome.

Bradua's accusation is so specific that we may assume that Herodes was acquitted only because he was protected by Marcus Aurelius. The correspondence of Marcus Aurelius and Fronto gives abundant evidence that the emperor cared deeply about his old tutor. Ties between their families went back three generations to the emperor's maternal grandfather and Herodes' paternal grandfather. The future emperor had grown up in the company of Herodes. Some twenty years before the trial, Marcus Aurelius had written to Fronto: "I love both of you, each for his virtues. And I remember that [Herodes] was raised in the home of my grandfather Publius Calvisius."[23] After the first son Regilla bore died, Fronto urged Herodes to take heart because of his love for Marcus Aurelius, telling him that this relationship was more important than anything else. Fronto twice uses unambiguous terms for love *(eras, anterastes)*. These words cover a wide range of possible relationships from spiritual to physical, but in this context are likely to refer to the bond between student and teacher. Doubtless this relationship exerted a decisive influence upon the outcome of the murder charges against Herodes. The senatorial court would not thwart the emperor's wishes.[24] That Herodes was found not guilty suggests that the emperor interfered. Power, personal connections, and politics triumphed over justice. The outcome of the trial is an example of the abuse of Roman law under the monarchy, especially when it concerned the upper echelons of society; the senatorial court bowed to the emperor's personal wishes. Insofar as the verdict favored a man born in Greece over a bona fide Roman aristocrat, this case may also be seen as part of the imperial policy to incorporate members of the foreign elite into the empire as equal to native-born Italians.

In court Herodes claimed that he had not ordered Alcimedon to do such a thing to Regilla and that his great grief was indicative of innocence.[25] The onus of guilt was placed on Alcimedon, but he does not appear to have suffered any punishment. It is difficult to imagine that an ex-slave would perpetrate such a crime against a kinswoman of the emperor's wife unless he had been asked to do so. Master and freedman were so close in reality that each was implicated in the criminal act of the other. Though Herodes was tried and freed, his subsequent behavior, not only excessive demonstrations of grief but also unprecedented generosity to his freedman's family, including raising the daughters of Alcimedon "as his own,"[26] suggests that he was guilty. Herodes' motivation is difficult to fathom. There is no apparent reason why he would have planned to murder Regilla or to have her murdered. He might well have been hoping that she was carrying another son. Thus a possible scenario is that Herodes had ordered Alcimedon to give Regilla a beating for a minor offense. She was pregnant and vulnerable, and because

Alcimedon was too enthusiastic about his task it went wrong and she died. This chain of events might account for Herodes' acquittal and Marcus Aurelius' leniency toward Alcimedon.

After the trial, Bradua would have served as proconsul, an office that conveniently got him out of Italy. Herodes was the ultimate victor in this rivalry with his brother-in-law. Bradua is not attested in historical sources after his defeat in court and his proconsulship, which was the pinnacle of his career. No marriage or offspring are recorded. His prosecution of the emperor's beloved tutor evidently ended his political career and public life. Bradua also relinquished any hope he may have cherished of regaining his family's ancestral property on the Appian Way. Perhaps he died soon after the trial. The minimum age for serving as consul was forty, and that was old by Roman standards, although many lived beyond it.

Cui bono? Who reaped the greatest benefit from Regilla's death? One answer is Alcimedon and his children. Though we do not hear about him before the events surrounding the murder, we may infer from subsequent events that Herodes and Alcimedon had a close relationship even when Regilla was alive. The freedman was not executed, perhaps as a favor of the emperor to Herodes. Many years after Regilla's death Alcimedon accompanied his patron to Sirmium in Pannonia, where he was summoned by the emperor in 174 to answer charges of seeking tyranny that had been brought against him by some Athenian politicians.[27] That Herodes still associated with Alcimedon and treated his children as though they were members of his own family suggests, variously, that he approved of the freedman's actions, or had forgiven him, or was in his power. That he did so in the presence of Marcus Aurelius indicates that the emperor went along with Herodes' decision. Alcimedon brought his twin daughters on the journey to Sirmium, but they died when lightning struck a tower in a suburban house where they were sleeping.[28] Herodes was so fond of them that he referred to them as his little daughters and loved them as if they actually were.[29] Philostratus had noted the same extension to the trophimoi of affection due to legitimate children.

The girls had been born around the time of Regilla's death, for they were of marriageable age on the trip to Sirmium. When they were born, they were probably a diversion from the murder charge and from the alienation of his own natural children. If Regilla's fetus had been born at the same time as the twins and lived, perhaps his own child would have monopolized Herodes' attention, and the twins would have been its playmates. As part of the household staff, twins were a novelty and thus a sign of conspicuous wealth. Infant and juvenile mortality made the survival of twins a much more rare occurrence than it is nowadays. Whether they were slave, or freed, or freeborn depended first upon the status of their mother: slave, freed, or freeborn. Herodes could have manumitted them when he freed their father, or Alcimedon could have purchased the girls from his master and then freed them if he so wished. Herodes had appointed the twin girls his cook and cupbearer. These were jobs which had brought him into daily contact with them, and he took his pets along on the journey.

In any case, it was advantageous to Herodes that he appear out of his mind with grief at the girls' death when he met with Marcus Aurelius to discuss the tyranny charges against him. At Sirmium the emperor pardoned Herodes and Alcimedon, but placed the burden of blame on some of Herodes' other freedmen.[30] He punished them as mildly as possible; this verdict is reminiscent of that following the trial for Regilla's death, when the emperor found Alcimedon guilty, though he evidently did not punish him. Marcus Aurelius continued to cover Herodes with an inviolable mantle of protection, rendering him virtually immune from private and public prosecution. In a lengthy Greek inscription displayed in the Roman marketplace in Athens dealing with appeals from that city, the emperor refers to

Herodes as his "own" *(ton emon)*.[31] The date of the inscription is probably 174/175.[32] Herodes was also selected to be a candidate for a second consulship.

When Regilla died in premature childbirth the fetus was said to be of eight months' gestation. Philostratus gives the age of the fetus because it supplied a reason for its death. Even if Regilla had not been kicked in the stomach, the chances that mother and infant would have survived childbirth were slim. Greek and Roman medical writers believed that a baby born at eight months would not live and that giving birth to such a baby could be fatal to the mother too. Birth weight was not viewed as the problem, for it was thought that a baby born after a seven months' gestation had a better chance to live than the child of eight months. The latter was viewed as unlucky.[33]

An issue worth considering is how anyone would know for certain that Regilla was in her eighth month. Medical texts of the time allow for some monthly blood loss in the first few months of pregnancy, when, as was believed, the fetus is not large enough to use up all the blood.[34] Furthermore, a child who died would be redefined as "an eight months' child." If the mother died in her eighth month together with her child, however, there is always the suspicion that the death was nudged into the eighth month to exonerate anyone involved with the termination of the pregnancy. In such unfortunate, even hopeless, circumstances Alcimedon's guilt might well have to be reconsidered.

A simple spontaneous miscarriage is unlikely in a woman who had survived at least five previous births. Nevertheless, there are conditions, for example, eclampsia (toxemia, convulsions, and coma), that could bring on such a disaster in an advanced pregnancy. Furthermore, Regilla was in her late thirties and about twenty years had passed since she bore her first child. Child bearing until forty was not considered abnormal, and by the age of forty some women had been pregnant more than a dozen times.[35] As a consequence of the state of ancient gynecology and general health practices, continuous pregnancies must have taken a heavy toll even on upper-class women.

Nowadays in the United States, the murder of a pregnant woman and her fetus may be prosecuted as a double murder, since some refer to an eight months' fetus as a "baby." In California in 2004, Scott Peterson was convicted of a double murder in the killing of his wife Laci, who was eight months pregnant. Their son was variously referred to as "their unborn child"[36] and "fetus."[37] In contrast, according to Roman law, the child belonged to its father who, wielding *patria potestas* (the legal power of the father), had the right to determine whether his offspring was to live or die. Under normal circumstances, this right was to be exercised after the infant was born, not by a kick while still *in utero*.

The Familia without Regilla

> Blessed is the person who has built a new city,
> giving it the name "Regilla's," he lives exulting.
> But I live grieving that this estate exists for me without my
>   dear wife and my home is half complete.
> Thus the gods mix a lifetime for mortals
> having both joys and sorrows as neighbors.

Herodes added these lines to the inscription on the Gate of Eternal Harmony. In this lugubrious poem Herodes suggests that at one time he was happily married, but then by losing Regilla his home is only half full. In such public ways, he made known his grief over his wife's death.

Other members of the familia perhaps did not grieve, at least privately. Nonrelated subordinates, including the trophimoi, freedmen's children, and adopted son, comprised another, more numerous part of Herodes' familia. This portion benefited from Regilla's death in that Alcimedon's children and the trophimoi also won a more secure place in their master's affections, exploiting the vacuum in Herodes' emotional life. Regilla's children were the most obvious losers. Not only had they lost their mother, but they also were obliged to continue to live with a father who had been charged with murdering her. Furthermore, without their mother to intercede, they now had to tolerate sharing family intimacy and privileges not only with the trophimoi but also with a freedman's children.

Did Herodes lavish affection on Alcimedon's children in order to secure his freedman's silence? We know that Marcus Aurelius condemned Alcimedon, but that Herodes did not punish him. It is clear that a freedman would hardly have dared to murder a woman of Regilla's status on his own initiative. On the other hand, during this period the freedmen of Athens were notably bold and exercised political clout. They had earlier attempted to deny Herodes much of his inheritance and future control over it by persuading his father Claudius Atticus to bequeath one *mina* annually to every Athenian citizen.[38]

After Regilla's death, Alcimedon remained in Herodes' household and his daughters continued to enjoy Herodes' favors. That their relationship remained as it had been, or became even warmer than before Regilla's death, would seem to indicate that Alcimedon had not displeased his master. An act of homicide in the presence of a crowd of slaves would not have posed a problem. Herodes owned many slaves, and in such a household there must have been witnesses. For example, there were the twenty-four boys he had bought in order to help Bradua learn to read. Among the slaves and freedmen some would surely have seen who had ordered the kick and who administered it, and whether the actual perpetrator was their master or his freedman. Alcimedon himself would have had enemies and rivals among the slaves who would have spoken if he had acted alone; but they would not have dared to accuse someone so close to their master who had acted at his behest. Herodes' household slaves were aware that he had had freedmen beaten, robbed, and killed.[39] If freedmen could be treated in this way, slaves (who were even lower on the social scale) could expect worse. Terror sealed their lips.

Regilla's children were old enough to understand the events surrounding their mother's death and they may have caught wind of the truth, but what could they do? They may even have witnessed the beating and heard their mother cry out as she expelled the fetus. *Patria potestas* was in force: testimony against one's own father was not acceptable in a Roman court.

Because she was eight months pregnant, it is unlikely that Regilla's provocation or infraction (if there was any) was sexual in nature. Philostratus reports that a certain wise man named Lucius, upon learning that slaves were preparing white radishes for Herodes, said "Herodes wrongs Regilla by eating white radishes in a black house."[40] Lucius alludes to the traditional Greek treatment of the adulterer by the cuckolded husband: pushing a long white radish up his anus. Adultery was a serious crime, but Philostratus describes the reason for the beating as "trivial" *(ouch hyper megalon)*. Anything that would impugn Herodes' honor would not be "trivial." Furthermore, inscriptions repeatedly praised Regilla for self-control (sophrosyne). Though this virtue was commonly ascribed to women, if Regilla's behavior was notoriously lacking in chastity, perhaps other ways would have been devised to praise her. It is likely that Regilla was well behaved, for her isolation in Greece meant that she had no convenient refuge from her husband. On the other hand, her upbringing had not prepared her to be totally submissive. Furthermore, she was in an advanced state of pregnancy, a time when many women do not sleep well and are vexed by other symptoms. We do not know the time of year when Regilla died, but if she had to endure a hot Athenian summer while eight months pregnant, then she may have been irritable and have demanded indulgences that she would not have dared to ask for normally. Herodes needed another son. With that son perhaps in her belly, Regilla may have thought the time was favorable to oppose her husband and make some demands on him.

It is believable that Herodes, though violent himself and incensed at some minor provocation, dispatched Alcimedon to inflict his deadly wife abuse. Here he behaved like Nero, who had twice ordered his subordinates to murder his mother. In a milieu where slaves and freedmen are always present, even impetuous acts, especially those that require physical activity, may well be carried out by subordinates who serve as the master's "right-hand man." According to Roman law, a slave or freedman could be found guilty of homicide, but the person who commanded that a murder be carried out was also considered a murderer.[41] The murder of Regilla followed the usual patterns of domestic abuse in the west: the husband abuses or murders the wife. In Rome most homicides occurred within the family.[42] The familia included not only blood relatives and adoptees; slaves and freedmen were also members, and in Herodes' familia the distinction between statuses was blurred.

The freedman Alcimedon was the obvious suspect, and Marcus Aurelius found him guilty of administering the lethal kick. Alcimedon had the most to gain from Regilla's death. She stood between his master and himself and his family. Iago-like, Alcimedon may have fed Herodes denigrating slander about her son Bradua when he was a child.[43] Herodes had been told that his son was foolish, had a poor memory, and could not learn to read. These accusations alienated him from his little boy, for they concerned talents that he, a man of learning, especially prized. Philostratus tells a similar story about Scopelianus, one of Herodes' teachers of declamation.[44] Scopelianus' cook, who was a slave, convinced the old man that his son was trying to murder him to gain his inheritance. Scopelianus thereupon rewrote his will, disinheriting his own son, appointing the slave as his heir, and calling him his son. Herodes thus ignored his own son and looked elsewhere in the younger generation for children upon whom he could pin his hopes. Alcimedon is likely to have been responsible for slandering Bradua and for manipulating his master so that he transferred his affections to Alcimedon's twin daughters. With Regilla out of the picture, Alcimedon was better able to wield his influence over Herodes. Subtle blackmail was a ready tool. Alcimedon knew too much about the murder and about Herodes' other transgressions.

Autopsy of the Marriage

The past was a powerful influence on Herodes' behavior. At Athens and Sparta there was a self-conscious revival of classical customs and culture. The first such revival had occurred during the Hellenistic period (323–30 B.C.). This Hellenistic version of the past was filtered through the Macedonian conquerors of Greece and their intellectual entourage, including Aristotle to some extent and later Peripatetics such as Demetrius of Phalerum. Important literary texts of archaic and classical Greece were also edited in the Hellenistic period and then read by Greeks and Romans alike. The revival in the imperial period was influenced as much by knowledge of classical Greece as by the Hellenistic interpretation of antiquity. That Herodes endeavored to recall, even to re-create, the archaic and classical periods of Greek history can be observed in a wide range of evidence, including the names he bestowed on his daughters, his blatant display of homoerotic affection for younger men, his revival of the Panathenaia, and his use of motifs from archaic and classical art and literature. Furthermore, upper-class Athenian women in the classical period were expected to be secluded and silent.[45] Perhaps Herodes expected such subdued behavior from Roman Regilla, but in times of stress she failed to conform to the ancient model.

The *oikos* (household) may be viewed as a microcosm of the *polis* (state); the private sphere a mirror of the public. According to Aristotle's neat analysis, the male citizen is in charge of both spheres.[46] The wife, however, is also a citizen, a passive citizen, but not a slave. Yet, within his own city Herodes behaved as a tyrant. His fellow citizens repeatedly complained to the emperor that Herodes was trying to become a tyrant. In the fourth century B.C. the Athenians had reenacted their ancestral legislation against tyranny and displayed the law prominently in the marketplace.[47] Humiliated by waves of conquest, first by the Macedonians and then by the Romans, the Athenians were nostalgic for the glorious days of Periclean democracy. Instead they had to tolerate Herodes, a capricious latter-day tyrant of sorts, who treated them like children, withholding the legacy bequeathed to them by his father, but then seducing them with lavish gifts. The tradition was well established in his family. Hipparchos, the name of Herodes' grandfather, was also the name of one of the most hated tyrants in Athenian history. The Athenians charged Herodes with tyranny. Such charges were not trivial, for the emperor at Rome usually tolerated petty monarchs and despots, as long as they were loyal to the central government.[48] Marcus Aurelius took the charge seriously enough to summon Herodes to Sirmium to face his accusers even though he held him in great affection personally. Sirmium was in Pannonia (Serbia), not an easy journey from Athens for a septuagenarian, and Marcus Aurelius must have thought the charge had enough merit to impose this burden on his old tutor.

For ideas about marriage in Roman Greece in the days of Regilla and Herodes, the best source is Plutarch. We do not know, however, whether Regilla and Herodes read these works. Plutarch emphasizes the importance of persuasion in creating a harmonious marriage.[49] Herodes was a teacher of rhetoric. Nevertheless, he frequently resorted to physical violence rather than persuasion. Though contemporaries who wrote about the proper relationships within marriage believed that the wife should be subordinate to her husband, they did not advocate that the husband exercise tyrannical power over an unwilling wife.[50] Greeks generally assumed that the male would dominate the female, but Plutarch advised that a husband must not humiliate a noble wife; he must not break her spirit. Surely wife abuse in the form of a kick to a pregnant abdomen runs counter to this advice.

A contemporary of Plutarch, the Stoic Musonius Rufus, took an even more radical position than Plutarch on gender relations. He believed that the education of girls and boys should be the same and he rejected the double standard in sexual behavior.[51] He wrote that the purpose of marriage is a partnership in living and creating children *(What Is the Goal of Marriage?)*. Musonius thought that men no less than women should control their appetites and suppress anger. This view was consistent with the Socratic idea that sophrosyne (self-control) is a virtue of men as well as of women. It ran counter to Herodes' rejection of the *apatheia* (lack of emotion) of the Stoics. Because the emperor Marcus Aurelius was a Stoic and most Roman statesmen were too, more or less, these beliefs were not only theoretical but served as a practical guide to life. Herodes was aware of the new conjugal ideal and advertised it on the Gate of Eternal Harmony. In the inscription added after Regilla's death he refers to his marriage and to the division of his estate as a new polis.[52] This metaphor suggests orderliness and civic government according to Greek law and custom. The Greek word for "harmony" is *homonoia,* literally "being of the same mind." In view of the gender politics of the period, it is fair to say that to achieve this goal, the wife was the partner who would have to make her mind conform to her husband's. In any case, for Regilla and Herodes, ironically, harmony was not eternal.

There is no evidence that Bradua had taken any interest in his sister before her death. He was too involved in his own political career. In the larger context, the case of Bradua acting in behalf of Regilla by bringing suit against Herodes may be understood as a struggle for power between a Roman and a Greek. Ethnic identities and economic and social status were underlying issues. With Regilla dead, of course, ongoing gender difference did not play a part in this rivalry. Bradua and Herodes were each stereotypical upper-class representatives of their ethnic groups. Bradua was a Roman of Italy. His benefactions were confined to a single city in Italy. In contrast, though Herodes boasted that evidence for his euergetism (philanthropy) could be found all over the world, in truth his gifts were to be found in areas frequented by the Greeks or colonized by them, including southern Italy, Asia Minor, and the Greek mainland.[53]

Herodes was the wealthiest private citizen of his day in the empire and he did not conceal his wealth. With Regilla dead, he readily shifted the focus to himself as the grieving husband.[54] Using his fortune to proclaim his innocence, he changed the archaeological landscape in Rome and Athens. Monuments on the Appian Way and at the foot of the Acropolis still stand to shape our historical memory of the wife Herodes claimed he had loved and of the time when they lived. If an educated and cultivated Roman woman and a Greek man could not enjoy a harmonious marriage, was the Pax Romana fact or fiction in an empire peopled with barbarians who could not even speak to each other in Greek or Latin?

Traditionally Greek husbands married very young women in the expectation that they would be able to teach them and to mold them into the sort of wife they wanted. Herodes continued this process after Regilla's death. Rid of her corporeal presence and her clothing, he shaped her into an appropriate recipient of his mourning and adulation. Certainly Herodes found the Regilla of memory far easier to manipulate and control than any living wife.

CHAPTER 5

REGILLA'S FINAL RESTING PLACE

Appia Annia Regilla, wife of Herodes, the light of the house,
by the gods and heroes, whoever possesses this place,
whoever disturbs any part of these things, including the
    images and the honors of the statues,
for him may the earth not bear crops, nor the sea be
    navigable. May he and his kinsmen perish evilly.[1]

THE INSCRIPTION ABOVE was purportedly found on a marble
base of a dedicatory altar in the remains of a temple-tomb in
Marousi, a suburb of Athens.[2] Either Herodes composed the ep-
igraph himself, or he paid a poet to write it and dictated the
content. As restored, it presents the same image of Regilla as
"[the light of the] house" that occurs in two other inscriptions at
Marathon and Rome.[3] The inscription goes on to include allusions to Herodes, and devotes many lines to the curses that he
habitually added to such monuments in a vain attempt to preserve the monument for posterity.

Yet where the remains of Regilla were placed has not been established beyond doubt. Because of the violence of her death
and the accusations surrounding it, it is likely that at first Herodes disposed of her corpse quickly and without public commemoration, though such unseemly haste might aggravate suspicion. Although he chose to inter his children in sarcophagi (as

was customary at the time), he may have had Regilla cremated. In any case, as a result her brother Bradua was not able to produce any material evidence such as a bloodied dress to support his accusation in court.

Many Romans devoted a great deal of attention to the location and decor of their tombs, for most believed in some sort of survival after death.[4] Furthermore, even if they were buried in private tombs, which only their descendants would visit, they cared about the image they would present to posterity. It is obvious, however, that Regilla died suddenly, before completing her expected span of years, and before choosing her final resting place or her last images. Herodes, although some twenty-four years her senior, outlived Regilla by about seventeen years. He had deployed his wife while she was alive as his link to superior beings, both imperial and divine, and he did so even more after her death when he had plenty of time to determine her final destination and shape her image for eternity. This he did with deliberate ambiguity. It is not clear whether she came to rest in Greece or Rome, nor whether she was alone, or with some of her children, or with her husband. Furthermore, the location may have changed over time. Regilla had been elevated to the status of a heroine. Divinities and other superhuman beings are not confined to a single geographical context; their temples are found in many places.

In 1866 four sarcophagi were found in a marble tomb in Kephisia and were identified by their location and decorative motifs as the graves of Herodes' and Regilla's family.[5] As was usual in the second century A.D., the burial had been in a private structure to be visited only by the family who presumably knew the names of the deceased; therefore no inscriptions identifying them were provided. It is conceivable that Regilla's remains were placed in this tomb, at least immediately following her death. Three of the sarcophagi probably held the bodies of Regilla's children. Athenais, who seems to have died by 161 just after her mother, was not buried at Kephisia but within the city walls.[6] Therefore the children in the sarcophagi were: Regillus, who had died during his mother's lifetime; Elpinike, who died around 165; and perhaps the unnamed child whom Regilla was carrying when she died. Even if this premature infant had lived outside the womb for a while rather than dying with Regilla, it would not have required elaborate mourning and burial because dead infants did not cause ritual pollution. Nevertheless, in view of Herodes' extravagant indulgence in displays of emotion when an opportunity presented itself, it is quite possible that the third burial is of Regilla's and Herodes' last child. Apparently the infant died when it was three months old, just before it would have participated in the hair-cutting ceremony of the Apatouria, a festive occasion when Herodes would have introduced the baby to his phratry ("brotherhood"), a social and political unit that validated an individual's membership in the citizen body. Herodes alludes to the death of a three-month-old in a poem that was discovered inscribed near the family tomb. As usual, in this poem he draws attention to himself, rather than to the untimely death, but much of the text is ambiguous:

> Herodes dedicates this hair, not for a whole year
> having let his hair grow, nor, dear child, cutting yours in the
>   third month
> did he put it in the depths of the earth.
>
> Herodes soaked the ends of his hair with tears,
> a sure indication to the three souls of his children
> that sometime you will welcome the body of your father
>   among your coffins.[7]

There are other candidates. Herodes was audacious and indiscreet; therefore he may have dared to entomb one of his foster sons along with his natural children, and Achilles, Memnon, or Polydeukion may have occupied one of the sarcophagi.[8] There were many Roman precedents for joint burial of members of the familia of every status. Thus huge *columbaria* (communal tombs with niches like a dovecot) often housed the ashes of the elite, and of their slaves and freedmen. Whether Regilla's surviving children (and Regilla herself—if she was buried with them) found the presence of Herodes' trophimos irritating is not known; they may have had to endure the presence of one of their father's darlings by their side forever. In the inscription just translated above, Herodes promised three children that he would join them when he died. Therefore we may deduce that the fourth sarcophagus was designated either for another child or for himself. In this inscription, Herodes does not mention joining his wife in death. We may speculate that he avoided proximity to his murdered wife's avenging ghost which would have hovered around her physical remains, just as he sent her clothing to be dedicated at Eleusis, and later located her cenotaph in Rome far from his villa.

The sarcophagus was historically a Roman rather than a Greek form of disposing of the dead, but it became popular in the second century A.D. outside of Italy.[9] The decor of sarcophagi can provide clues about the occupants and survivors, especially when the purchaser was Herodes Atticus, a person not likely to buy something ready-made, unless he was in a hurry. Two of the sarcophagi are decorated with conventional themes of the time; one is not decorated. These may have held the younger children who died suddenly. The fourth is elaborately adorned with sculpture on all four sides, and for that reason especially it is thought to have held the body of Herodes' older daughter, Elpinike, whose death was particularly poignant. Because her younger sister married while Elpinike remained unwed, it is possible to speculate that the older sister was ill for a long time, and that the sarcophagus was designed with care.

Consistent with the taste Herodes displayed in other artistic efforts, the style of the sculpture on the sarcophagus is archaizing, reminiscent of archaic and classical Greek art. The motifs are carefully selected to recall Greek and Roman myths, in particular myths connected with Sparta. On one long side of the sarcophagus, Helen is shown flanked by her brothers Polydeukes and Kastor. Karyatids stand on all four corners of the sarcophagus. The best-known karyatids are those in the Porch of the Maidens in the Erechtheion, the temple of Poseidon on the Athenian Acropolis. The Erechtheion karyatids support the entablature of a roof upon their heads.

Though karyatids are a decorative and architectural element, they are also an illustration of women's servitude and immobility. In the fifth century B.C. when the Erechtheion was constructed, women did carry urns of water and other heavy burdens on their heads publicly, while respectable women remained under the roof of their home. An elite Roman woman could consider this image as a representation of the real work of slaves and lower-class women who were obliged to perform menial labor. The heads of Regilla's daughters, of course, never carried more of a burden than a heavy wig. Herodes liked to use karyatids; they also appear in his constructions at Loukou and at Regilla's estate on the Via Appia.

The sculptural program on the sarcophagus alludes to the alleged Trojan ancestry of Elpinike's mother and the connections with Sparta on her father's side. This putative genealogy remained vital some fourteen hundred years after the Trojan War.[10] Eros is carved on one of the short sides. On the opposite short side, a swan rapes a struggling Leda (see fig. 5.1). Zeus had disguised himself as a swan in order to accost the innocent girl. It is evident that the arrows shot by Eros reached only Zeus. From this union Leda gave birth to Helen, Kastor, and Polydeukes.[11] Whether the occupants of the tomb considered rape scenes repugnant, or whether they accepted or ignored them as ancient myths or fiction, this scene was imposed on them for eternity.[12] In mythology, rape was also a metaphor for marriage. For women to die unwed was considered pitiful, since marriage was

Fig. 5.1.   Sarcophagus at Kephisia showing Leda and the swan. Nude, and trying to cover herself with a cloth, Leda struggles in vain against Zeus, who is disguised as a swan. He is equipped with a sharp beak and ferocious feet, while she is weaponless. Though she pushes him away with her arm, his long curved neck extends easily to her.

their major goal in life. Thus the rape imagery and allusions to Eros may have been an effort to provide Elpinike in death with the marriage that she did not attain in life.

The disposal of Regilla's corporeal remains epitomizes the enduring dilemma of the identity of a married woman in antiquity. Was she still considered a member of her natal family? Or was she a member of her husband's family and kin to her children, with a good likelihood of being buried with them?

Most upper-class Roman women married *sine manu* (without the husband's power over a wife).[13] In this type of marriage the woman and her property belonged legally to her natal family and were in the power of her own father or his successor as head of the household, but her children belonged to their father's family. Thus the mother was not legally a member of the same familia as her children. She was attached to her children by sentiment, and in cases like Regilla's, by matrilineal naming, but not by law. Cremated remains are easily transported and easily concealed. Was Regilla united in death with her children in Greece? Or was she cremated and were her ashes transported to her ancestral estate near Rome? She had lived twenty years in Italy and fifteen years in Greece, where she met a violent death. It is not possible for us to know what kind of burial she would have preferred, but apparently Herodes was uncertain as well.

Despite his inscribed vow to join his children in Kephisia after he died, Herodes left instructions that he himself should be buried at Marathon.[14] After he died, however, the Athenians displayed their gratitude for his benefactions with an enthusiasm that they had usually withheld from him during his lifetime. Though burial within the city walls was no longer practiced, the Athenians had buried Athenais within the city and eventually buried Herodes in the Panathenaic stadium that he had built.[15] In this way, Herodes' tomb was juxtaposed to the temple of Tyche he had built for Regilla. He was thus doomed to be reminded of her forever. The onlooker, unaware that Herodes himself had requested burial at Marathon, would have imagined that he had been close to his wife.

If Regilla's remains were entombed at Kephisia or Marousi, archaeologists have been unable to identify them securely. Admittedly, most of the material traces of ancient Athens have perished or lie unexcavated beneath the modern city, but on the other hand the vast majority of what Herodes himself had constructed survives sufficiently to be studied today. Herodes built a cenotaph for Regilla at her estate on the Appian Way perhaps because he was troubled by her unquiet spirit that wanted to be free of Greece, where she had met an untimely death, and that longed to return to the place where she had been born. Or perhaps the estate at Rome simply offered Herodes an opportunity to construct another monument in a central location in the hope of silencing rumors of wife murder by advertising his grief on stone.

After Regilla's death, Herodes dedicated her clothing to Demeter at Eleusis, a site of political interest to him. Marcus Aurelius, who was Herodes' friend and protector, followed Hadrian in showing special favor to the sanctuary, establishing it as a center of an imperial cult in Attica and endowing it with monuments.[16] Members of the Eumolpidai and Kerykes clans monopolized the priesthoods; Herodes claimed descent from the latter. Although Regilla was disqualified by her Roman birth from holding a priesthood at Eleusis, gifts of her property were acceptable.

Cult centers often were storehouses of treasures donated by the pious; functioning almost like museums, their ancient, valuable, unusual, or artistic possessions attracted visitors to the sites. Regilla's clothing must have been valuable, and would have been testified to by items inventoried on inscriptions. A wealthy woman could dress in linen, or in superb Apulian wool, or in silk from Kos or even China. Thus this dedication was not only an act of piety, but of ostentation. At the same time, Herodes divested himself of reminders of Regilla, including outfits associated with special memories and cloth imbued with her personal scents.

Perhaps it was because Demeter was equated with Ceres, the ancient Italian goddess of marriage, that Herodes needed to be generous to her. Ceres was a protector of wives, and the penalties for wife abuse were severe. In early Rome a husband who sold his wife was consecrated to the infernal deities and executed.[17] Furthermore, if a husband divorced his wife for any reason other than adultery, poisoning his children, or counterfeiting his keys, she took half his property; the other half was consecrated to Ceres.[18] Demeter and Ceres were also assimilated to Isis, an Egyptian goddess who enjoyed great popularity in the Roman Empire. Egyptian artistic and religious motifs have been discovered on the estates of Regilla and Herodes at Marathon and the Via Appia.[19]

Odeion

Herodes dedicated an odeion, or recital hall, to Regilla at the foot of the south slope of the Athenian acropolis (see fig. 5.2).[20] This elaborate building was constructed in less than fourteen years and finished by A.D. 174, when Pausanias mentions it as completed after he had written his account of Athens in his first book.[21] It was the largest odeion in Greece, and could hold an audience of 5,000. The structure was massive and richly adorned. The seats, pavement, and walls were covered with white marble, but ancient commentators were especially impressed by the expensive cedar roof that spanned the huge area by means of some remarkable feat of engineering.[22] Many of the bricks are inscribed with an ideogram of Theta, Eta, and Rho, possibly for "Theater of Herodes and Regilla" or "to Regilla." The interlocking letters—if they in fact refer to the initials of Regilla and Herodes ("Herodes" in Greek starts with an aspirated Eta)—are an emblem of an intimate embrace.[23]

The odeion occupied space that had been sacred since the earliest days of the city, a place abounding in mythological and divine associations.[24] The odeion was not a purely secular space: the musical and theatrical arts were traditionally sacred to Dionysus and Apollo. The back wall towered so high that it threatened to compete with the acropolis itself, or at the very least to share the sacred aura. Thus Regilla was installed among the

Fig. 5.2.   Odeion auditorium with the acropolis in the background. The odeion was dedicated to Regilla. Perhaps as a tribute to ethnicity of the dedicatee, it was built like a Roman theater, in contrast to the neighboring theater of Dionysus and to Herodes' Panathenaic stadium. The towering wall behind the stage associates the odeion with the acropolis and divinities above.

immortals, and Herodes himself was elevated to superhuman status by association with a wife who had become divine. The emperor tolerated the pretensions of his old tutor and his construction of a minor ruler cult replete with human divinities and monuments. Herodes was not the first nonroyal person to heroize members of his family, but his great wealth allowed him to translate his pretensions into public monuments.[25]

Herodes was in a great hurry to build this monument. Was it so that he could have a public icon testifying to his love for his wife, and a bribe to quiet gossiping tongues in Athens? The same question might be asked about his addition of an epigram on the Gate of Eternal Harmony at Marathon to advertise his grief.

Regilla's Property

Regilla died suddenly; she could not have expected to die. Had she been a man of the same economic status, a will would have been available for just such an emergency. But we do not know whether elite women like Regilla generally made wills as men in their class did, or whether it was normal for them to die intestate. According to the Law of Three Children *(ius iii liberorum)*, a freeborn woman who bore three children was released from male guardianship. Thus Regilla had the right to devise her property as she wished, free from the control of her husband or brother, so long as she followed the strictures of Roman law.

The laws on succession, however, are ambiguous. There were legal obstacles that discouraged women from making wills.[26] In a *sine manu* marriage, it was assumed that the property would revert to the woman's family who had furnished it, and that a will would be written only to the disadvantage of the agnates (relatives by blood through the father). Regilla's brother Bradua was her closest agnate, and thus in the absence of a will his claim to her estate was valid. On the other hand, Regilla may have made a will directing that her children inherit her property. When she died, her children Bradua, Elpinike, and Athenais were alive. It must have been apparent to Regilla that her husband favored his daughters, but disliked their son Bradua, and that if he disinherited him, her property would be all that Bradua would have. We do not know the intentions of Regilla, and can only attempt to deduce them from the arrangements later made regarding her property.

Whatever Regilla's intentions, Herodes seized control of her estate. Elpinike was alive at her mother's death, but died soon after. Eventually Regilla's only surviving child, Bradua, inherited her property on the Via Appia. Because he was young when his mother died and evidently not emancipated from his father's guardianship *(patria potestas)*, Herodes managed it and built on it without inhibition as though it were his own.[27] In A.D. 178, the law changed. The *Senatus Consultum Orfitianum* allowed children a right to succeed to their mother's property in preference to her agnates.[28] In any case, Herodes was dead by A.D. 177, thus freeing Bradua from *patria potestas*—if he had not already been freed from his father's control—and Bradua inherited Regilla's property. Since he had been disinherited in his father's will, his mother's property must have constituted the total or at least a substantial portion of whatever fortune he had, though one doubts that he had the means to continue to build on the property on the same scale as Herodes did. Thus the major renovations on this lavish estate must be attributed to Herodes.

Regilla's untimely death followed by Herodes' defeat of her brother in court enabled the widower to take possession of her land. Since Herodes was so much older than Regilla, in the natural course of events he would have died, leaving his wife a widow. Eventually the estate would have passed to their children. Aside from sentimental value, the property on the Via Appia was worth a substantial amount. If Regilla's brother had not pursued his case against Herodes, and if there had been goodwill among the parties concerned, Bradua the elder, who lived at Rome, could have managed the estate until the younger Bradua came of age. At least the property of the Annii Regilli would not have fallen into the hands of a despised foreigner who had been accused of murdering the previous owner.

At her death, Regilla's property consisted largely, or entirely, of her estate on the Via Appia that she had received from her father. Whether any of the family property at Canosa was in her name is not known. The land at Marathon that was Herodes' marriage gift to his wife was surrounded by his own property and readily absorbed back into it. For generations, the Annii Regilli had owned a suburban estate at the third milestone of the Via Appia. The value of the property was enhanced by its proximity to the city of Rome, an easy journey when the heat of the city became intolerable, and a short return trip for political duties and social obligations. It was common for senators to have an urban residence and additional property in rural locations.[29] This suburban villa was ideal for a senator and had served many generations of the Annii Regilli. Regilla's brother may well have been using it in the absence of his sister.

The estate was vast.[30] The country villa with its surrounding gardens and huge elaborate nymphaeum occupied a small portion. The remainder of the property was devoted to gardens, farmland, woods, pastures, orchards, wheat fields, outdoor pavilions, sacred precincts, and other buildings. Some land remained uncultivated so that the Annii Regilli and their guests could hunt.[31] The area even now teems with birds, snakes, foxes, rabbits, and other smaller mammals. Domestic animals and birds were raised and fish swam in fishponds.

Slaves lived on the estate in their own enclave. They cultivated fruit, olives, grain, and vegetables. Good wine is produced in the Castelli nowadays and was then on the estate, at least for everyday consumption. Buildings were decentralized and scattered artfully around the estate. Discreetly hidden service structures included cisterns, drainage canals, and whatever else was needed on an estate with a large population of slaves and with owners accustomed to rustic luxury. Water flowed abundantly as the estate was able to tap aqueducts leading to the city, including the Aqua Claudia and the Aqua Marcia. The property was particularly lovely in the spring.

Here on the land that had been in their family for generations, the Annii Regilli children spent many of the happiest times of their youth. Perhaps because of Regilla's special affection for the place, her parents gave it to her as part of her dowry. It is unlikely that she ever saw it again after she sailed for Athens. Herodes' marital gift to Regilla of rugged, inhospitable property at Marathon was a poor substitute for her verdant estate at Rome.

The biographies of Herodes and Regilla and the archaeological remains suggest two starting points for Herodes' building projects on Regilla's estate. Herodes may have begun work soon after their marriage, before the couple left for Athens.[32] Yet, considering that his construction at the property destroyed much of the earlier villa and completed the transformation of simple farmland, fields, vineyards, and olive groves into highly cultivated property crammed with richly adorned structures, it is difficult to imagine that even he would have been so arrogant as to have started it while his father-in-law was alive and his marriage just begun. Therefore it is more likely that Herodes carried out his plans after Regilla's death, perhaps beginning when he was recalled to Rome for the homicide trial.

This chronology is consistent with the consecutive pattern of Herodes' expensive building projects, with the Panathenaic stadium and the aqueducts at Alexandria Troas (a Roman colony near ancient Troy in Asia Minor), Canusium, and Olympia built before Regilla's death, and the odeion and the construction at the Via Appia after. Regilla's property was valuable, and her husband benefited financially from it. Even though Herodes was extremely wealthy, his ambitions were boundless.

A preliminary appraisal suggests that Herodes' posthumous portrayal of Regilla and their family varies according to the ideal audience envisioned and the regional context in which the artifact would be viewed. He was an expert in visual propaganda. Herodes' monuments in Greece include several public structures that refer to the Greek artistic achievement in theater and sculpture and draw the attention of a vast audience to Regilla's interest in music and her religious activities. Those near Rome seem more private and removed from a potentially hostile audience that Herodes must have despaired of seducing with public benefactions and laments. For example, any casual passerby might examine the inscription at the Gate of Eternal Harmony, but only invited guests were intended to read the inscriptions at the estate on the Via Appia.

Herodes obliterated the Republican villa at the Via Appia by siting his own on top of the earlier building, which itself had undergone some renovation in the early empire. Malice may not have been his sole inspiration. Not only the existing infrastructure, but also the excellent location of the earlier villa encouraged subsequent builders to choose the same site, looking over to the Castelli Romani, still a weekend retreat southeast of Rome. As was the case with Nero's Golden House and other substantial buildings, part of the earlier structure was hidden beneath the superimposed buildings and some of it has survived. But Nero had suffered *damnatio memoriae* and his extravagant palace was infamous. Though it is fair to acknowledge that it doubtless needed major improvements, Regilla's family villa (like Regilla herself) was eradicated by Herodes' desires. That Regilla's ancestral estate is usually known as Herodes' contributes as well to her invisibility to posterity.[33]

Revenge on Regilla's brother Bradua for the murder trial was surely a motive in Herodes' plans for total renovation. He may also have felt that his own son, Bradua, was too inept and inexperienced to do anything worthwhile with the property. In addition, Herodes had some history of not venerating old objects simply because of their antiquity. For example, he had dared to replace the images of Demeter and Kore at Olympia and to substitute new sculptures made of Pentelic marble.[34] Since pagan worship centered, in part, on the image as a form of divine incarnation, this substitution could have been interpreted negatively as irreverence.

The cryptoporticus (vaulted corridor, see fig. 5.3) and other structures of the Republican villa were preserved as a foundation under the new building to raise it and improve the panoramic views. Even in the oppressive summer heat the cryptoporticus offered cool rooms for an afternoon nap. Since the older rooms were used only for sleeping or as a passageway, and not for entertaining guests, they were not highly decorated.

In contrast to the earlier villa, Herodes' edifice seemed more like a palace, and the style may be described as ostentatious, competitive, and pedantic, reflecting his imperious, tyrannical personality. Rome had long since assimilated the language, culture, and religion of the Greeks. Despite the fact that Rome conquered Greece, Herodes' estate, as much as he dared, gives the opposite impression. His version of the estate is not merely an objective correlative of the poet Horace's dictum: *Graecia capta ferum victorem cepit* ("a conquered Greece conquered its savage victor").[35] Herodes' visible use of the Greek language in inscriptions, of Greek building elements, of Greek building materials, and of Eastern religion seems to flaunt his foreignness in this venerable Roman landscape. Philhellenism was fashionable among the Roman elite, but they did not reject their Roman identity. In contrast, Herodes' disdain for Latin and for Roman traditions was obvious. Yet his visual propaganda reminded the Roman visitor in various ways that he was not an interloper, but rather occupied the site legitimately as the surviving husband of

Fig. 5.3. Cryptoporticus at Regilla's estate. This structure was retained from the old villa. The frescoes, though poorly preserved, appear to be simple, restful, and conventional, and include candelabra, garlands, and branches with leaves.

the rightful owner. The image of Regilla that Herodes created and perpetuated at her estate gives information about himself, and exploits her *Romanitas* while shaping her into the appropriate consort for a Greek potentate who was a citizen of Rome.

Looming over the landscape was the huge tomb of Caecilia Metella, constituting an edifying contrast. Like Regilla, Caecilia Metella was descended from numerous consuls and heroes of the Republic. Caecilia Metella had married a Roman, the son of M. Licinius Crassus, a triumvir who had defeated the slave rebellion under Spartacus. Her tomb was built around 50 to 40 B.C.[36] Looking at this tomb in the distance as a young girl, Regilla doubtless thought that, like Caecilia Metella, she would marry a Roman aristocrat and live and die in Rome.

By the second century A.D., despite the Metelli and others like them, the Appian Way was no longer reserved for Roman families with historic pasts who could trace their lineage back to heroes of the early Republic. Herodes' neighbors at the fourth milestone included the Quintilii brothers, Sextus Quintilianus Condianus and Sextus Quintilianus Valerius Maximus, members of a vastly wealthy family from Alexandria Troas.[37] They were descended from a *novus homo*. Nerva (emperor A.D. 96–98) had elevated their father to the Senate, and like Herodes they had not been born in Italy.

Herodes, when he served as governor of the free cities of Asia, had improved the water supply at Alexandria Troas largely at his own expense.[38] He denigrated the Quintilii as "Trojans."[39] Well-educated, both Quintilii were authors of technical manuals and had held governmental posts in the empire. In the private sphere, the brothers' fraternal concord was well known and easily deduced from the facts that their villas were on the same property and they shared imperial posts. When the Quintilii served as proconsuls of Greece and constituted the highest court there, they had supported a faction of Athenians who were Herodes' political opponents and who accused him of tyranni-

Fig. 5.4.   Tomb of Caecilia Metella. This tomb of an upper-class woman of the late Republic is visible from Regilla's estate.

cal behavior.[40] Like Herodes, they were held in high regard by the emperor.[41] Marcus Aurelius refers to them as his "own" in the same Athenian inscription where he uses similar language about Herodes.[42] The Quintilii mocked Herodes for indulging his affection for his *trophimoi*, Achilles, Polydeukion, and Memnon, by erecting marble statues of them getting ready to hunt, hunting, and after the hunt.[43] Herodes could envy Maximus his son, Sextus Condianus, who excelled in talent, training, and cleverness, while he despised his own son Bradua for lack of intellectual ability and for dissolute behavior and had turned to foster sons and adopted sons instead. The huge estate of the Quintilii on the Via Appia was doubly grandiose because the brothers owned it together. Their estate was competitive with Herodes' in luxury, with its own hippodrome, nymphaea, large and small baths, and two cisterns. That the Quintilii were his rivals and critics and his next-door neighbors on the Via Appia must have riled Herodes. But he had not chosen the location of the estate; he acquired the property through marriage.

Regilla's Refuge

Regilla's cenotaph is located on the edge of her estate at the Via Appia (see fig. 5.5).[44] Perhaps Herodes wanted to provide a refuge for his wife's restless, vengeful spirit, raging about her murder and resentful at her husband's opportunistic usurpation and transformation of her property. It is understandable that he would place her cenotaph as far as possible from the main villa so that he could avoid looking at it. Nevertheless, he was able to exploit the occasion of Regilla's death to advance his image of devoted husband. The building is located on or near the site of the venerable temple of the Deus Rediculus (God of Return), and is now known in Italian as the Deo Redicolo.[45] The traveler leaving Rome would pray to the Deus Rediculus for a safe return. Regilla's bodily remains were probably in Greece; nonetheless a staircase leads to a burial chamber within.[46]

An inscription, ostensibly honoring Regilla, but also shedding glory on Herodes, was found in the gardens of the Palatine, and taken to England. It was described and published in 1676, but is now lost.[47] The content suggests that the stone originally stood at Regilla's cenotaph at the Deus Rediculus:

> Herodes dedicated this monument also to commemo-
> rate his misfortune and his wife's virtue.
>
> 5   But this is not a burial. Her body is in Greece and now
> beside her husband.

Fig. 5.5.   Cenotaph of Regilla at Deus Rediculus. This building is a small temple-like jewel built in the Italian temple or podium style, but adorned with Greek ornament such as the egg and dart that are still visible. It was constructed of polychrome brick with some Proconnesian marble. Colors distinguished the various architectural elements.

10   The Emperor Antoninus, called "Pius" by his country
         and everyone, proposed to the Senate that her son be
         enrolled among the Patricians in Rome,

15   and by decree he was enrolled.

Regilla's *arete* (virtue) is mentioned in lines 3–4. This idea of virtue is general, but similar to the praise of her sophrosyne (modesty) in Greece. An underlying message could be that since so perfect a woman could not deserve a kick in the abdomen, she died in some other way that could not possibly involve Herodes. If, as is likely, Regilla's son Bradua erected the monument when he inherited the property, he may have wanted to quiet nasty gossip about his parents and impose a post-mortem reconciliation between them. Furthermore, the statement in line 7 that Regilla was now beside her husband suggests that her ashes had been moved to Herodes' burial place next to the Panathenaic stadium across from the temple of Tyche where she had served as priestess. Or, at least from the point of view of the Via Appia, a tomb in Marousi could be loosely referred to as "beside her husband," since both were in Attica.

Herodes also constructed a temple known as the temple of Faustina dedicated to Demeter and Faustina the Elder (wife of Antoninus Pius), adjacent to the Via Latina (see fig. 5.6). In this way he continued to associate himself with the imperial family through his wife and to earn their gratitude. The New Demeter *(Deo nee)* and the Old *(Deo palaie)* were both honored in this temple. Faustina was titled "the New Demeter." Herodes dedicated a statue of Regilla as priestess of the Old Demeter there.[48] The cult of the Roman emperors and their families was long established. Thus, for example, Marcus Aurelius and Faustina were themselves considered divine and were also thought to incarnate various divinities.

Faustina's cult was especially associated with Ceres. Her proximity in the temple drew attention to Regilla's family connection with the imperial house. Ceres was goddess of marriage: the temple could be seen as constituting Herodes' continuing homage to the goddess of marriage, who demanded payment for the abuse of wives. On the other hand, although Ceres was seen as the Roman version of Demeter, it does not follow that all of Ceres' characteristics and attributes were grafted onto Demeter. Thus, by referring to Demeter rather than Ceres, Herodes may have attempted to avoid the punitive aspects of Ceres as goddess of marriage and protector of abused wives that were enshrined in Roman law. In any case, Regilla was associated with the goddess and with an empress who had joined the gods.[49] Faustina was divine, therefore her kin could not be mere mortals. As a distant relative of the deified Faustina, Regilla partook of the divine. It follows that Herodes, widower of Faustina's heroized kinswoman, was more than mortal.

Medallions on the barrel-vaulted ceiling (see fig. 5.7) and a

Fig. 5.6. Temple of Faustina: exterior. Originally a tetrastyle temple, in the seventeenth century the colonnade was walled in and today the building is known as the church of San Urbano.

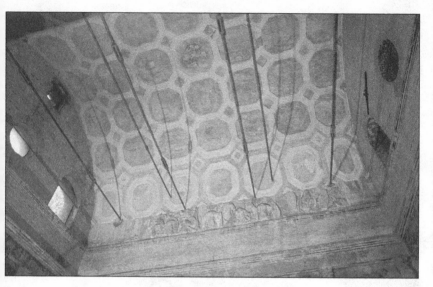

Fig. 5.7.   Temple of Faustina: interior fresco. The frieze depicts armor and
the ceiling is adorned with medallions.

frieze just below the ceiling on the north side, both in stucco relief, are generally in poor condition; however, two women are
depicted in a well-preserved section. One woman, thought to be
Faustina, holds two ducks and another, preserved only from the
waist down, holds another bird in her right hand. The latter has
been identified as Regilla.[50] The identifications are not secure
since both are now headless. But because Regilla and Faustina
are honored in this temple, there is a strong likelihood that
they are the women who are represented. In that case, the armor draws attention to the military triumphs of Regilla's ancestors. The array of armor represents various trophies.[51] These
include Gallic equipment which may allude to the cognomen
of Regilla's father Appius Annius Gallus. The motif is the apo-
theosis of Regilla, and the bird and ducks may be construed as
a sacrifice.[52] This interpretation is consistent with the efforts
of Herodes elsewhere to emphasize Regilla's connections with

Demeter, her lineage and kinship with the imperial family, and his own gratitude to the emperor for many favors including exonerating him from the charge of murdering his wife.

The Via Appia estate has also yielded another image of a woman thought to be Regilla. A sculpture in the round made of Greek marble showing a seated woman has been excavated, but the face has been restored. For these reasons, the portrait cannot be compared to the known representation of Regilla from her nymphaeum at Olympia.[53] The seated figure may be the one that had been placed in Regilla's shrine in the Triopeion and is referred to in Marcellus' poem about her.[54]

Immortal Regilla

Herodes endeavored to transform his dead wife into a benevolent spirit. He created new images and contexts for the wife he had destroyed. He appropriated and exploited Regilla's intimate connections with Roman history, while attempting at the same time through Greek cult and visual monuments to shape her into a wife who suited his image of himself.

The cult of Regilla is a theme that inspired and unified much of the building program at the Via Appia estate.[55] The cenotaph at the Deus Rediculus temple offered a resting place if her spirit desired to leave Greece and visit her sacred precinct in Italy.[56] Regilla's cult had many associations with Demeter and Ceres and with her distant kinswoman Faustina. Regilla's close relationship to Demeter, a reward for her service as priestess of the goddess, was also commemorated. She herself had expressed this preference at Olympia where she had chosen to identify herself simply as "Regilla, priestess of Demeter." Various members of her family fostered this special relationship with the goddess over many years. Herodes had also cultivated favor with Demeter in Greece by dedicating Regilla's clothing at Eleusis after she died, and at least two of their children had served at Eleusis as "child of the hearth."

Next to the temple of Demeter/Faustina at the Via Appia site was the Triopeion, a sacred precinct housing an esoteric Eastern cult connected with Demeter. The original Triopeion was located in Knidos. Herodes had probably become acquainted with the cult when he was governor of the Free Cities of Asia Minor before his marriage. Triopas was an old Thessalian hero who was turned into a dragon after he displayed hubris by cutting down a grove sacred to Demeter.[57] He went into exile and founded Knidos. The Triopeion designed by Herodes paid special homage to Demeter, Persephone, Minerva, and Nemesis.[58] Persephone is naturally paired with Demeter, while Athena was important to Herodes who was an Athenian, but the explanation for the inclusion of Nemesis (Retribution) is less obvious.

While it is true that Herodes had an interest in the cult of Nemesis at Rhamnous, the modern scholar cannot but think that Herodes would need to cultivate and placate Nemesis, for revenge was due him from Regilla, her brother Bradua, and her son Bradua. Nemesis was also associated with Tyche in art: Herodes had instituted the cult of Tyche at Athens and Regilla served as her first priestess.[59] The Triopeion offered the learned Herodes an opportunity to make a wide range of historical and mythical allusions. These identified him as an erudite foreign intellectual to those visitors who understood them.[60] This foreign cult associated with Thessaly and Knidos must have seemed strange in Rome, but the taste of the time recognized innovation as a goal. There was so much wealth in evidence on the Via Appia that one of the few ways for property owners to distinguish themselves was by a novel display. Foreign cults from the East were fashionable in the empire. There was also a sanctuary of the Egyptian gods on the estate of Herodes and Regilla at Marathon. We do not know if Regilla would have been interested in these divinities apart from the assimilation of Demeter to Isis.

The estates of Regilla and of the Quintilii became imperial property at the end of the second century. Just as Herodes had reused the foundations of Regilla's family home for the palatial villa he erected, so in the first quarter of the fourth century the emperor Maxentius built his palace on top of Herodes' structures. It is reasonable to assume that much of the sculpture in the palace that can be dated to the middle of the second century had belonged to Herodes and perhaps to Regilla as well.[61] We have already mentioned the seated figure of a woman who is thought to be Regilla.[62]

Though Maxentius was a contemporary of Constantine, the first Christian emperor, he was a pagan who endeavored to restore the past. In fact, he named his son Romulus, after the legendary founder of Rome. Displaying the antiquities of paganism was thus crucial to Maxentius' political agenda, just as alluding to the antiquities of classical Athens had been part of Herodes'.

Many of the freestanding sculptures excavated at the palace of Maxentius and datable to the second century A.D. copy or echo Athenian sculpture of the classical period, and many are carved from Pentelic marble.[63] Some commemorate great Athenians of the past, for example Demosthenes and Epicurus, whom Herodes regarded as his intellectual forebears.[64] Remains of five karyatids, four torsos and one head, have been found in the area of Regilla's estate. They are sculpted from different kinds of white marble. Displaying a wide variety of marbles was a characteristic of wealth and conspicuous consumption. The origin of one type has been identified, and it is Greek.[65] Greek marble was popular in Rome, but one wonders whether Herodes was deliberately making a lavish display of Greek marble to remind the viewer of his own origins.[66]

An inscription behind the head of another karyatid records that the Athenians Kriton and Nikolaos were the sculptors.[67] Once again, as in the Kephisia sarcophagus, the obvious prototypes are the Erechtheion maidens.[68] We note the accumulation of Greek or Eastern elements in the religious themes; in the reference to Faustina as "Demeter" rather than the Roman equivalent "Ceres"; in the neo-Attic sculptural motifs; in the use of Greek marble; and in the prominence of the Greek language. Any one or two of these elements would not be obtrusive on the estate of an elite, well-educated family in Italy, but their accumulation in a location associated with early Roman history draws attention and must have been part of a deliberate intellectual design and building program. Herodes was grafting Hellenism onto his Roman wife and her property and leaving a record visible to Romans.

Herodes commemorated Regilla not only with material monuments but also with words. Inscriptions on carved monuments are stationary and communicate words visually to a literate viewer, but the poems that were written also circulated orally and in writing on papyri beyond the site where they were originally inscribed. Regilla's death served as the major inspiration for Herodes' poetry. All his poems may be dated to 160 and later.[69] His maudlin elegy at the Gate of Eternal Harmony was followed by another, even more self-pitying, composed at the death of a child, either a child born of Regilla, or one of his foster children.[70]

When epigrams of this period mention a marriage in retrospect, they always describe it as harmonious and successful.[71] Sometimes this evaluation reflects the author's idea of the truth. In prose, Plutarch describes his marriage this way, and though we do not have his wife's words, his own appear to convey her acquiescence.[72] Conjugal idealism was official policy. Coins issued by Marcus Aurelius, both while Faustina was living and after her death, advertised their relationship as congenial, depicting them holding hands with legends like "Concordia," despite salacious gossip about her disloyalty to her husband.[73] Thus, in keeping with the mood of the period, Herodes repeatedly announced that his marriage to Regilla had been perfect, and that consequently he was miserable and pitiable as a widower.

In Greece, Herodes was content to seize the opportunity to write elegies himself but even he had to recognize that his amateur efforts could attract scorn in the sophisticated neighborhood of the Via Appia. Perhaps (like his statues of the trophimoi hunting) they already had. Furthermore, if an outsider—even a well-paid professional—described his marriage as harmonious and Herodes as a heartbroken widower, the words would be more persuasive than if he had written them himself. Therefore it is understandable that Herodes engaged a poet, Marcellus of Side, to compose the poem commemorating Regilla inscribed at the Via Appia property.

Though in some inscriptions it is not easy to distinguish Greek and Roman alphabets immediately, the appearance of a few letters can alert a reader to the difference. The use of the Greek language for the inscriptions at Regilla's estate was not a casual choice, but a deliberate act of sexual and public politics. It is true that after living twenty years in Greece, Regilla (or her ghostly spirit) would understand Greek perfectly well. Nevertheless, these inscriptions seem incongruous on her ancestral estate. Herodes' preference is obvious in a bilingual inscription:[74]

> [In Greek] Annia Regilla
>
> Herodou gune, to phos
>
> tes oikias, tinos tau-
>
> ta ta choria gegonan.
>
> 5 [In Latin] Annia Regilla
>
> Hirodis uxor

lumen domus

cuius haec

praedia

10   fuerunt.

[Trans.] Annia Regilla, wife of Herodes, the light of the
house, whose estate this was.

Although the inscription was erected on Regilla's property in
Rome, the Greek version is written first. *Praedia,* the Latin used
for "estate," refers to property that constitutes a dowry.[75] Since
this property was in Italy and had belonged to Regilla, it would
seem more natural to begin with Latin. Was this hierarchy of
language an intentional and arrogant mockery of Bradua and of
the senatorial trial? Was it demeaning to Regilla, or testimony to
her unusual facility in both Greek and Latin?[76]

Furthermore, the letters are inscribed in the archaic Attic
script and alphabet (pre-403 B.C.), and in the laconic style that
Herodes sometimes preferred.[77] Even Athenians who were
Herodes' contemporaries would have found this archaic script
difficult to decipher. The reader in Rome surely would have experienced the letter shapes and literary style as pedantic and
strange. The Latin is a poorly spelled translation.[78] The Italian
stonecutter misspelled his employer's name in the Latin version.
The perfect tense *(gegonan, fuerunt)* in both the Greek and
the Latin can be interpreted as deliberately ambiguous: Regilla
owned the land in the past, but she can still be considered the
owner. Therefore there was no need for her spirit to rage against
her husband for appropriating her property after her murder.

Two columns of Roman cipollino marble inscribed with the
same words in Greek emphasize by repetition that the Triopeion
is dedicated to Demeter, Kore, and the chthonian (underworld)
gods.[79] These stood at the entrance. A curse is leveled on anyone
who would move them:

1   These columns are dedicated to Demeter and Kore

5   and the chthonian gods and

     it is not lawful

     for anyone to move anything

10   from the Triopeion which is at the third milestone

15   in the Appian Way in the land of Herodes.

     Nor is it very good

20   for the person who moves something.

     The witness is the daemon Enhodia.

Demeter and Kore are mother and daughter. The old woman Enhodia (an epithet of Hecate, goddess of the crossroads and of witchcraft) is invoked to enforce the curse. Just as the monuments to Regilla on her Roman estate were more impressive than those at Kephisia, so the curses invoked on anyone who would injure the monuments were at least as strong. As in the bilingual inscription above, the letters are written in the archaic Attic alphabet,[80] strange, perhaps incomprehensible, to most viewers even if they could read Greek. If Herodes had not wished to flaunt his Hellenism and his pedantry and had displayed the curses in Latin, they might have been more effective. In fact, the columns were moved several times and now are in the National Museum in Naples.

Herodes commissioned Marcellus of Side in Asia Minor to write a panegyric about Regilla. Marcellus was known for lengthy works, and this poem is so long that it is tempting to suppose that he charged Herodes by the line, as it were. In any case, there were Roman precedents for huge inscriptions praising dead wives, perhaps a development from the eulogy delivered at funerals. These eulogies were not always private speeches addressed only to members of the family and close friends. The man speaking might use the occasion of the funeral for personal and political gains. Thus the young Julius Caesar's speech at the funeral of his aunt Julia in 69 B.C. provided a podium for him to launch his political career.[81] A similar self-serving dynamic may be detected in the panegyric of Regilla. Herodes exploits the text as an opportunity to depict himself not as a murderer, but as a mourner devoted to his wife's memory. The most obvious example of a long inscription written by a husband about his dead wife is the "Laudatio Turiae" of the late Republic. This comprised about 180 lines of prose. The husband himself is the speaker of the inscription. He praises his wife for the heroism and self-sacrifice she displayed for his benefit.[82] For example, because the marriage was sterile, she had offered to divorce him and continue in a caring relationship with him and his new (and presumably fertile) wife. The husband depicts himself as vehemently rejecting this idea. The inscription is written in straightforward Latin, meant to be read by members of the public who passed by casually. In contrast, Herodes engaged a respected professional poet to compose an esoteric Greek inscription in honor of Regilla, though he certainly was responsible for the general content. The poem, of course, reflects favorably on the poet's patron. Marcellus was not an obvious choice, for he was best known for his didactic poems about medical matters. Herodes may have known Marcellus from the time when he was Corrector of the Free Cities in Asia, or he may have been familiar with his works, which Hadrian and Antoninus had ordered to be available in libraries in Rome.[83]

The poem was inscribed on two slabs. One stele is 1.22 meters high and 0.54 meters wide. The other is 1.17 meters high and 0.37 meters wide. The poem opens with an exhortation to Roman women, followed by a reference to Regilla's descent from the founder of Rome, but it is written in Greek. Though some of the Roman women invoked in the first sentence could read this poem and understand the literary allusions, most would have been more comfortable with Saturn, Minerva, and Ceres than with Kronos, Athena, and Demeter, to mention the more obvious differences. Furthermore, the Greek is often rather odd, and not readily understood.[84] Echoes of earlier poets including Homer and Callimachus have been identified, but some of our current difficulty in interpretation may be due to the loss of ancient literature to which this poem alludes. As Regilla had been excluded by birth from some aspects of religious life when she lived in Greece, so the choice of the Greek language in this poem isolates her from much of her natural audience on the Via Appia, though they are asked participate in her cult.

Cults of heroes and heroines originally centered on the burial place of their human remains. Though Regilla's remains were in Greece, Herodes had provided a cenotaph in the Deus Rediculus. It is clear that her cult is based on the premise that she is a heroine, less than a full-fledged goddess, but more than mortal.[85] The poem gives the impression of a hymn, and is written in hexameters, as was traditional for this genre.[86] Whether it was ever performed orally is not known, but it is conceivable that Marcellus or Herodes read it aloud or that musicians were engaged to present it at a dedicatory event before a select audience. After it was inscribed, it was meant to be read by visitors to the Triopeion.

The addressees change from "women of the Tiber" in the first line to a singular "dear friend" in line 40. This address is consistent with the traditional style of Roman tombstones which were erected along the roads: with their inscriptions they summoned the people who passed by to pause and consider the dead. The gender of the participles in the next line shows that this friend is considered to be male, or, knowing that the male may include the female in general statements in Greek, we understand that the addressee is no longer limited to women of the Tiber. The poem contains ninety-four lines. The first seventy-four lines, which include information about the cult of Regilla and give a description of her estate, are translated below. The inscription concludes with the curses that Herodes customarily added to prevent vandalism, the reuse of the property, or removal of his monuments.

1   Come here to this shrine surrounding the seated statue

2   of Regilla, women of the Tiber, bringing sacred offer-
     ings.

3   She was descended from the prosperous line of Aeneas,
     the renowned blood of

4   Anchises and Idaean Aphrodite.

5   She married into [a family at] Marathon.

6   The heavenly goddesses honor her, both the New Deo
     [Faustina the Elder/Demeter] and the Old [Demeter].

7   To them the sacred image of the well-girt wife is conse-
     crated.

8   She, however, has been allocated a place among the her-
     oines

9   in the islands of the blessed, where Kronos is king.

10   This she has received as her reward for her noble mind.

11   Thus Zeus had pity on the grieving spouse

12   lying in the middle of his widower's bed in harsh old
     age,

13   since from his blameless house

14   the black Harpy Fate-Spinners carried off half of his
     many children.

15   Two young children are still left,

16   innocent of harm, still completely unaware

17   that a pitiless fate seized their mother

18   before she had reached the years when old women
      spin.[87]

19   To him, grieving without respite, Zeus

20   and the emperor, who is like Zeus in nature and intelli-
      gence, has given

21   consolation. Zeus ordered that his [Herodes'] fertile
      wife[88] be brought

22   to the Ocean stream on the Elysian [paradisiacal]
      breezes of Zephyr.

23   Caesar [Antoninus Pius] granted his son [Bradua] the
      privilege of wearing on his feet the sandals decorated
      with stars

24   which they say Hermes too wore

25   when he led Aeneas from the war against the Achaians

26   through the dark night; around his feet was set,

27   shining as a protecting savior, the [half] globe of the
      moon.

28   The descendents of Aeneas once stitched this on the
      sandal

29   to be an honor for the noble Ausonians [Italians].

30   Not begrudged to him, a descendent of Kekrops,

31   is this old gift of Tyrrhenian men [Etruscans] on his
      ankle

32   if truly born of Hermes and Herse was

33   Keryx, ancestor of Herodes, descended from Theseus
      [i.e., an Athenian].

34   Therefore he is honored and gives his name to the
      year.[89]

35   He is included at the lordly Senate in the front row of
      seats.

36   In Greece there is no family or reputation more royal
      than

37   Herodes'. They call him the voice of Athens.

38   But she [Regilla] of the beautiful ankles was descended
      from Aeneas

39   and was of the race of Ganymede, for she is of the
      Dardanian race from Tros,

40   the son of Erichthonios. As for you, dear friend [the
      reader], please go and make sacrifices

41   and burn them. But it is necessary that the one who sac-
      rifices be not unwilling.

42   It is good for the pious to also care about heroes.

43   For she [Regilla] is neither mortal, nor divine.

44   Therefore she has neither sacred temple nor tomb,

45   neither honors for mortals, nor honors like those for the
      divine.

46   In a deme of Athens is a tomb for her like a temple,

47   but her soul attends the scepter of Rhadamanthys.

48   This image of her so gratifying to Faustina has been
      erected

49   in the area of the Triopeion, where there were formerly
      broad fields,

50   rows[90] of cultivated vines, and acres of olive trees.

51 Nor would the goddess, queen of women [Faustina], disdain her,

52 who was a priestess for her [Faustina's] sacrifices and an attendant in her [Regilla's] youth.

53 The archeress with the beautiful throne [Artemis] did not disdain Iphigeneia

54 nor did fierce-eyed Athena disdain Herse.[91]

55 The grain-giving mother of powerful Caesar [Domitia Lucilla],

56 who rules over the heroines of the past, will not despise her

57 as she goes to the chorus of earlier semi-divine women,

58 and with her Alkmene, whose lot is to rule over Elysian choruses of women,

59 and the blessed daughter of Kadmos [Semele].

60 Powerful ruler of Athens, born of Triton [Athena],

61 and you who see the deeds of mortals from your look-out at Rhamnous [Nemesis],

62 next-door neighbors of hundred-gated Rome,

63 goddesses, honor also this fruitful estate

64 of Deo [Demeter] of the Triopeion, a place friendly to strangers.

65 So long may the Triopeion goddesses be honored among immortals,

66 surely as when you came to Rhamnous and to Athens of the broad streets

67 leaving the homes of your loud thundering father.

68   So surely make this vineyard flourish rich in grapes
         throughout,

69   taking care of the crop of grain and vines with clusters
         of fruit

70   and tresses of grasses in the soft meadows.

71   For you Herodes sanctified the land

72   and built a rounded wall encircling it

73   not to be moved or violated, for the benefit of future
         generations.

CHRONOLOGICAL CHART

NOTES

ACKNOWLEDGMENTS

ART CREDITS

INDEX

CHRONOLOGICAL CHART

(Some of the dates pertaining to private life are approximate)

27 B.C.	Greece becomes Roman province of Achaea
A.D. 101	Birth of Herodes Atticus
110	Faustina the Elder marries Antoninus Pius
117–138	Reign of Hadrian
125	Birth of Regilla
126	Death of Plutarch
130	Birth of Faustina the Younger
138/9	Regilla marries Herodes Atticus
138–161	Reign of Antoninus Pius
138	Antoninus Pius adopts M. Aurelius and L. Verus
140	Death of Faustina the Elder
141	Birth and death of infant Claudius
142	Birth of Elpinice
143	Herodes Atticus and Fronto consuls
143/44	Birth of Athenais; Panathenaic stadium rebuilt
145	Birth of Bradua, Faustina the Younger marries M. Aurelius
149 to 153	Regilla constructs nymphaeum at Olympia
150	Birth of Regillus
155	Death of Regillus

160	Death of Regilla
160/61	Death of Athenais
165	Death of Elpinice
161–180	M. Aurelius reigns with L. Verus, then alone
169	Death of L. Verus
170	Birth of Philostratus; Herodes completes odeion
174	Athenians charge Herodes with tyranny
175	Death of Faustina the Younger
177	Death of Herodes*

* For the date of Herodes' death see Simon Swain, "The Promotion of Hadrian of Tyre and the Death of Herodes Atticus," *CP* 85 (1990), 214–216, esp. 214 and 216.

NOTES

I have translated all the ancient evidence I present in order to make it accessible to the reader; my translation of the long poem composed by Marcellus of Side in honor of Regilla is the first to be published in English. Line numbers in my English translations correspond to the line numbers of the original Greek and Latin inscriptions. Square brackets indicate a scholarly restoration, usually, based on similar passages in other texts. Photos show the relevant archaeological evidence. With a few obvious exceptions, journal titles are abbreviated according to the forms in *L'année philologique* and the list published online by the *American Journal of Archaeology*. Accepted abbreviations are used for standard works. Lists of standard abbreviations may be found in reference books such as the *Oxford Classical Dictionary*, edited by Simon Hornblower and Antony Spawforth, 3rd ed. (Oxford, 2003) and in the major Greek and Latin dictionaries. Works of Plutarch are referred to by the English titles given by Donald Russell, *Plutarch: Selected Essays and Dialogues* (Oxford [World's Classics], 1993), xxii–xxix. Inscriptions that are published in Walter Ameling, *Herodes Atticus* (Hildesheim, 1983), are cited as referred to in that work, although Ameling's system is not always consistent with the method of citation in other epigraphical publications. "Ps." preceding an author's name means that scholars have doubted the attribution of a work to the author named; however, such works were usually written by a less distinguished contemporary of the author named. Emphasizing that the focus of this study is on a woman, I will cite Marie-Thérèse

Raepsaet-Charlier, *Prosopographie des femmes de l'ordre sénatorial (Ier–IIe s.)* (Louvain, 1987), in preference to other standard prosopographical works such as the *Prosopographia imperii Romani (saec. I. II. III)*, 2nd ed., edited by E. Groag et al. (Berlin, 1933–1987).

INTRODUCTION

1. Edward Gibbon, *History of the Decline and Fall of the Roman Empire* (1782, 1845), vol. 1, ch. 1.
2. Fictitious and drawn from her own writings which the biographers assumed were autobiographical: see Mary Lefkowitz, *The Lives of the Greek Poets* (London, 1981), 36–37, 64.
3. Tim Whitmarsh, *The Second Sophistic, G&R* New Surveys in the Classics, 35 (Oxford, 2005), 34.
4. The genealogy is not clear. See further Marie-Thérèse Raepsaet-Charlier, *Prosopographie des femmes de l'ordre senatorial (Ier–IIe s.)* (Louvain, 1987), vol. 1, 71–72, no. 56.
5. G. Anderson, *Philostratus: Biography and Belles Lettres in the Third Century A.D.* (London, 1986), 80, 112.
6. They are limited to the following: a joke about a fat wife; a concubine who behaves as an evil stepmother; whether the baby born to a raped girl belongs to the maternal or paternal grandfather; a concubine endowed with every feminine weakness; an ugly and unpleasant bride; and whether marriage brings good fortune or unhappiness. See Philostr. *VS* 485, 516–517, 569, 603–604, 611, 625. Only one woman mentioned by Philostratus is presumably good, for her husband dedicated a portico to her: *VS* 605.
7. Simon Swain, "The Reliability of Philostratus' Lives," *Cl.Ant.* 10 (1991), 148–163, esp. 163 n.76.
8. In contrast, Emily A. Hemelrijk, *Matrona Docta: Educated Women in the Roman Elite from Cornelia to Julia Domna* (London, 1999), 1–2, finds she cannot trace chronological

change in the education of Roman women and uses evidence
from many centuries synchronically.

9. See the caveats of M. I. Finley cited in the Preface, above,
concerning the limitations of archaeological evidence in historical reconstruction: "Archaeology and History," in *The Use
and Abuse of History* (London, 1975), 87–103, esp. 92–93,
originally published in *Daedalus* 100.1 (Winter 1971), 168–
186. The threat of the American Institute of Archaeology to
hold its annual meeting separately from the American Philo-
logical Association constitutes recent evidence for the widen-
ing gulf between classicists and archaeologists.

10. See Jennifer Tobin, *Herodes Attikos and the City of Athens*
(Amsterdam, 1997), with appendices on monuments outside
Athens.

11. L. Quilici, "La valle della Caffarella e il triopio di Erode
Attico," *Capitolium* 9–10 (1968), 329–346 and 3 figs. In his
various discussions of Regilla's estate over the past thirty-
some years, Quilici has not altered his report. Indeed, only
the excavations scheduled for the near future under the supervision of Gianni Ponti will provide new information. My
description of the estate in ch. 5 is also based on archaeological finds at neighboring estates on the Via Appia and general
information in John R. Clarke, *The Houses of Roman Italy 100
B.C.–A.D. 250: Ritual, Space, and Decoration* (Berkeley, 1991),
esp. ch. 1.

12. *Un Milliardaire antique: Hérode Atticus et sa famille* (Cairo,
1930).

13. G. Pisani Sartorio and R. Calza, *La Villa di Massenzio sulla
via Appia* (Rome, 1976).

14. Thus Gianni Ponti in a personal communication of Feb. 3,
2004.

15. Despite the contemporary interest in the history of ancient
women and in the Roman family and childhood, no historian (including me) has ever before written a coherent chapter-

length narrative on "Growing up Female in Rome," as I have in chapter 1, by using both archaeological and written sources. For a similar reconstruction, see Daniel Stern, *Diary of a Baby: What Your Child Sees, Feels, and Experiences* (New York, 1990, 1998), 1.

16. Robert Darnton, "It Happened One Night," *New York Review of Books,* June 24, 2004, 60–64.

17. S. Hornblower and A. Spawforth (eds.), *The Oxford Classical Dictionary,* 3rd ed. (Oxford, 1996), 338, 695.

18. Although *The Cambridge Ancient History,* vol. 11: *The High Empire A.D. 70–192,* 2nd ed. (Cambridge, 2000), has appeared, the situation has not changed significantly since it was noted by Susan E. Alcock, *Graecia Capta: The Landscapes of Roman Greece* (Cambridge, 1993), 1–3.

19. See further Michael Hoff and Susan Rotroff (eds.), *The Romanization of Athens: Proceedings of an International Conference Held at Lincoln, Nebraska (April 1996),* Oxbow Monograph, 94 (Oxford, 1997), Preface.

20. For the appearance of the new Sophists: Whitmarsh, *The Second Sophistic,* 27–29.

21. Barbara Levick, "Greece and Asia Minor," in *The Cambridge Ancient History,* vol. 11, 604–634, esp. 630.

22. See Ewan Bowie, "Greeks and Their Past in the Second Sophistic," *Past and Present* 46 (1970), 3–41, republished in M. I. Finley (ed.), *Studies in Ancient Society* (London, 1974), esp. 194–195.

23. "Greeks and Their Past in the Second Sophistic," 197.

24. An anonymous reviewer of Bowie's article reiterates: "[This] survey of the literary works of sophists and historians of the period shows a marked tendency to adopt the conventions and attitudes of classical Greece." *L'année philologique* 41 (1972), 368.

25. Ps.-Demosthenes 59.122.

26. See, e.g., Xen. Oec. 7–10 and Sarah B. Pomeroy, *Xenophon,*

Oeconomicus: A Social and Historical Commentary (Oxford, 1994), ad loc.

27. Sarah B. Pomeroy, "Reflections on Plutarch, A Consolation to His Wife," in Sarah B. Pomeroy (ed.), *Plutarch's Advice to the Bride and Groom and A Consolation to His Wife* (New York, 1999), 75–81, esp. 78–80.

28. Marco Galli, *Die Lebenswelt eines Sophisten: Untersuchungen zu den Bauten und Stiftungen des Herodes Atticus* (Mainz, 2002).

29. Of the total of thirty-one editors and authors of *The Cambridge Ancient History,* vol. 11, only three are female.

30. Bernadette Puech, *Orateurs et sophistes grecs dans les inscriptions d'époque impériale* (Paris, 2002), includes some women, but omits Herodes Atticus from her survey because of the existing study by Walter Ameling, *Herodes Atticus* (Hildesheim, 1983), vol. 1: Biographie; vol. 2: Inschriftenkatalog.

31. See further Pomeroy (ed.), *Plutarch's Advice to the Bride and Groom and A Consolation to His Wife,* 33–42.

32. See ch. 1.

1. Girlhood in Rome

1. Marie-Thérèse Raepsaet-Charlier, *Prosopographie des femmes de l'ordre sénatorial (Ier–IIe s.)* (Louvain, 1987). For Regilla: vol. 1, pp. 83–84, no. 66; vol. 2, stemma xxvii.

2. For a Greek woman we do not even need her name: David M. Schaps, "The Woman Least Mentioned: Etiquette and Women's Names," *CQ* n.s. 27 (1977), 323–330. What follows is an example of the construction of the biography of a woman primarily from prosopographical ("writing down of persons," i.e., the study of the families, careers, and relationships of individuals) and archaeological evidence. I have based my description of Regilla's background and social context on what is known about her family and about other

upper-class women in imperial Rome. The following narrative of Regilla's youth in Rome is based on historical evidence for the rearing of girls in elite Roman familes. While much of this story of girlhood cannot be specifically ascribed to Regilla, there is no reason to believe that her experience was anomalous. Hence in this chapter I will not over-burden the reader with frequent caveats such as "it is likely that . . . ," or "Regilla probably . . ."

3. The abundant commemoration of men who were active in politics makes it possible to date female members of their families and situate them in the social hierarchy.

4. The terminology of the Lex Julia et Papia indicates that daughters and wives of men of senatorial status were legally classified as members of the senatorial class: Raepsaet-Charlier, *Prosopographie des femmes de l'ordre sénatorial,* vol. 1, esp. pp. 1–7. Juv. *Sat.* 6.385 uses a woman from the Appian family as an example of wealthy women who squander their money and attention on musicians.

5. "Gallus" in Regilla's father's name could simply have meant "cock" or "rooster," and may have been an ancestor's cognomen or nickname distinguishing him from kinsmen with praenomina and nomina similar to his own. "Gallus" also suggests descent from a Gallic ancestor (see ch. 5, below). According to Larissa Bonfante and Rex Wallace, in a personal communication of May 1, 2004, the name of Regilla's brother, Bradua, is certainly neither Latin nor Etruscan, but perhaps Celtic.

6. Plin. *HN* 35.2.6–7, and see further Harriet J. Flower, "Were Women ever 'Ancestors'?" in Jakob Munk Højte (ed.), *Images of Ancestors* (Aarhus, 2002), 159–184, esp. 165.

7. For the identity of Regilla's mother, see Raepsaet-Charlier, *Prosopographie des femmes de l'ordre sénatorial,* vol. 1, p. 190, no. 202.

8. Caucideius/Caucidia may be Etruscan: see W. Schulze, *Zur*

Geschichte lateinischer Eignennamen (Berlin, 1904), 213, 348. I am grateful to Michael Peachin, in a personal communication of May 3, 2004, for this reference.

9. Plut. *Quaest. rom.* 102.

10. Sor. *Gyn.* 2.12.20, adapted from Owsei Temkin, *Soranus' Gynecology* (Baltimore, 1956), 94.

11. Sor. *Gyn.* 2.12.19, adapted from Temkin, *Soranus' Gynecology,* 90–91.

12. See further Sarah B. Pomeroy, *Xenophon, Oeconomicus: A Social and Political Commentary* (Oxford, 1994), 275.

13. To prevent too many slaves from being manumitted, there was an age minimum of twenty for the owner who wished to manumit a slave; however, there was an exemption in the case of the owner manumitting a slave who cared for children. Such an owner could manumit at the age of eighteen: *Dig.* 40.2.13, and see Keith R. Bradley, *Discovering the Roman Family: Studies in Roman Social History* (New York, 1991), esp. 27.

14. Plin. *Ep.* 5.16 mentions a number of nurses, pedagogues, and tutors for an only daughter in northern Italy. We must suppose even more for the daughter in an elite family in Rome.

15. See further Keith R. Bradley, "Wet-Nursing at Rome: A Study in Social Relations," in Beryl Rawson (ed.), *The Family in Ancient Rome: New Perspectives* (Ithaca, N.Y., 1986), 201–229, and "The Nurse and the Child at Rome: Duty, Affect, and Socialisation," *Thamyris* 1 (1994), 137–156.

16. Thus Plutarch's daughter commanded *(keleue)* her nurse: *Cons.* 2.

17. For the ivory doll, see Ida Anna Rapinesi, "Il lusso a Roma," in Daniela Candilio (ed.), *Moda costume e bellezza nella Roma antica* (Rome, 2004), 33–40, esp. 34, Pl. 2.

18. W. V. Harris, *Ancient Literacy* (Cambridge, Mass., 1989), 248–253.

19. Hor. *Epist.* 2.1.156.

20. Quint. *Inst.* 1.1.126.

21. Quint. *Inst.* 1.1.12.

22. As in Plin. *Ep.* 5.16.3.

23. For female pedagogues: Beryl Rawson, *Children and Childhood in Roman Italy* (Oxford, 2003), 166–167, 198.

24. Emily A. Hemelrijk, *Matrona Docta: Educated Women in the Roman Elite from Cornelia to Julia Domna* (London, 1999), 50.

25. See further T. C. Brennan, "The Poets Julia Balbilla and Damo at the Colossus of Memnon," *CW* 95 (1998), 215–234, and ch. 3, below.

26. Bradua served as consul in 160, so he must have been born by A.D. 127. On his career see ch. 4, below.

27. E.g., C. Musonius Rufus, frs. 3 and 4, and *Should Daughters Receive the Same Education as Sons?* and *That Women Should Do Philosophy.* See also ch. 4 n. 51, below. On the education of upper-class women in Regilla's time and their interaction with male intellectuals, see Hemelrijk, *Matrona Docta,* esp. 72, 116–122.

28. Front. *Ep.* 2 = C. R. Haines, *Marcus Cornelius Fronto,* 2 vols. (Cambridge, Mass., 1982 and 1988) (henceforth referred to as "Haines"), vol. 1, p. 148, para. 2. See further below on Domitia Lucilla.

29. Plut. *Advice to the Bride and Groom* 48. Plutarch does not explain his proscription of dancing. The choreography of dancing was expressed in geometrical patterns. Presumably women who study mathematics and geometry will understand the dance patterns as unchangeable philosophical abstractions rather than as mere shifting corporeal shapes.

30. See Rawson, *Children and Childhood in Roman Italy,* 171–172.

31. See Richard P. Saller, "Men's Age at Marriage and Its Consequences in the Roman Family," *CP* 82 (1987), 21–34, esp. 29–30, and B. Shaw, "The Age of Roman Girls at Marriage," *JRS* 77 (1987), 30–45, esp. 43–44.

32. Hemelrijk, *Matrona Docta,* 236 n. 53, and Susan Treggiari, *Roman Marriage: Iusti Coniuges from the Time of Cicero to the Time of Ulpian* (Oxford, 1991), 402.

33. *Dig.* 50.17.30, Ulpian 1.12.

34. Raepsaet-Charlier, *Prosopographie des femmes de l'ordre sénatorial,* vol. 1, p. 83.

35. Raepsaet-Charlier, *Prosopographie des femmes de l'ordre sénatorial,* vol. 1, p. 84, no. 66.

36. Front. *Ep. 3.2* (M. Caes. ad Front.) = Haines, vol. 1, p. 61, and see just above.

37. Front. *Ep. 1* = Haines, vol. 1, pp. 130–137; Front. *Ep. 2* = Haines, vol. 1, pp. 146–151, and see further Hemelrijk, *Matrona Docta,* 199.

38. SHA *Verus* 2.4, etc.

39. He married in the same year as his rival Fronto: *The Cambridge Ancient History,* vol. 11: *The High Empire A.D. 70–192,* 2nd ed. (Cambridge, 2000), 1012. For the date: Walter Ameling, *Herodes Atticus* (Hildesheim, 1983), vol. 1, p. 78, and Francesco Grelle, *Canosa romana* (Rome, 1993), 126. Bernadette Puech, *Orateurs et sophistes grecs dans les inscriptions d'époque impériale* (Paris, 2002), 56–57 n. 57, argues that Herodes must have been born no later than A.D. 101.

40. M. Aurelius may have also wished to prevent the rise of sons-in-law who could be rivals to his own sons and heirs. I am grateful to Barbara Levick for this observation.

41. Georgia Tsouvala in a personal communication of Mar. 20, 2005, citing chronology in Miriam Griffin, "The Elder Seneca and Spain," *JRS* 62 (1972), 1–19, esp. 7.

42. Hemelrijk, *Matrona Docta,* 236 n. 57.

43. Sor. *Gyn.* 1.34.

44. Pers. 2.70. She also dedicated other items appropriate to girlhood: see further D. P. Harmon, "The Family Festivals of Rome," *ANRW* II.16.2 (1978), 1592–1603, esp. 1598.

45. See below and n. 65.

46. Philostr. *VS* 548–549.

47. Philostr. *VS* 555–556.

48. Philostr. *VS* 547.

49. Thus John Day, *An Economic History of Athens under Roman Domination* (New York, 1942), 243–246.

50. Philostr. *VS* 547–548, and see L. Quilici, *La via Appia: regina viarum* (Rome, 1997), 39.

51. Michael Woloch, "Four Leading Families in Roman Athens," *Historia* 18 (1969), 503–512. Herodes' immediate ancestors held priesthoods, including the prestigious imperial priesthood, at an early age.

52. Raepsaet-Charlier, *Prosopographie des femmes de l'ordre sénatorial,* p. 84, no. 66.

53. *Idelos* VI 2630, Ameling, *Herodes Atticus,* vol. 2, pp. 36–39, nos. 1–3, and see ch. 2 n. 121, below.

54. See further Sarah B. Pomeroy, "Family Values: The Uses of the Past," in T. Engberg-Pedersen and L. Hannestad (eds.), *Conventional Values of the Hellenistic Greeks* (Aarhus, 1997), 204–219.

55. See further A. J. S. Spawforth, "Symbol of Unity? The Persian Wars Tradition in the Roman Empire," in Simon Hornblower (ed.), *Greek Historiography* (New York, 1994), 233–247.

56. Plut. *Mor.* 349e, and see N. Hammond, "The Campaign and the Battle of Marathon," *JHS* 88 (1968), 13–57, esp. 40, and Basil Petrakos, *Marathon* (Athens, 1996), 38.

57. *SEG* 13, 479; G. Pfohl, *Griechische Inschriften* (Munich, 1966), 87; Kaibel, *Epigr. Gr.* 1087. This herm is now in Ravenna. On this herm and on the late traditions about Miltiades, see Petrakos, *Marathon,* 40, 42, who mistakenly refers to the "Villa" Strozzi (p. 40).

58. Ameling, *Herodes Atticus,* vol. 2, no. 186, and see further Ewan Bowie, "Greek Sophists and Greek Poetry in the Second Sophistic," *ANRW* II.33.1 (1989), 209–258, esp. 232–233.

59. A. J. S. Spawforth, "Families at Roman Sparta and Epidaurus: Some Prosopographical Notes," *ABSA* 80 (1985), 191–258, esp. 225, for the Spartan brother-in-law Claudius Aristocrates, and Spawforth, "Sparta and the Family of Herodes Atticus: A Reconstruction of the Evidence," *ABSA* 75 (1980), 210–217 and Pl. 23a, followed by Ameling, *Herodes Atticus,* vol. 2, no. 68.

60. This was the educational system for the citizen-cadet around seventeen or eighteen to twenty. Ameling, *Herodes Atticus,* vol. 2, pp. 98–101, no. 70, argues (p. 70) that *IG* V 1 45, mentioning a *sunephebe* of Herodes Atticus, must be dated between 117 and 123 and that the ephebe was Herodes, not his son. Ameling is now followed by A. J. S. Spawforth, review of J. von Freeden, D. E. E. Kleiner, S. Follet, and W. Ameling, *JRS* 74 (1984), 214–217, esp. 217, and "Families at Roman Sparta and Epidaurus," 191–258, esp. 226. Cf. Spawforth's previous view that the ephebe was Herodes' son: "Sparta and the Family of Herodes Atticus," 203–220.

61. Philostr. *VS* 554. Free cities *(civitates liberae)* enjoyed certain privileges and the right to conduct some of their local affairs. The provincial governor usually was not in charge of the free cities, though of course geography assured that their political, economic, and military circumstances were intertwined.

62. Front. *Ep. 3.3* (ad M. Caes.) = Haines, vol. 1, pp. 62–67. See further Jennifer Tobin, *Herodes Attikos and the City of Athens* (Amsterdam, 1997), 30–31.

63. Front. *Ep. 3.3.3.* (ad M. Caes.) = Haines, vol. 1, p. 66. Hadrian was also called *Graeculus* in connection with his Greek studies, not his sexuality: SHA *Hadrian* 1.5, and see further Craig Williams, *Roman Homosexuality: Ideologies of Masculinity in Classical Antiquity* (New York, 1999), 68, 294 nn. 35–36.

64. M. Hammond, "Composition of the Senate, A.D. 68–235," *JRS* 47 (1957), 74–81, esp. 77, notes that slightly over half the

senators under Hadrian, Antoninus Pius, and Marcus Aurelius whose origins are known are of Italian origin. See also Introduction, above.

65. Modern scholars do not like him either. Paul Graindor, Herodes' first modern biographer, describes him as a husband who was a "despote irascible": *Un milliardaire antique: Hérode Atticus et sa famille* (Cairo, 1930), 99. Rawson refers to him as "pragmatic, often ruthless," *Children and Childhood in Roman Italy*, 349. Barbara Levick, "Greece and Asia Minor," *The Cambridge Ancient History*, vol. 11, 604–634, esp. 613, describes Herodes' family as "turbulent," and see Robert Lamberton, below, ch. 2 n. 69, on the death of Polydeucion.

66. Plut. *Cimon* 3.3, 4.3, 10.5–6.

67. Plut. *Cimon* 4.9, and see ch. 5, below.

68. See most recently Amy Richlin, "Fronto + Marcus: Love, Friendship, Letters," in M. Kuefler, *The Boswell Thesis: Essays on Christianity, Social Tolerance and Homosexuality* (Chicago, 2006), 111–129.

69. Philostr. *VS* 554.

70. Philostr. *VS* 561, and see ch. 4, below.

71. See further John Clarke, *The Houses of Roman Italy, 100 B.C.– A.D. 250: Ritual, Space, and Decoration* (Berkeley, 1991), 156–157, 367–368.

72. Catullus 61.6–10.

73. This dress, by coincidence, was known as a "regilla," so called because the cloth of this tunic was woven vertically by a weaver who stood up: *OLD* s.v. *rectus* 6.

74. Harmon, "The Family Festivals of Rome," 1592–1603, esp. 1595.

75. Spawforth, "Families at Roman Sparta and Epidaurus," 191–258, esp. 192.

76. Plut. *Quaest. Rom.* 108 = *Mor.* 289d–e; see also *Quaest. Rom.* 6 = *Mor.* 265d–e.

77. Pliny the Younger, e.g., *Ep.* 5.11, 6.12, 8.10.

78. There was a notorious precedent at the end of the Republic: the marriage of the Ptolemy Cleopatra VII and the Roman Mark Antony in Egypt. Their case, however, was unique. The marriage was chosen by the spouses themselves, who were mature and had been previously married to others. In fact, Antony was still married to Octavia, but polygyny was characteristic of the Ptolemies. Cleopatra ruled in her own country. Antony was the outsider.

79. Thus Michael Woloch, *Roman Citizenship and the Athenian Elite, A.D. 96–161* (Amsterdam, 1973), 169.

80. Gell. *NA* 1.2.6. See further N. Horsfall, "Doctus sermones utriusque linguae," *EchCl* 23 (1979), 85–95; Michel Dubuisson, "Problèmes du bilinguisme romain," *ÉtCl* 49 (1981), 27–45; Michel Dubuisson, "Utraque lingua," *AntCl* 50 (1981), 274–286.

81. See ch. 5 n. 76, below.

82. Philostr. *VS* 564.

83. See above and Jorma Kaimio, *The Romans and the Greek Language* (Helsinki, 1979), 190, 249–520, 319. Juvenal (6.184–196) rants about pedantic women who can use their knowledge of Greek for dubious sexual purposes.

84. Fronto *Ep. 1* and 2 *metri Kaisaros* 1 = Haines, vol. 1, pp. 130–136, 146–150.

85. See the praetor's edict (a fundamental statement on law) issued under Hadrian on births by pregnant widows, when the dead husband's family doubts the legitimacy of the unborn child: *Dig.* 25. 3–4, translation and commentary in Rawson, *Children and Childhood in Roman Italy,* 100. I am grateful to Ann Ellis Hanson, in a personal communication, Nov. 24, 2003, for advice on the circumstances of giving birth.

86. E.g., the ex-consul Flavius Boethus had asked Galen to take on the care of his wife: Galen, *De praenotione ad Posthumum* 641.

87. See T. G. Parkin, *Demography and Roman Society* (Baltimore, 1992), 92–94, and Richard Saller, "*Patria Potestas* and the Stereotype of the Roman Family," *Continuity and Change* 1 (1986), 7–22, esp. 12.

88. Seneca, *Ad Marciam de consolatione* 9.2.

89. Arist. *Pol.* 1335a–b.

90. Sor. *Gyn.* 1.33 and see further Rawson, *Children and Childhood in Roman Italy,* 96.

91. Plut. *Lyc.* 15.3 and see Plato, *Rep.* 5.452–460E.

92. See further Rawson, *Children and Childhood in Roman Italy,* 343, and Jean-Pierre Néraudau, *Être enfant à Rome* (Paris, 1984), 375–376.

93. Ulpian, *Frag. Vat.* 321 = *FIRA*² 2, p. 536, Plut. *Numa* 12.2, and see further Rawson, *Children and Childhood in Roman Italy,* 104, 346, and Keith Bradley, "Images of Childhood: The Evidence of Plutarch," in Sarah B. Pomeroy (ed.), *Plutarch's Advice to the Bride and Groom and A Consolation to His Wife* (New York, 1999), 183–196, esp. 183–184.

94. Maternal care and close supervision could have increased the infant's chances of survival.

95. Plin. *Ep.* 5.16.

96. Front. *Ep. 1.6.7* (ad M. Caes.) = Haines, vol. 1, p. 154. *Hodie mortuus* is a restoration: see M. P. J. van den Hout, *M. Cornelii Frontonis epistulae* (Leiden, 1954), 13, *ad loc.,* dated Sept. 143 by Edward Champlin, *Fronto and Antonine Rome* (Cambridge, Mass., 1980), 131.

97. Front. *Ep. 3* = Haines, vol. 1, pp. 169–170.

98. Scholars may ask, "Did the Ancients Care When Their Children Died?" (thus the title of an article by Mark Golden, *G&R* 35 [1988], 152–63). This question cannot be adequately answered for we do not have direct information about what the mothers thought. Nevertheless, restraint was a common theme in letters of consolation to women: e.g., Seneca in *Ad Helviam de consolatione* 16.7 wrote a letter of consolation to his mother reminding her that Cornelia, mother of the

Gracchi, had lost ten children and Rutilia had lost an adult
son, and in *Ad Marciam de consolatione* 2.3 he cites the examples of Octavia and Livia, who had also lost grown sons.

99. Herodes later spent time there in exile from Athens. Cf. the
suggested itinerary of a subsequent journey of Herodes to
Sirmium in Pannonia: Ameling, *Herodes Atticus*, vol. 1,
p. 145.

100. E.g., Cic. *Fin.* 5.1.2, and see Susan E. Alcock, *Graecia Capta:
The Landscapes of Roman Greece* (Cambridge, 1993), 226.

101. Horace had described it as "gritty, not enriched by an urn of
water" (*lapidosus, aquae non ditior urna: Sat.* 1.5.91).

102. Philostr. *VS* 551, and see further Giuseppe Morea, *Canosa:
dalle origini all'ottocento* (Barletta, 1968), 51–52, 55, and figs.
XI and XII. Pieces of lead pipes from the aqueduct are displayed in the Museo Civico Archeologico at Canosa.

103. Philostr. *VS* 551.

104. See further Grelle, *Canosa romana*, 121–123. Grelle, 128–131,
dates Herodes' activities in Canosa between 143 and 146 just
after his consulship and marriage.

105. See the names listed in Marcella Chelotti, Rosanna Gaeta,
Vincenza Morizio, and Marina Silvestrini, *Le epigrafi romane
di Canosa,* vol. 1, Università degli Studi di Bari,
Dipartimento di Scienze dell'antichità, Sez. Storica,
Documenti e Studi, no. 4 (Bari, 1985; repr. 1990), 369, and
Raffaella Cassano, *Principi imperatori vescovi: duemila anni di
storia a Canosa* (Marseilles, 1992), 796–797. Ameling, *Herodes
Atticus,* vol. 1, p. 88, hypothesizes that Herodes' father may
have acquired land there when he was a senator.

106. Above, n. 63. For "Herodes" misspelled in an inscription on
the Via Appia see ch. 5, below.

2. A Roman Matron in Imperial Athens

1. See further T. Leslie Shear, Jr., "Athens: From City-State to
Provincial Town," *Hesperia* 50 (1981), 356–377, esp. 374.

2. Paus. 1.18.9.

3. Ps.-Demos. 59.118–122.

4. From Sophocles, *Tereus,* in *Sophocles: Fragments,* ed. and trans. Hugh Lloyd-Jones (Cambridge, Mass., 1996), 293–295, fr. 583.

5. Plut. *Advice to the Bride and Groom* 14 = *Mor.* 139–140.

6. Sarah B. Pomeroy, *Xenophon, Oeconomicus: A Social and Historical Commentary* (Oxford, 1994), 214.

7. E.g., Tac. *Germ.* 19. Favorinus, an associate of Herodes, advocated breastfeeding: see further Leofranc Holford-Strevens, *Aulus Gellius: An Antonine Scholar and His Achievement,* rev. ed. (Oxford, 2003), 41, 114, 304, 308. According to Plut. *Cons.* 2 and 5, Timoxena did not nurse her last child, a daughter, but she had nursed Chaeron and developed a blister or abscess on her nipple: see further Sarah B. Pomeroy, "Reflections on Plutarch, *A Consolation to His Wife,*" in Sarah B. Pomeroy (ed.), *Plutarch's Advice to the Bride and Groom and A Consolation to His Wife* (New York, 1999), 75–81, esp. 79–80. Marcus Aurelius (*Med.* 5.4) refers to his own wet nursing.

8. See, e.g., Arist. *Hist. an.* 587b, *Gen. an.* 777a, Ps.-Plut. *Lib. Educ.* 3d.

9. Bruce W. Frier, "Demography," in *The Cambridge Ancient History,* vol. 11: *The High Empire* A.D. *70–192,* 2nd ed. (Cambridge, 2000), 787–816, esp. 797.

10. Marie-Thérèse Raepsaet-Charlier, *Prosopographie des femmes de l'ordre sénatorial (Ier–IIe s.)* (Louvain, 1987), vol. 1, pp. 71–73, no. 56.

11. Plut. *Cimon* 10.7, 16.2–4, 17.2, and ch. 1, above.

12. Plut. *Cimon* 16.1.

13. Plut. *Cimon* 4.7, 15.3.

14. Philostr. *VS* 561, and see further J. F. Gilliam, "The Plague under Marcus Aurelius," *AJP* 82 (1961), 225–251, esp. 231. R. J. Littman and M. L. Littman, "Galen and the Antonine

Plague," *AJP* 94 (1973), 243–255, esp. 245, 254, postulate smallpox.

15. Raepsaet-Charlier, *Prosopographie des femmes de l'ordre sénatorial,* vol. 1, pp. 70–71, no. 55.

16. See further Sarah B. Pomeroy, *Women in Hellenistic Egypt from Alexander to Cleopatra* (New York, 1984; pb. with new foreword, Detroit, 1990; ACLS History E-Book, 2004), 9.

17. Ps.-Plut. *Vit. orat. Lyc.* 841d, 852c; Philostr. *VS* 549–550.

18. Philostr. *VS* 557; Walter Ameling, *Herodes Atticus* (Hildesheim, 1983), vol. 2, p. 124, no. 106; p. 134, no. 127; pp. 141–142, no. 137; and p. 142, no. 138.

19. G. di Vita-Evrard, "Le proconsul d'Afrique polyonyme *IRT* 517: une nouvelle tentative d'identification," *MÉFR* 93 (1981), 183–226, esp. 197; I. Kajanto, "On the Peculiarities of Women's Nomenclature," in M. Hans-Georg Pflaum and M. Noël Duval (eds.), *L'onomastique latine* (Paris, 1977), 147–159, esp. 157; and G. Daux, "L'onomastique romaine d'espression grecque," in Pflaum and Duval (eds.), *L'onomastique latine,* 405–417, esp. 406.

20. See ch. 1 n. 1, above.

21. Richard Saller, "Family and Household," in *The Cambridge Ancient History,* vol. 11, 855–874, esp. 856, 872.

22. Philostr. *VS* 558.

23. *IG* V 1.45.9–10.

24. See ch. 1 n. 59.

25. See further Nigel M. Kennell, *The Gymnasium of Virtue: Education and Culture in Ancient Sparta* (Chapel Hill, N.C., 1995).

26. Though this work has been attributed to Plutarch, it is generally believed that it is spurious. Nevertheless, the information therein is valid for Plutarch's time and the work is preserved under Plutarch's name.

27. Philostr. *VS* 558, and see ch. 4, below. According to A. J. Papalas, "Herodes Atticus and His Son," *Platon* 24 (1972),

244–251, Philostratus did not wish to antagonize his patron Gordian; therefore he did not emphasize the differences between Herodes and his son Bradua. Papalas argues that Bradua was the link between Herodes and the emperor's family, but see Introduction, above, n. 4.

28. Philostr. *VS* 558.

29. Ameling, *Herodes Atticus,* vol. 2, pp. 151–152, no. 145, and pp. 153–160, no. 146, esp. p. 158, note to pp. 23ff.

30. T. D. Barnes, "Philostratus and Gordian," *Latomus* 27 (1968), 581–597, esp. 583, argues that Bradua was born in 152, thus making his birth later than most scholars understand it to be. For the archonship see Susan J. Rotroff, "An Athenian Archon List of the Late Second Century After Christ," *Hesperia* 44 (1975), 402–408, esp. 405, 407.

31. There is disagreement about whether there are one or two Braduas who may be dated to the second half of the second century A.D. and who also held proconsulships in the provinces of Asia and Africa. See I. Avotins, "Bradua Atticus, the Consul of A.D. 185, and Bradua Atticus, the Proconsul of Africa," *Phoenix* 27 (1973), 68–76; Vita-Evrard, "Le proconsul polyonyme *IRT* 517," 187, 198, 216; and G. di Vita-Evrard, "Contribution de la Tripolitaine à la prosopographie de deux sénateurs, proconsuls d'Afrique," *Tituli* 4 (1982), 467–470, esp. 469–470. Raepsaet-Charlier, *Prosopographie des femmes de l'ordre sénatorial,* vol. 1, p. 73 n. 1, follows Vita-Evrard.

32. *IG* II² 3978, *IG* II² 1077.

33. According to H. Solin, "Latin Cognomina in the Greek East," in O. Salomies (ed.), *The Greek East in the Roman Context: Proceedings of a Colloquium Organised by the Finnish Institute at Athens, May 21 and 22, 1999* (Helsinki, 2001), 189–202, esp. 197–198, the names of Herodes and his father may be understood as either Greek or Roman.

34. See Brent Salway, "What's in a Name? A Survey of Roman

Onomastic Practice from *c.* 700 B.C. to A.D. 700," *JRS* (84 (1994), 124–145, esp. 130.

35. Ameling, *Herodes Atticus,* vol. 2, pp. 19–20, argues that Bradua was younger than Regillus, because Bradua's name has more matrilineal components, assuming incorrectly in this case that the mother is less important.

36. A. J. Marshall, "Roman Women and the Provinces," *Anc. Soc.* 6 (1975), 109–127, esp. 125.

37. Philostr. *VS* 557–558, and n. 17, above.

38. See Pomeroy, *Women in Hellenistic Egypt,* 108–110, 121–124.

39. Vita-Evrard, "Le proconsul d'Afrique polyonyme *IRT* 517," 198.

40. Plut. *Advice to the Bride and Groom* 36 = *Mor.* 143b. Evidently Plutarch observed family dynamics, but was not thinking about Oedipus or Electra.

41. Scholars have adopted Philostratus' (*VS* 558) assessment; thus, e.g., I. Avotins, "Bradua Atticus, the Consul of A.D. 185, and Bradua Atticus, the Proconsul of Africa," 70, uses the terms "degenerate," "foolishness," and "debauchery" in connection with Bradua.

42. Plut. *Advice to the Bride and Groom* 35 = *Mor.* 143a–b.

43. Plut. *Advice to the Bride and Groom* 36 = *Mor.* 143b.

44. From Cephisia (an Athenian suburb), Ameling, *Herodes Atticus,* vol. 2, no. 174, and see further Jennifer Tobin, *Herodes Attikos and the City of Athens* (Amsterdam, 1997), 216–217.

45. Although this is an argument *ex silentio* and we do not know when Alcia died, we note her failure to commemorate Regilla, Regillus, Athenais (whom she probably outlived), and perhaps Elpinice.

46. Jane F. Gardner, *Women in Roman Law and Society* (London, 1986), 8, 144.

47. Philostr. *VS* 558.

48. T. G. Nani, "Threptoi," *Epigraphica* 5–6 (1943–1944), 45–84, and see now B. Levick, S. Mitchell, et al., *Monumenta Asiae Minoris antiqua,* 9: *Monuments from the Aezanitis Rceorded by C. W. M. Cox, A. Cameron, and J. Cullen, JRS* Monographs, no. 4 (London, 1988), esp. lxv.

49. Jane F. Gardner, "Status, Sentiment, and Strategy in Roman Adoption," in Mireille Corbier (ed.), *Adoption et fosterage* (Paris, 1999), 63–80, esp. 65.

50. Xen. *HG* 5.3.9, and see further (including the possibilities for female children born of helot men and Spartan men) Sarah B. Pomeroy, *Spartan Women* (New York, 2002), 64, 70, 95–98, 102.

51. "Copronyms and the Exposure of Infants in Egypt," in Roger Bagnall and William Harris (eds.), *Studies in Roman Law in Memory of A. Arthur Schiller* (Leiden, 1986), 147–162; abstract in *Atti del XVII congresso internazionale di papirologia* (Naples, 1984), 1341.

52. Philostr. *Apollonius* 3.11.

53. Ewan Bowie, "Greek Sophists and Greek Poetry in the Second Sophistic," *ANRW* II.33.1 (1989), 205–298, esp. 211.

54. A. and É. Bernand, *Les inscriptions grecques et latines du Colosse de Memnon* (Paris, 1960), 149–151, no. 61, line 1, an epigram by Falernus.

55. Philostr. *VS* 558.

56. E. Gazda, "A Portrait of Polydeucion," *Bulletin of the Museum of Art and Archaeology* (University of Michigan) 3 (1980), 1–13, esp. 2.

57. *IG* II² 3970 = Ameling, *Herodes Atticus,* vol. 2, pp. 163–164, no. 161.

58. Ameling, *Herodes Atticus,* vol. 2, p. 167: "irgendeiner Form."

59. I am grateful to Barbara Levick for this last suggestion. Louis Robert took him for some sort of kinsman of Herodes who could have been freeborn: "Deux inscriptions de l'époque

imperiale en Attique: un concours et Hérode Atticus," *AJP*
100 (1979), 153–165, esp. 164.

60. See Peter M. Fraser and Elaine Matthews (eds.), *A Lexicon of Greek Personal Names,* vol. 3A: *The Peloponnese, Western Greece, and Magna Graecia* (Oxford, 1997).

61. Sarah B. Pomeroy, "Copronyms and the Exposure of Infants in Egypt," in Bagnall and Harris (eds.), *Studies in Roman Law in Memory of A. Arthur Schiller,* 147–162, esp. 159; abstract in *Atti del XVII congresso internazionale di papirologia* (Naples, 1984), 1341.

62. Beryl Rawson in a personal communication, Nov. 14, 2003, and see further Beryl Rawson (ed.), *The Family in Ancient Rome: New Perspectives* (Ithaca, N.Y., 1986), 176.

63. *IG* II² 13194 = Ameling, *Herodes Atticus,* vol. 2, p. 163, no. 158.

64. For the pairing of portraits of Polydeucion and Herodes, see Hans Rupprecht Goette and Thomas Maria Weber, *Marathon: Siedlungskammer und Schlachtfeld-Sommerfrische und Olympische Wettkampfstätte* (Mainz, 2004), 122.

65. Around 173, according to Bowie, "Greek Sophists and Greek Poetry in the Second Sophistic," 234. Most recently Holford-Strevens, *Aulus Gellius,* 143 n. 72, and 144, citing Ameling, *Herodes Atticus,* vol. 2, p. 171, nos. 174–175, maintains that Polydeucion died 147/148–153/154 (excluding 150/151), and see n. 97, below.

66. Gell. *NA* 19.12.

67. A. R. Birley, "Hadrian to the Antonines," *The Cambridge Ancient History,* vol. 11, 132–194, esp. 144. For Antinous as the artistic prototype of Polydeucion: Hugo Meyer, *Antinoos* (Munich, 1991), 28, 29, 129, 214, 219.

68. Meyer, *Antinoos,* 28, 29, 129, 214, 219.

69. Robert Lamberton, in a personal communication of Sept. 27, 2003, points to parallels between the mysterious death of

Hadrian's beloved youth Antinous and the fate of Polydeucion.

70. See Lucian *Demon.* 24, and for honorific inscriptions for Polydeucion: Ameling, *Herodes Atticus,* vol. 2, pp. 163–173, nos. 158–78. See esp. *SIG³* 861 = Ameling, *Herodes Atticus,* vol. 2, p. 172, no. 176, with praise for his sophrosyne.

71. Plutarch likewise suppresses information about Alexander's and Caesar's sexual exploits because he is interested in emphasizing their political ambition: see J. Beneker, "No Time for Love: Plutarch's Chaste Caesar," *GRBS* 43 (2002/2003), 13–29.

72. Protogenes in Plut. *Erot.* 750C–751B, and Pausanias in Pl. *Symp.* 178D–180B.

73. See Gretchen Reydams-Schils, *The Roman Stoics* (Chicago, 2005), 116–119.

74. Frank M. Snowden, Jr., *Blacks in Antiquity: Ethiopians in the Greco-Roman Experience* (Cambridge, Mass., 1970), xviii, 96, fig. 73, and 187–188, and Karl Schefold, *Die Bildnisse der antiken Dichter, Redner und Denker,* 2nd ed. rev. by A.-C. Bayard, H. A. Cahn, M. Guggisberg, M. J. Jenny, and Ch. Schneider (Basel, 1997), 334–335.

75. Tobin, *Herodes Attikos,* 74–75, 214.

76. "Youth from Cephisia," originally published by D. Kazianis, "Agalma Romaiokaratias apo ten Kephisia," *AAA* 15 (1982), 130–141, and see Perry, *Artistic Imitation and the Roman Patron,* 132–133 and fig. 10.

77. See Introduction, above.

78. This relationship is not explicit in Homer. Later authors and artists interpreted it in various ways ranging from carnal to chaste: see further K. J. Dover, *Greek Homosexuality* (Cambridge, Mass., 1978), 41, 130, 197–199, and David M. Halperin, *One Hundred Years of Homosexuality* (New York, 1990), ch. 4.

79. Pind. *Nem.* 3.43–52.

80. Sappho fr. 1, 21.
81. Plut. *Cimon* 16, for naked boys and young men exercising together, and boys rushing out of the gymnasium to chase a hare. See further Judith M. Barringer, *The Hunt in Ancient Greece* (Baltimore, 2001), 95.
82. See further Barringer, *The Hunt in Ancient Greece,* esp. ch. 2 and 206–207.
83. Gell. *NA* 19.12; see also above and ch. 5, below.
84. Gell. *NA* 19.12.
85. On conjugal love as superior to homosexual love see, e.g., Musonius Rufus (14 Lutz), Plutarch in Plut. *Erot.,* Reydams-Schils, *The Roman Stoics,* 148, 152–153, and see above.
86. Sen. *Helv.* 16.1–2, 5.
87. Lucian *Demon.* 24, and see further C. P. Jones, *Culture and Society in Lucian* (Cambridge, Mass., 1986), 94.
88. Now in the Brauron Museum. For this hero relief: Tobin, *Herodes Attikos,* 103, 282, and see below.
89. Lucian *Demon.* 25, 33.
90. Tobin, *Herodes Attikos,* 157–160.
91. See further Eva Cantarella, *Bisexuality in the Ancient World,* trans. C. Ó Cuilleanéan from *Secondo natura* (Rome, 1988; New Haven, 1992), 171–172, and Craig Williams, *Roman Homosexuality: Ideologies of Masculinity in Classical Antiquity* (New York, 1999), 48, 50, 62–64.
92. See above, n. 65.
93. Lucian *Demon.* 33. Robert, "Deux inscriptions de l'époque imperiale en Attique," 164, hypothesizes that Herodes sponsored grand funeral games for Polydeucion, modeling them on the games Achilles celebrated for Patroclus.
94. See further Sarah B. Pomeroy, *Xenophon, Oeconomicus,* passim.
95. See further Pomeroy, *Women in Hellenistic Egypt,* chs. 1 and 2.
96. Bowie, "Greek Sophists and Greek Poetry in the Second Sophistic," 211.

97. Tobin, *Herodes Attikos,* 107–109, 157–158, and see n. 65, above. Most recently Bernadette Puech, *Orateurs et sophistes grecs dans les inscriptions d'époque impériale* (Paris, 2002), 63, agreeing with Ameling, *Herodes Atticus,* vol. 2, pp. 168–169, argues that the three trophimoi died in quick succession between 165 and 168.

98. Paul Graindor, *Un milliardaire antique: Hérode Atticus et sa famille* (Cairo, 1930), 115. Some portraits that may be derived from the Polydeucion model were also found more widely spread in the empire: Gazda, "A Portrait of Polydeucion," 6–7.

99. See the survey in Tobin, *Herodes Attikos,* 297, 299. Th. Stephanidou-Tiveriou, "Paratereseis ste stele tou kynegou tes Korinthou," *AE* (1977 [1979]), 23–28 and Pl. 8, compares a second-century Roman relief from Corinth portraying a hunter in a chlamys with a dog at his feet to a sculpture of Polydeucion at Brauron dating between 147/148 and 177. According to Stephanidou-Tiveriou (26), the hunter in the Corinth relief is heroized. The relief may have been dedicated by Herodes to Polydeucion after the youth died (27). See also E. M. Gardiner, "A Series of Sculptures from Corinth: I. Hellenic Reliefs," *AJA* 13 (1909), 158–169, esp. 165–168.

100. *IG* II² 3969. According to M. Woloch, *Roman Citizenship and the Athenian Elite, A.D. 96–161: Two Prosopographical Catalogues* (Amsterdam, 1973), 119–120, no. 5 (2), a few equites probably preceded Polydeucion, though they are not recorded. The sons of senators were ipso facto equites, and there had been Athenian senators since Herodes' father.

101. *IG* III 814 = Ameling, *Herodes Atticus,* vol. 2, p. 172, no. 177, and see further H. T. Westbrook, "A Herm Dedicated by Herodes Atticus," *AJA* 33 (1929), 402–404, esp. 403. The inscription does not specify the type of baths, but Westbrook describes Polydeucion as having "a benefactor's interest" in

public baths. Tobin, *Herodes Attikos,* 280–281 (and sim. 313) observes that Polydeucion "had a specific connection with some local baths" and conjectures that the herm served a protective purpose for the baths.

102. See n. 65, above.

103. *IG* II² 3979, and see Ameling, *Herodes Atticus,* vol. 2, p. 141, and A. J. S. Spawforth, "Families at Roman Sparta and Epidaurus: Some Prosopographical Notes," *ABSA* 80 (1985), 191–258, esp. 232.

104. See n. 97, above.

105. Juv. *Sat.* 6.398–412, and see further Emily A. Hemelrijk, *Matrona Docta: Educated Women in the Roman Elite from Cornelia to Julia Domna* (London, 1999), passim.

106. Plin. *Ep.* 4.19, 6.7. Pliny published his letters.

107. Plut. *Advice to the Bride and Groom* 48.

108. Hemelrijk, *Matrona Docta,* 47–49 and 248 n. 125.

109. See further Keith Bradley, "The Roman Family at Dinner," in Inge Nielsen and Hanne Sigismund Nielsen (eds.), *Meals in a Social Context: Aspects of the Communal Meal in the Hellenistic and Roman World* (Aarhus, 1998), 36–55, esp. 38, and Hanne Sigismund Nielsen, "Roman Children at Mealtimes," in Nielsen and Nielsen (eds.), *Meals in a Social Context,* 56–66.

110. Plut. *Advice to the Bride and Groom* 15, 19.

111. Plut. *Advice to the Bride and Groom* 32 = *Mor.* 142d.

112. *Aphrodite . . . hermosmenen* and see further Pomeroy (ed.), *Plutarch's Advice to the Bride and Groom and A Consolation to His Wife,* 45.

113. Philostr. *VS* 1.521, and see ch. 1.

114. See further Lisa Nevett, "Continuity and Change in Greek Households under Roman Rule: The Role of Women in the Domestic Context," in Erik Nis Ostenfeld (ed.), *Greek Romans and Roman Greeks: Studies in Cultural Interaction* (Aarhus, 2002), 81–96, esp. 94–95. Nevett's examples, how-

ever, are not the grand houses of the super-rich like Herodes
or even like Plutarch.

115. H. A. Thompson and R. E. Wycherley, *The Agora of Athens:
The History, Shape, and Uses of an Ancient City Center*
(Princeton, 1972), 185 and fig. 46.

116. *CIL* III 549.

117. Thorough investigations of the site have not yet been published. See further Tobin, *Herodes Attikos,* passim, and T.
Spyropoulos and G. T. Spyropoulos, "The Villa of Herodes
Atticus at Eva (Loukou) in Arcadia," unpublished paper
(1996).

118. Tobin, *Herodes Attikos:* Memnon, 97–99, 256, 338;
Polydeucion, 338, 346–347; and Achilles, 347. For the females: 342–344, 351.

119. Gell. *NA* 18.10, 1.2. For the date: Leofranc Holford-Strevens,
"Towards a Chronology of Aulus Gellius," *Latomus* 36
(1977), 93–109, esp. 97.

120. Holford-Strevens, *Aulus Gellius,* 141, suggests that the description by Gellius is typical of a *locus amoenus.*

121. Domingo Plácido, "Emperadores y sofistas: Herodes Ático y
Roma," in E. Falque and F. Cascó (eds.), *Graecia capta: de la
conquista de Grecia a la helenización de Roma* (Huelva, 1995),
193–200, esp. 197.

122. See further Susan Treggiari, *Roman Marriage: Iusti Coniuges
from the Time of Cicero to the Time of Ulpian* (Oxford, 1991),
366–371.

123. J. G. Frazer, *Pausanias's Description of Greece,* 6 vols., 2nd ed.
(London, 1913), vol. 1, p. 437, and see further Tobin, *Herodes
Attikos,* 241–283.

124. Tobin, *Herodes Attikos,* fig. 80. Goette and Weber, *Marathon,*
112, find the Marathon property more attractive.

125. Juv. *Sat.* 6.149–150 for a woman who asks her husband for
Canusian sheep, and see ch. 5, below.

126. Plut. *Advice to the Bride and Groom* 20, in Pomeroy (ed.),

Plutarch's Advice to the Bride and Groom and A Consolation to His Wife, 8. Similarly Antipater, *SVF* 3.62–63.

127. J. G. Frazer notes that the title "Gate of Immortal Unanimity" is "pompous," and illustrative of the "decline in good taste": *Pausanias's Description of Greece,* vol. 1, p. 438.

128. *IG* II² 5185.

129. See most recently Goette and Weber, *Marathon,* who survey the archaeological evidence for Herodes at Marathon (106–126). They devote four and a half pages (122–126) to the trophimoi, and less than a total of two pages to Regilla (110 fig. 131, 111, and part of 112).

130. See further Graindor, *Un milliardaire antique,* 115 n. 1; Tobin, *Herodes Attikos,* passim.

131. Plut. *De glor. Ath.* 7 = *Mor.* 349d, and see further R. W. Macan, *Herodotus,* vol. 2 (London, 1895), 223–224.

132. Frier, "Demography," 788–789.

133. Richard Chandler, *Travels in Asia Minor and Greece,* vol. 2 (Oxford, 1825, pb. repr. Chestnut Hill, Mass., 2004), ch. 36, pp. 207–208.

3. PUBLIC LIFE

1. John Day, *An Economic History of Athens Under Roman Domination* (New York, 1942), 238–241, 248.

2. *IG* II–III² 2776. See further *SEG* 43 (1993), 58; *SEG* 45 (1995), 161 and 232; Day, *An Economic History of Athens Under Roman Domination,* 232–233; Riet van Bremen, *The Limits of Participation: Women and Civic Life in the Greek East in the Hellenistic and Roman Periods* (Amsterdam, 1996), 83, 263 n. 90; and Stephen G. Miller, "A Roman Monument in the Athenian Agora," *Hesperia* 41 (1972), 50–95 and Pls. 13–18.

3. For a similar phenomenon in Hellenistic Egypt, see Sarah B. Pomeroy, *Women in Hellenistic Egypt from Alexander to Cleo-*

patra (New York, 1984; pb. with new foreword, Detroit, 1990; ACLS History E-Book, 2004), 108–110, 119, 121–124.

4. Note the dismay of Septimius Severus at the presence of his sister, who could scarcely speak Latin: SHA *Sev.* 15.

5. See J. N. Adams, *Bilingualism and the Latin Language* (Cambridge, 2003), 383, 751–753, and Eleanor Dickey, "Ancient Bilingualism," review of J. N. Adams, *Bilingualism and the Latin Language,* and J. N. Adams et al., *Bilingualism in Ancient Society: Language Contact and the Written Text, JRS* 93 (2003), 295–302, esp. p. 298. Unfortunately, though Adams considers the relationship between bilingualism and class, he does not discuss the influence of gender, but see the survey by Otta Wenskus, "Wie schriebt man einer Dame? Zum Problem der Sprachwahl in der römischen Epistolographie," *WS* 114 (2001), 215–232.

6. Plut. *Sull.* 6.12, 13.1, 221, Sen. *De matrim.* 63, and Plut. *Ant.* 33.3.

7. Suet. *Tit.* 6.2, Dio Cass. 54.7.2.

8. Suet. *Aug.* 24.1, and see further A. J. Marshall, "Roman Women and the Provinces," *Anc. Soc.* 6 (1975), 109–127.

9. See further A. J. S. Spawforth, "Balbilla, the Euryclids, and Memorials for a Greek Magnate," *ABSA* 73 (1978), 249–260 and Pls. 34–35; T. C. Brennan, "The Poets Julia Balbilla and Damo at the Colossus of Memnon," *CW* 95 (1998), 215–234; Sarah B. Pomeroy, *Spartan Women* (New York, 2002), 128–129; ch. 1 n. 25, above; and this chapter below.

10. Miller, "A Roman Monument in the Athenian Agora," 86–87. See Brennan, "The Poets Julia Balbilla and Damo at the Colossus of Memnon," for the identification of the poet with the landowner in *IG* II–III² 2776, lines 57–59.

11. For this date see G. W. Bowersock, "The Miracle of Memnon," *BASP* 21 (1984), 21–32, esp. 21. The dating of Amenhotep's reign is approximate. L. M. Berman, "Overview of Amenhotep III and His Reign," in D. O'Connor and

E. H. Cline, *Amenhotep III: Perspectives on His Reign* (Ann Arbor, 1998), 1–15, esp. 1, gives "ca. 1391–1353." Most recently C. H. Roehrig, with R. Dreyfus and C. A. Keller (eds.), *Hatshepsut: From Queen to Pharaoh* (New Haven, 2005), 6, give ca. 1390–1352.

12. Adams, *Bilingualism and the Latin Language,* 546–55.

13. Philostr. *VA* 6.4.3.

14. A. and É. Bernand, *Les inscriptions grecques et latines du Colosse de Memnon* (Paris, 1960), no. 83, trans. by Brennan, "The Poets Julia Balbilla and Damo at the Colossus of Memnon," 228 (adapted).

15. See further, e.g., the women in C. P. Jones, "A Leading Family of Roman Thespiae," *HSCP* 74 (1970), 223–255, and Sarah B. Pomeroy, "Commentary on Plutarch, *Advice to the Bride and Groom,*" in Sarah B. Pomeroy (ed.), *Plutarch's Advice to the Bride and Groom and A Consolation to His Wife* (New York, 1999), 42–57, esp. 44.

16. The situation in Roman Sparta was similar: Pomeroy, *Spartan Women,* 123–128.

17. *Pais aph' hestias, IG* II² 3608; Walter Ameling, *Herodes Atticus* (Hildesheim, 1983), vol. 2, p. 139, no. 134; and see further Kevin Clinton, "Inscriptions from Eleusis," *Arch. Eph.* (1971), 81–136, esp. p. 132, no. 28, and "The Sacred Officials of the Eleusinian Mysteries," *Transactions of the American Philosophical Society* n.s. 64.3 (1974), pp. 8, 110, nos. 34 and 35. Herodes' paternal aunt Claudia Alcia had also held this office ca. 50–70: Clinton, "The Sacred Officials," p. 108, no. 15. Claudia Alcia is not listed in Marie-Thérèse Raepsaet-Charlier, *Prosopographie des femmes de l'ordre sénatorial (Ier–IIe s.)* (Louvain, 1987), but she does appear in the stemma in Ellen E. Perry, "Iconography and the Dynamics of Patronage: A Sarcophagus from the Family of Herodes Atticus," *Hesperia* 70 (2001), 461–492, esp. 488 fig. 17.

18. See further Werner Eck, "Die Präsenz senatorischer Familien

in den Städten des Imperium Romanum bis zum späten 3. Jahrhundert," in W. Eck, H. Galsterer, and H. Wolff (eds.), *Studien zur Antiken Sozialgeschichte: Festschr. Friedrich Vittinghoff* (Cologne, 1980), 283–322, esp. 293, and 313 n. 34.

19. His predecessor Alexander I, who reigned ca. 495–450 B.C., claimed Greek lineage and may have also been admitted to the competition. For the opening of the games to non-Greeks see M. Finley and H. Pleket, *The Olympic Games: The First Thousand Years* (London, 1976), 62.

20. Paus. 6.21.2, and see L. Robert, "Les femmes théores à Éphèse," *CRAI* (1974), 176–181, esp. 180.

21. Paus. 6.20.9.

22. Paus. 6.21.1.

23. See *LSJ* s.v. *chasko.*

24. L. Farnell, *The Cults of the Greek States,* vol. 3 (Oxford, 1907), and vol. 4 (London, 1913), 86 n. 21. In vol. 3, p. 30, Farnell refers to the priestess as "a semi-divine personage."

25. Robert, "Les femmes théores à Éphèse," 180 n. 1. According to Paus. 5.6.8, in the fourth century B.C. a woman who disguised herself as a man sneaked in to watch. When she was detected, she gained admission on the grounds that she was a daughter, sister, aunt, and mother of Olympic victors.

26. Augustus had been prudish in not allowing women and girls to see competitions in which the males were unclothed, but they continued to attend: Suet. *Aug.* 44.3, Plin. *Ep.* 4.22.

27. According to Paus. 6.20.9, unmarried girls were allowed to attend. It is difficult to speculate about the social classes of such girls, if in fact any actually did attend. In general in Greece unmarried girls stayed close to home and their parents guarded their virginity. It would appear that traveling without adult female chaperones to attend games where the audience consisted primarily of boisterous men would not have any purpose and could compromise a girl's reputation. Ulrich Sinn, *Olympia: Cult, Sport, and Ancient Festival*

(Princeton, 2000), 74, hypothesizes that unmarried girls had been attached to an earlier cult of Demeter Chamyne predating the construction of the Olympic facilities around 700 B.C. and that the girls continued to be allowed to be admitted "as a sign of penance."

28. Epictet. *Diss.* I.6.23–29, in Robert F. Dobbin (trans.), *Epictetus, Discourses Book 1* (Oxford, 1998), 14. Dobbin (p. xiii) gives Epictetus a floruit of ca. A.D. 100.

29. *IOlymp.* no. 610 = Ameling, *Herodes Atticus,* vol. 2, pp. 127–128, no. 112. Ulrich Sinn, "Olympias Spätgechichte im Spiegel des Demeterkults," in Helmut Kyrieleis (ed.), *Olympia 1875–2000: 125 Jahre deutsche Ausgrabungen: Internationales Symposion, Berlin 9.–11. November 2000* (Mainz am Rhein, 2002), 371–376, argues that the post of priestess of Demeter was not primarily religious, but a way of honoring a generous benefactor.

30. See further K. W. Arafat, *Pausanias' Greece: Ancient Artists and Roman Rulers* (Cambridge, 1996), 37–38, 212, and S. Walker, "Roman Nymphaea in the Greek World," in S. Macready and F. S. Thompson (eds.), *Roman Architecture in the Greek World,* Society of Antiquaries Occasional Papers 10 (London, 1987), 60–71.

31. See further Pomeroy, *Spartan Women,* 155.

32. Lucian *De mort. Peregr,* 19.

33. Sinn, *Olympia,* 107–108, followed by Betsey Ann Robinson, "Fountains and the Culture of Water at Roman Corinth" (Ph.D. diss., Univ. of Pennsylvania, 2001), 354 and n. 90. For the attribution to Herodes, see, e.g., Walker, "Roman Nymphaea in the Greek World," 60–61 and fig. 20, who also refers to the sculpture of Hygieia (see below) as a dedication by Herodes and Regilla (61); R. A. Tomlinson, *Greek Sanctuaries* (New York, 1976), 45, 64; Jennifer Tobin, *Herodes Attikos and the City of Athens* (Amsterdam, 1997), Preface; and the currently definitive work, Renate Bol, *Das*

*Statuenprogramm des Herodes-Atticus-Nymphäeums,
Olympische Forschungen,* vol. 15 (Berlin, 1984). A. Mallwitz,
Olympia und seine Bauten (Munich, 1972), 108–109, 152,
calls it "das Nymphäum der Regilla," but also asserts that
Herodes built it in his wife's name. E. Norman Gardiner,
Olympia: Its History and Remains (Oxford, 1925, repr. Wash-
ington, D.C., 1973), refers constantly to Herodes as the au-
thor of the exedra, but (299) suggests that "the Eleans con-
ferred this honour [i.e., the priesthood] upon Regilla in
gratitude for the exedra." I. Avotins, "On the Dating of the
Exedra of Herodes Atticus at Olympia," *Phoenix* 29 (1973),
244–249, attributes the nymphaeum to Herodes in his title,
but in his opening sentence notes that Regilla dedicated it.
Most recently Rachel L. Meyers presented a paper titled
"Representing Antonine Imperial Woman at Olympia: The
Case of the Nymphaeum of Herodes Atticus," at the Annual
Meeting, Archaeological Institute of America, Jan. 8, 2005,
Session 3D.

34. Philostr. *VS* 551.

35. H. W. Pleket (ed.), *Epigraphica,* vol. 2: *Texts on the Social
History of the Greek World* (Leiden, 1969), no. 5 = *I. Priene,*
no. 208.

36. This monument may also have served as Balbilla's tomb. See
the definitive publication on this monument: Diana E. E.
Kleiner, *The Monument of Philopappos in Athens* (Rome,
1983), 52, 95.

37. Spawforth, "Balbilla, the Euryclids, and memorials for a
Greek Magnate," 260.

38. See, e.g., M. L. West, "Erinna," *ZPE* 25 (1977), 116–119; in
rebuttal, see Sarah B. Pomeroy, "Supplementary Notes on
Erinna," *ZPE* 32 (1978), 17–22.

39. Bol, *Das Statuenprogramm des Herodes-Atticus-Nymphäeums,*
98–101, 139–140.

40. Lucian *De mort. Peregr.* 19.

41. *IOlymp.,* no. 288 = Ameling, *Herodes Atticus,* vol. 2, p. 127, no. 111.

42. Philopappus, however, was royal, the son of Epiphanes, and the grandson of Antiochus IV, the last king of Commagene. According to Plutarch, Philopappus was still referred to as a king (Plut. *Quaest. conv.* 628a, *Friends and Flatterers* 27). See further Kleiner, *The Monument of Philopappos in Athens,* esp. 9–10, 78, 95.

43. Bol, *Das Statuenprogramm des Herodes-Atticus-Nymphäeums,* 190, for sculptures of Zeus. I have followed Bol's reconstruction, but see also S. Settis, "'Esedra' e 'ninfeo' nella terminologia architettonica del mondo romano: dall'età repubblicana alla tarda antichità," *ANRW* I.4 (1973), 661–745, who distinguishes public fountains from nymphaea, for the latter included fountains but also had religious connotations: see 709–712 for the reconstruction by Settis. See also A. Mallwitz, *Olympia und seine Bauten* (Munich, 1972), 20 fig. 8 (reconstruction with sculpture on roof), 145–155.

44. This reconstruction follows Bol, *Das Statuenprogramm des Herodes-Atticus-Nymphäeums,* Pl. 4.

45. Thorsten Opper in "Appia Annia Regilla: Hairstyle and Status in Antonine Female Portraiture," paper delivered Jan. 28, 2006 at the symposium "Reading the Roman Portrait," Emory University, Atlanta, Georgia, argued that the head which is usually identified as Regilla's is the head of her mother. Dr. Opper proposed that a portrait type thought to be of Faustina the Younger represents Regilla. I am grateful to Dr. Opper for discussing his unpublished work with me at the British Museum, Jan. 24, 2006.

46. Bol, *Das Statuenprogramm des Herodes-Atticus-Nymphäeums,* 25, 101, 105, 134–135.

47. I am grateful to Larissa Bonfante and Christopher Ratté for this interpretation in a personal communication of Nov. 28, 2005. Bol, *Das Statuenprogramm des Herodes-Atticus-*

Nymphäeums, appendix 4, nos. 14 and 47, shows the fragmentary figure of Bradua dressed as a Roman.

48. Thus Meyers, "Representing Antonine Imperial Woman at Olympia: The Case of the Nymphaeum of Herodes Atticus," following Bol, *Das Statuenprogramm des Herodes-Atticus-Nymphäeums,* 106.

49. See Katherine Welch, "Greek Stadia and Roman Spectacles: Asia, Athens, and the Tomb of Herodes Atticus," *JRA* 11 (1998), 117–145, esp. 135.

50. Some of the sculpture and architectural elements were moved to a fifth-century basilica across the Altis.

51. The attribution of the temple to Herodes is secure: Philostr. *VS* 2.550, and *IG* II–III² 3607.

52. Dated by *IG* II–III² 351, an inscription of 330/329. See further John Travlos, *Pictorial Dictionary of Ancient Athens* (New York, 1971), 498, and ch. 2, above.

53. See further A. J. S. Spawforth and Susan Walker, "The World of the Panhellenion I: Athens and Eleusis," *JRS* 75 (1985), 78–104, esp. 91.

54. Pleket, *Epigraphica,* vol. 2, p. 26, no. 9.

55. See Stephen V. Tracy and Christian Habicht, "New and Old Panathenaic Victor Lists," *Hesperia* 60 (1991), 187–236, esp. 213–214, for eight women whose teams of horses were victorious at Athens. None of these women can be identified as Athenian.

56. Carlo Gasparri, "Lo stadio Panatenaico: documenti e testimonianze per una riconsiderazione dell'edificio di Erode Attico," *ASAtene* 36–37 (1974–1975), 313–392, esp. 316.

57. Gasparri, "Lo stadio Panatenaico," 367–75.

58. See Ameling, *Herodes Atticus,* vol. 2, pp. 109–110, no. 90 (a dedication by twenty-seven *pragmateutae* of Peiraeus in Regilla's honor as first priestess), for comparable priesthoods held for life.

59. Philostr. *VS* 550.

60. Paul Graindor, *Un milliardaire antique: Hérode Atticus et sa famille* (Cairo, 1930), assumes that Herodes' Tyche was also sculpted in gold as well as the ivory mentioned by Philostratus.

61. Gasparri, "Lo stadio Panatenaico," 390, posits that Herodes was following Hadrian's mandate in erecting a new Acropolis.

62. Philostr. *VS* 566, and see ch. 5.

63. Spartianus, *Hadrian,* 19, and see further J. G. Frazer, *Pausanias's Description of Greece,* 2nd ed., 6 vols., vol. 2 (London, 1913), 206–207.

64. For the Greek text: *SEG* XIII 226, and J. H. Kent, *The Inscriptions 1926–1950: Corinth,* vol. 8, pt. 3 (Princeton, 1966), pp. 59–60, no. 128. J. Bousquet, "Regilla à Corinth," *BCH* 88 (1964), 609–613, esp. 610, and Ameling, *Herodes Atticus,* vol. 2, no. 100, restore the beginning of some of the lines differently. See also Tobin, *Herodes Attikos,* 298–299. The base was found separated from the statue, but Bousquet and Kent associated them and identified the sculpture as Regilla.

65. Marco Galli, *Die Lebenswelt eines Sophisten: Untersuchungen zu den Bauten und Stiftungen des Herodes Atticus* (Mainz, 2002), 102, differentiates between the artificiality of the new cult of Tyche at Athens, and the organic pre-existing cult at Corinth.

66. Apul. *Met.* 10.18, and see Susan E. Alcock, *Graecia Capta: The Landscapes of Roman Greece* (Cambridge, 1993), 133.

67. Aur. Vict. *Caes., Ep.* 14.2; *SHA* "Verus" 6.9; Apul. *Met.* 10.18–11.25; Plut. *Quaest. conv.* 8.4 = *Mor.* 723.

68. E.g., B. H. Hill, *The Springs—Peirene, Sacred Spring, Glauke: Corinth,* vol. 1, pt. 6 (Princeton, 1964), 103. One inscription in Corinth raises the additional possibility of a Roman donor whose name is fragmentary, but this man may be responsible only for the marble paving, some of the construction, and a restoration of some architectural elements, rather than for

the original concept: James Wiseman, "Corinth and Rome I: 228 B.C.–A.D. 267," *ANRW* II.7.1 (1979), 438–548, esp. 526, and for the nymphaeum at Olympia see above.

69. Robinson, "Fountains and the Culture of Water at Roman Corinth," 354. Robinson (355) suggests that if Herodes was involved at all in construction in the area, he may have been the donor of a monumental sculptural complex including a figure of Scylla in the courtyard. See Robinson for detailed discussion of relevant archaeological material. In the present discussion, I have generally followed Robinson.

70. Hill, *The Springs,* 103.

71. Mary Sturgeon, "Sculpture at Corinth, 1896–1996," in Charles K. Williams II and Nancy Bookidis (eds.), *Corinth: Results of Excavations Conducted by the American School of Classical Studies at Athens,* vol. 20: *Corinth, the Centenary 1896–1996* (Athens, 2003), 351–368, esp. 353.

72. Thus M. Edwards, "Tyche at Corinth," *Hesperia* 59 (1990), 529–542, Pls. 83–88, esp. 537. See also B. S. Ridgway, "Sculpture from Corinth," *Hesperia* 50 (1981), 422–448, esp. 436–439. Ridgway sees a connection between the Antonine sculpture at Corinth and neo-Attic sculpture in Athens.

73. Edwards, "Tyche at Corinth," 537–538 n. 44. R. L. Scranton, *Monuments in the Lower Agora and North of the Archaic Temple: Corinth,* vol. 1, pt. 3 (Princeton, 1951), p. 70, Pl. 28a–b, refers to a head found in the northwest Stoa as "a head of Tyche (Nemesis)."

74. See further Franklin P. Johnson, *Sculpture 1896–1923: Corinth,* vol. 9, pt. 1 (Cambridge, Mass., 1931), p. 20, Pl. 10, and C. E. De Grazia, "Excavations of the American School of Classical Studies at Corinth: The Roman Portrait Sculpture" (Ph.D. diss. Columbia, 1973), 299–301, no. 98, for a larger-than-life-size figure of a woman wearing chiton and himation dated to the Antonine period.

75. Ridgway, "Sculpture from Corinth," 436, and see further Robinson, "Fountains and the Culture of Water at Roman Corinth," 98–100.

76. See further O. Broneer, "Excavations in Corinth, 1934," *AJA* 39 (1935), 53–75, esp. 67, and Pl. XX.

77. See further Benjamin Powell, "Greek Inscriptions from Corinth," *AJA* 7 (1903), 26–71, esp. p. 43, no. 21, and a sketch of the relief in Hill, *The Springs,* 102–103.

78. I am grateful to Dr. Ioulia Tzonou-Herbst, Curator, Corinth Excavations, who examined the sculpture and the base on Mar. 14, 2006, and looked for any signs of workmanship that could tell us if the two faces were carved at a different time, but she could not see anything: personal communication of Mar. 15, 2006.

79. See, e.g., grave stele of Nico showing a slave offering a lyre to a woman (Cairo, Egyptian Museum C.G. 9259), and wall painting of woman holding a writing implement and tablets from Pompeii (Naples, Museo Nazionale Archeologico). See further Pomeroy, *Women in Hellenistic Egypt,* 60–72.

80. *IG* IV 1599; B. D. Merritt, *Greek Inscriptions, 1896–1927: Corinth,* vol. 8, pt. 1 (Cambridge, Mass., 1931), p. 64, no. 86 = Ameling, *Herodes Atticus,* vol. 2, pp. 122–123, no. 102, and see further Hill, *The Springs,* 102–103. In this extremely brief inscription, the Council manages to boast of their mythological connections to Sisyphus.

81. On the exedra see Tobin, *Herodes Attikos,* 304–305.

82. *IG* II–III² 12568 (Cephisia); *IG* II–III² 4072 (Eleusis); Antony E. Raubitschek, "Greek Inscriptions. The American Excavations in the Athenian Agora: Twenty-Third Report. (Jan.–Mar., 1943)," *Hesperia* 12.1 (1943), 12–88, esp. 73–76, no. 22; FD III (3), 67 (Delphi) = Ameling, *Herodes Atticus,* vol. 2, pp. 123–126, nos. 104–109; W. Dittenberger and K. Purgold, *Die Inschriften von Olympia* (Berlin, 1896), no. 612,

lines 1–6 (Olympia); and see further J. H. Oliver, *Athenian Expounders of the Sacred and Ancestral Law* (Baltimore, 1950), 111–13.

83. FD III (3) 71 = Ameling, *Herodes Atticus,* vol. 2, pp. 125–126, no. 108, and see further Tobin, *Herodes Attikos,* 79, 304–305.

84. FD III (3) 72 = Ameling, *Herodes Atticus,* vol. 2, p. 126, no. 109.

85. Parallel athletic competitions for women were held at Elis at a festival of Hera: see Pomeroy, *Spartan Women,* 24–25.

86. Pomeroy, *Spartan Women,* 123–127.

4. Death in Athens and Murder Trial in Rome

1. Philostr. *VS* 555.

2. See further P. R. C. Weaver, *Familia Caesaris* (London, 1972).

3. Juv. *Sat.* 6. 146–149.

4. Emily A. Hemelrijk, *Matrona Docta: Educated Women in the Roman Elite from Cornelia to Julia Domna* (London, 1999), 188–200, and see ch. 1, above.

5. Front. *Ep. 3.3* (ad M. Caes.) = Haines, vol. 1, p. 62, and see ch. 1, above.

6. Philostr. *VS* 554, and see ch. 1, above.

7. Sarah B. Pomeroy, "The Relationship of the Married Woman to Her Blood Relatives in Rome," *Anc. Soc.* 7 (1976), 215–227.

8. Val. Max., *Memorable Deeds and Words,* 6.3.9

9. *Plagarum vestigia:* August. *Conf.* 9.9, cited by Jo-Ann Shelton, *As the Romans Did,* 2nd ed. (Oxford, 1998), p. 48, no. 67.

10. Plut. *Quaest. rom.* 108.

11. Suet. *Ner.* 34–35. R. Mayer, "What Caused Poppaea's Death?" *Historia* 30 (1982), 248–249, compares Poppaea and Melissa (not Regilla). A similar image occurs when Nero sent assas-

sins to kill his mother Agrippina and she offered her womb
to their dagger: Tac. *Ann.* 14.8.

12. Hdt. 3.50.

13. Hdt. 5.92.

14. Hdt. 3.50.

15. Philostr. *VS* 556.

16. Contemporary scholars are quite willing to believe Bradua's
accusation: e.g., William V. Harris, *Restraining Rage: The Ideology of Anger Control in Classical Antiquity* (Cambridge,
Mass., 2001), 228.

17. Plut. *Quaest. rom.* 108 = *Mor.* 289d–e; see also *Quaest. rom.* 6
= *Mor.* 265d–e, Susan Treggiari, *Roman Marriage: Iusti
Coniuges from the Time of Cicero to the Time of Ulpian* (Ox-
ford, 1991), 112, and ch. 1, above.

18. For the composition of the court and procedure, see Richard
J. A. Talbert, *The Senate of Imperial Rome* (Princeton, 1984),
ch. 16.

19. Philostr. *VS* 555.

20. The Latin of a Greek scholar could be mocked as barbaric:
Lucian *Salt.* 24.

21. Philostr. *VS* 555.

22. *Eudokimotatos:* Philostr. *VS* 555.

23. Front. *Ep.* 3.2 (ad M. Caes.) = Haines, vol. 1, pp. 58–63, esp.
p. 60. The date of the letter is controversial. Haines gives
?140–143, but see Edward Champlin, *Fronto and Antonine
Rome* (Cambridge, Mass., 1980), 63–64, and Walter Ameling,
Herodes Atticus (Hildesheim, 1983), vol. 2, p. 31, for a later
date. On the implications of "love" between the emperor and
his old tutors see ch. 1.

24. Talbert, *The Senate of Imperial Rome*, 295.

25. Philostr. *VS* 556.

26. Philostr. *VS* 560.

27. Philostr. *VS* 559–560. For the date 169–170 see A. R. Birley,

"Hadrian to the Antonines," *The Cambridge Ancient History,* vol. 11: *The High Empire* A.D. *70–192,* 2nd ed. (Cambridge, 2000), 132–194, esp. 170, but for the date 174, see James H. Oliver, *Marcus Aurelius: Aspects of Civic and Cultural Policy in the East, Hesperia* suppl. 13 (Princeton, 1970), 83, and Barbara Levick, "Greece and Asia Minor," *The Cambridge Ancient History,* vol. 11, 604–634, esp. 628.

28. Philostr. *VS* 560.

29. Philostr. *VS* 560.

30. Philostr. *VS* 561.

31. Oliver, *Marcus Aurelius,* p. 8, line 93 = *SEG* 29 (1979), no. 127; see also *SEG* 46 (1996), no. 145. Nigel M. Kennell, "Herodes Atticus and the Rhetoric of Tyranny," *CP* 92 (1997), 346–362, argues that Herodes attempted to win access to governing bodies including the Areiopagus, Boule, and the Panhellenion for his freedmen supporters.

32. Oliver, *Marcus Aurelius,* 34–35. Most recently Kennell, "Herodes Atticus and the Rhetoric of Tyranny," 346, dates it to the mid-170s.

33. Ann Ellis Hanson, "The Eight Months' Child and the Etiquette of Birth: *Obsit Omen!*" *BHM* 61 (1987), 589–602, esp. 601, and personal communication of Nov. 24, 2003.

34. I am grateful to Helen King for her comments in a personal communication of Nov. 28, 2003.

35. Soranus (1.9.34) wrote that the appropriate years of conception for women were fifteen to forty. According to Anthony R. Birley, *Marcus Aurelius: A Biography* (paperback reprint of rev. ed., New York, 2000), 35, 162, 191, 239, Faustina was pregnant when she died in 175 at the age of forty-five, having given birth at least twelve times, including two sets of twins, and having borne her first child in 147. Her daughter Lucilla was pregnant in 165 at the age of fifteen, before Faustina had given birth to her last daughter, Vibia Aurelia Sabina, in 170.

On Faustina's children see further Birley, *Marcus Aurelius,* 241 and App. F (247–248).

36. E.g., Carolyn Marshall, "Peterson Defense Questions Prosecution's Star Witness," *New York Times,* August 24, 2004, A, 13.

37. Carolyn Marshall, "Jury Finds Scott Peterson Guilty of Wife's Murder," *New York Times,* Nov. 13, 2004, A, 8, see also A, 1.

38. Philostr. *VS* 549.

39. Front. *Ep. 3.3* (ad M. Caes.) = Haines, vol. 1, pp. 62–66, esp. 64, dated A.D. ?140–143 by Haines; 150s by Champlin, *Fronto and Antonine Rome,* 158.

40. Philostr. *VS* 557.

41. O. F. Robinson, *The Criminal Law of Ancient Rome* (London, 1995), 44.

42. Robinson, *The Criminal Law of Ancient Rome,* 41.

43. Philostr. *VS* 558, writes that Bradua had been slandered to his father: *diabebleto.*

44. Philostr. *VS* 517.

45. Sarah B. Pomeroy, *Goddesses, Whores, Wives, and Slaves: Women in Classical Antiquity* (New York, 1975), 79–81, and Sarah B. Pomeroy, *Xenophon, Oeconomicus: A Social and Political Commentary* (Oxford, 1994), 269–270, 272.

46. Arist. *Pol.* 1259a37, 1260a9.

47. The decree of the *nomothetai* (SEG 12.87), 337/336, confirming an earlier law.

48. *SEG* 29 (1979), no. 127, and see further Kennell, "Herodes Atticus and the Rhetoric of Tyranny," 351.

49. See further Emma J. Stafford, "Plutarch on Persuasion," in Sarah B. Pomeroy (ed.), *Plutarch's Advice to the Bride and Groom and A Consolation to His Wife* (New York, 1999), 162–172.

50. Treggiari, *Roman Marriage,* 209–210.

51. See ch. 1, above. For a recent analysis of Musonius' views see Martha C. Nussbaum, "The Incomplete Feminism of Musonius Rufus, Platonist, Stoic, and Roman," in Martha C. Nussbaum and Juha Sihvola (eds.), *The Sleep of Reason: Erotic Experience and Sexual Ethics in Ancient Greece and Rome* (Chicago, 2002), 283–326.

52. See this chapter, above, and D. J. Geagan, "A New Herodes Epigram from Marathon," *AM* 79 (1964), 149–156, esp. 153.

53. Philostr. *VS* 556.

54. Compare the spotlight on O. J. Simpson and the obscurity of the murder victims, his wife Nicole Brown and her friend Ronald Goldman, during the trial in California in 1995.

5. Regilla's Final Resting Place

1. *IG* II/III² 13200 = *IG* III 1417; Walter Ameling, *Herodes Atticus* (Hildesheim, 1983), vol. 2, p. 160, no. 147; and M. Guarducci, *Epigrafia greca,* 4 vols. (Rome, 1967–78), vol. 4, pp. 230–235.

2. Jennifer Tobin, *Herodes Attikos and the City of Athens* (Amsterdam, 1997), 125–126, 236–237, suggests that the tomb in Marousi may have been Regilla's. In that case she would have been isolated from both her children and husband, but see this chapter, below. See now Georgios N. Pallis, "*IG* ii (2) 13, 2000 kai to taphiko mnimeio tis Rigillis," *Horos* 14–16 (2000–2003), 191–195 and Pls. 47–48, who argues that the association of the monument at Marousi with the funeral monument of Regilla is based on nineteenth-century evidence that cannot be confirmed.

3. See below, and F. Lenormant, "Inscriptionum graecarum ineditarum centuria secunda et tertia," *RhM* 21 (1866), 362–404, esp. 383–384, no. 193, for an inscription found between Marathon and Probalinthos on a marble base that is now

lost. Lenormant reports it as: (1) Regilla (2) . . . kias. He restores as: (1) [Appia Anna] Regilla (2) [to phos tes oi]kias.

4. See, e.g., the excessive attention paid to his tomb by Trimalchio in Petron. *Sat.* 71.

5. In this chapter the Greek spelling is retained for Greek words and Latin for Latin words to draw attention to the two parts of Regilla's life and commemoration in Greece and Italy.

6. Philostr. *VS* 558.

7. *SEG* XXVI 290 = Ameling, *Herodes Atticus,* vol. 2, pp. 143–146, no. 140, and see further Tobin, *Herodes Attikos,* 225–227.

8. Thus Ellen E. Perry, "Iconography and the Dynamics of Patronage: A Sarcophagus from the Family of Herodes Atticus," *Hesperia* 70 (2001), 461–492, esp. 486.

9. See further Ellen E. Perry, "Artistic Imitation and the Roman Patron, with a Study of Imitation in the Ideal Sculptures of Herodes Atticus" (Ph.D. diss., Univ. of Michigan, 1995), 123–135, and Perry, "Iconography and the Dynamics of Patronage."

10. Perry, "Iconography and the Dynamics of Patronage," 470, and see ch. 1, above.

11. Klytemnestra, the fourth child, who died in ignominy murdered by her son, is not represented.

12. The fourth side is not finely carved. It shows clichéd figures of Triton and a Nereid, apparently not integral to the myth on the other three sides.

13. See further Sarah B. Pomeroy, "The Relationship of the Married Woman to Her Blood Relatives in Rome," *Anc. Soc.* 7 (1976), 215–227.

14. Philostr. *VS* 565.

15. Philostr. *VS* 557.

16. See further Kevin Clinton, "Eleusis and the Romans: Late Republic to Marcus Aurelius," in Michael Hoff and Susan Rotroff (eds.), *The Romanization of Athens: Proceedings of an*

International Conference Held at Lincoln, Nebraska (April 1996) (Oxford, 1997), 161–181, esp. 176–177.

17. The penalty for such wife abuse is similar to the one ordained for the man who pastures his cattle on someone else's land and steals crops by night: such a thief is put to death as a sacrifice to Ceres. See Pomeroy, "The Relationship of the Married Woman to Her Blood Relatives in Rome," 215–216, and ch. 4, above.

18. Plut. *Rom.* 22.3.

19. See further Ifigenia Dekoulakou, "Nea Stoixeia apo ten anaskafe tou ierou ton Aigyption theon ston Marathona," *AAA* (1999–2001), 113–126, with English summary on 126: "New Evidence from the Excavation of the Egyptian Gods at Marathon;" and below, this chapter. There also seems to have been a shrine to the Egyptian gods at Herodes' villa at Loukou.

20. On the possible commemoration of Regilla's musical talents at Korinth in her lifetime, see ch. 3, above.

21. Paus. 7.20.6.

22. *The Souda, s.v.* Herodes Ioulios, Philostr. *VS* 551, Paus. 7.20.6, and see John Travlos, *Pictorial Dictionary of Ancient Athens* (New York, 1971), 378.

23. K. Pittakis, "Peri theatrou Hrodou tou Attikou," *AE* (1858), 1707–1714, esp. 1712. Some tiles also found at the odeion had only Theta on them (possibly for Theater) or Eta (possibly for Herodes). It is also possible that they have nothing to do with the words "Theater," "Herodes," and "Regilla," but are simply stamp-marks of the people who made them. I am grateful to Georgia Tsouvala for this observation in a personal communication of Apr. 17, 2005.

24. Paus. 1.21, and see further Marco Galli, *Die Lebenswelt eines Sophisten: Untersuchungen zu den Bauten und Stiftungen des Herodes Atticus* (Mainz, 2002), 44–47.

25. See Henning Wrede, *Consecratio in formam deorum:*

Vergöttlichte Privatpersonen in der römischen Kaiserzeit (Mainz, 1981), 160, 172.

26. See Pomeroy, "The Relationship of the Married Woman to Her Blood Relatives in Rome," 224.

27. A person under *patria potestas* could not inherit, as stated in Gaius 2. 87: *Igitur quod liberi nostri, quos in potestate habemus, item quod servi nostri mancipio accipiunt vel ex traditione nanciscuntur sive quid stipulentur vel ex aliqualibet causa adquirunt, id nobis adquiritur: ipse enim, qui in potestate nostra est, nihil suum habere potest; et ideo si heres institutus sit, nisi nostro iussu hereditatem adire non potest; et si iubentibus nobis adierit, hereditas nobis adquiritur, proinde atque si nos ipsi heredes instituti essemus; et convenienter scilicet legatum per eos nobis adquiritur.* "Therefore anything which our children who are under our authority acquire, just like anything which our slaves acquire by sale, delivery, or stipulation, or by any means whatsoever, is acquired by us: for the person who is subject to our authority can have nothing of his own. Therefore if he is designated an heir he cannot take his inheritance without our command: and if he takes it when we command the inheritance is acquired by us, just as if we ourselves had been appointed heirs. And accordingly in the same manner a legacy is acquired by us through such parties." See Plin. *Ep. 4.2* (A.D. 104) for an example of emancipation by a father for this purpose. See also A. J. S. Spawforth, "Families at Roman Sparta and Epidaurus: Some Prosopographical Notes," *ABSA* 75 (1980), esp. 228, for a case from the same period involving sons in *patria potestas* inheriting from their mother who was divorced from their father.

28. *Inst.* III 4; *Dig.* XXXVII 17; *Cod. Iust.* VI 57, Ulp. fr. 26.7. At the risk of reasoning *post hoc ergo propter hoc,* I raise the possibility that the case of Regilla's property, which was both valuable and visible, had legal repercussions, and that the notoriety of the parties concerned brought legal reform

whereby a mother's property could pass to her unemancipated son.

29. Richard J. A. Talbert, *The Senate of Imperial Rome* (Princeton, 1984), 58.

30. See Introduction, above. My description of Regilla's estate is also based on archaeological finds at neighboring estates on the Via Appia and general information in John R. Clarke, *The Houses of Roman Italy 100 B.C.–A.D. 250: Ritual, Space, and Decoration* (Berkeley, 1991), esp. ch. 1.

31. On Herodes' interest in hunting and Achilles as a hunter see ch. 3.

32. Thus conjecture G. Pisani Sartorio and R. Calza, *La villa di Massenzio sulla via Appia* (Rome, 1976), 140.

33. E.g., in L. Quilici, "La via Appia antica," in V. Calzolari and M. Olivieri (eds.), *Piano per il Parco dell'Appia Antica, Italia nostra: sezione di Roma* (Rome, 1984), 61–80. A notable exception is the work of a female scholar: Marion Elizabeth Blake, *Roman Construction in Italy from Nerva through the Antonines* (Philadelphia, 1973), 101–102, who refers to the "villa di Annia Regilla."

34. Paus. 6.21.2, and see ch. 3.

35. Hor. *Ep.* 2.1.156, and see ch. 1.

36. Thus L. Quilici, *La via Appia: regina viarum* (Rome, 1997), 43. The inscription is laconic, and Roman women in the same family all bore the same name. Therefore the identification of Caecilia Metella is not secure; nevertheless all the women of this name in the late Republic married upper-class Roman men.

37. SHA, *Comm.* 4.9; Cass. Dio 71–73; Amm. Marc. 28.

38. Philostr. *VS* 548.

39. Philostr. *VS* 559.

40. Philostr. *VS* 559.

41. James H. Oliver, *Marcus Aurelius: Aspects of Civic and Cultural Policy in the East* (*Hesperia,* suppl. 13) (Princeton, 1970), 24–25, 92–93, and see ch. 4, above.

42. Oliver, *Marcus Aurelius,* p. 5, lines 21, 25, 40, 84.

43. Philostr. *VS* 558–559.

44. See further H. Kammerer-Grothaus, "Der Deus Rediculus im Triopion des Herodes Atticus: Untersuchung am Bau und zu polychromer Ziegelarchitektur des 2 Jh.s. n. Chr. in Latium," *MDAI(R)* 81 (1974), 131–252.

45. The identity of this building is disputed: G. Pisani-Sartorio, "The Urban Segment from Porta Capena to Casal Rotondo," in I. Della Portella (ed.), *The Appian Way: From Its Foundation to the Middle Ages* (Los Angeles, 2004), 40–83, esp. 57.

46. F. Castagnoli, *Appia antica* (Milan, 1956), caption to photos 7, 8, 9.

47. *IGUR* I (Rome, 1972), pp. 45–46, no. 341 = Ameling, *Herodes Atticus,* vol. 2, pp. 151–152, no. 145.

48. *IG* XIV 1389.1.7–8 and 48–49, see this chapter, below.

49. *IGUR* I, p. 44, no. 341, and see further Guarducci, *Epigrafia greca,* vol. 4, p. 234.

50. See further P. Gros, "Un décor d'époque antonine et sa signification: les stucs du 'temple de Cérès et de Faustine,'" *MEFR* 81 (1969), 161–193, esp. 175–180. H. Mielsch, *Die Römische Stuckreliefs,* Mitteilungen des Deutsches Archaeologisches Instituts Rom, suppl. 1975, 21 (Heidelberg, 1975), 89 n. 372, suggests the two figures are seasons, and thus consistent with the mythology concerning Demeter/ Ceres. L. Quilici inspected the medallions on my behalf, but could not succeed in seeing the shoes of the figure thought to be Regilla and described by Gros: personal correspondence addressed to Larissa Bonfante, May 3, 2006.

51. Gros, "Un décor d'époque antonine et sa signification," 180–183.

52. Thus L. Accettella et al., *La Valle della Caffarella: la storia ci racconta* (Rome, 1994), with introduction by L. Quilici, 90. See below the poem of Marcellus treating the cult of Regilla.

53. Torlonia Museum, Inv. 77. The sculpture is categorized as the "Olympias-Aphrodite" type. The head of the Roman

Olympias type sometimes was a portrait. See further R. Calza, "Le opere d'arte della villa," in Sartorio and Calza, *La villa di Massenzio sulla via Appia,* 159–213, esp. 186–187, and Pl. 18, and Perry, "Artistic Imitation and the Roman Patron," 150–157, 210.

54. See this chapter, below.

55. Galli, *Die Lebenswelt eines Sophisten,* 112.

56. Calza, "Le opere d'arte della villa," 209, argues that the so-called "sarcophagus of Cecilia Metella," also known as the Farnese sarcophagus, was actually a sarcophagus-cenotoph for Regilla.

57. E.g., Callim. *Hymn* 6, Ov. *Met.* 8.738–878, Diod. Sic. 5.61, and see further E. Wüst, *s.v.* Triopas, *RE* VII A 1 (1939), 168, and W. Ruge, *s.v.* Triopeion, *RE* VII A 1 (1939), 175–176.

58. Cf. the possible allusions to Nemesis in the Tyche sculptures at Corinth: Ch. 4, above. See also Quilici, "La valle della Caffarella e il Triopio di Erode Attico," *Capitolium* 9–10 (1968), 339–341.

59. See ch. 3.

60. Galli, *Die Lebenswelt eines Sophisten,* 112, and see also U. v. Wilamowitz-Moellendorff, "Marcellus von Side," *SB* (Berlin, 1928), 3–30 = *Kleine Schriften,* vol. 2 (Berlin, 1941), 192–228, esp. 203–204.

61. For a catalogue see Calza, "Le opere d'arte della villa," 159–213.

62. Above, n. 53.

63. See above and, e.g., head of Omphalos Apollo, Capitoline Museums, Inv. 3046; herm of Demosthenes, Monaco, Inv. 292; herm of Epicurus (now missing); and Calza, "Le opere d'arte della villa," 183–184 and Pl. 16.

64. See preceding note.

65. British Museum, Inv. 1746.

66. Herodes used so much Pentelic marble that he may have owned his own quarries: see J. C. Fant, "Ideology, Gift, and

Trade: A Distribution Model for the Roman Imperial Marbles," in *The Inscribed Economy: Production and Distribution
in the Roman Empire in the Light of Instrumentum
Domesticum, JRA* suppl. 6 (Ann Arbor, 1993), 145–170,
esp. 167.

67. Villa Albani, Inv. 19.
68. See this chapter, above. For other possibilities associating the
Triopeion karyatids with Knidos, see Perry, "Artistic Imitation and the Roman Patron," 145–149.
69. Ewan Bowie, "Greek Sophists and Greek Poetry in the Second Sophistic," *ANRW* II.33.1 (1989), 231, and ch. 3, above.
70. Above, n. 7.
71. See Bowie, "Greek Sophists and Greek Poetry in the Second
Sophistic," 240, 247, and ch. 4, above.
72. See Simon Swain, "Plutarch's Moral Program," in Sarah B.
Pomeroy (ed.), *Plutarch's Advice to the Bride and Groom and
A Consolation to His Wife* (New York, 1999), 85–96, esp. 93–
94.
73. For the gossip see SHA, *M. Ant.* 19, 23.7, *Verus* 10.1. Scholars
reject this gossip: see, e.g., Anthony R. Birley, *Marcus
Aurelius: A Biography* (pb. repr. of rev. ed., New York, 2000),
182, 224–225, 250.
74. Ameling, *Herodes Atticus,* vol. 2, pp. 150–151, no. 144.
75. Pisani Sartorio and Calza, *La villa di Massenzio sulla via
Appia,* 138.
76. Jorma Kaimio, *The Romans and the Greek Language,*
Commentationes Humanarum Litterarum 64 (Helsinki,
1979), 176, argues that such bilingual inscriptions were intended to draw attention to the eminent person who was
commemorated.
77. *IGUR* II (Rome, 1972), p. 45, no. 340 = Ameling, *Herodes
Atticus,* vol. 2, pp. 150–151, no. 144, and Guarducci, *Epigrafia
greca,* vol. 1, 389.
78. According to Martti Leiwo, "From Contact to Mixture: Bi-

lingual Inscriptions from Italy," in J. N. Adams, Mark Janse, and Simon Swain (eds.), *Bilingualism in Ancient Society. Language Contact and the Written Text* (Oxford, 2002), 168–194, esp. 174, the writer spoke Latin, but only colloquial Greek. Nevertheless, Leiwo postulates linguistic reasons for the misspelling.

79. *IGUR* I, pp. 41–46, no. 339 = Ameling, *Herodes Atticus,* vol. 2, pp. 149–150, no. 143.

80. Guarducci, *Epigrafia greca,* vol. 4, 233.

81. Plut. *Caes.* 5.

82. See further Marcel Durry, *Eloge funèbre d'une matrone romaine* (Paris, 1950), esp. li.

83. Marcellus, *AP 7.158.*

84. According to L. Moretti, *IGUR* III (Rome, 1979), 19, no other Greek poem inscribed in Rome has received as much scholarly attention as this one.

85. See bibliography in Ameling, *Herodes Atticus,* vol. 2, p. 153, no. 146. My translation follows Ameling's text with one change in line 50. Cf. the comments of Wilamowitz-Moellendorff, "Marcellus von Side." The inscription is in the Louvre, Inv. 1160.

86. See Ewan Bowie, "Poetry and Poets in Asia and Achaia," *BICS* suppl. 55 (1989) = Susan Walker and Averil Cameron (eds.), *The Greek Renaissance in the Roman Empire* (London, 1989), 198–205, esp. 201, who considers it one of the best works of the period.

87. Following W. Peek, "Zu den Gedichten des Marcellus von Side auf Regilla und das Triopion des Herodes Atticus," *ZPE* 33 (1979), 76–84, esp. 80.

88. Regilla was eight months pregnant when she died.

89. As eponymous archon in Athens.

90. Reading *choros* with Moretti and Peek.

91. Putative ancestor of Herodes.

ACKNOWLEDGMENTS

This book covers a wide range of subjects, including literature, art, and archaeology, and political, social, and intellectual history. I am grateful to have been able to discuss some of these subjects with other scholars. I wish to thank Judith Hallett, Barbara Levick, and Philip Stadter for their lucid and incisive comments on the entire manuscript and Beryl Rawson for her generous advice on the first two chapters. Special thanks to Jorgen Mejer for suggesting the subject of Regilla when he was Director of the Danish Institute for Classical Studies in Athens and for advice on the manuscript and photographs. Thanks are due to Sinclair Bell for various suggestions; to Elaine Baruch, Susan Merrell, Lee Foster, and Laurie and John Adams for editorial advice and support; to Lee Pomeroy for help with the photographs; to the Family History Group for their comments; to Malcolm Davies for advice on my translation of the poem by Marcellus of Side; and to Larissa Bonfante for consultations on the archaeological evidence. I am grateful to Barbara McManus for her keen remarks throughout the writing of this book and for supplying the photo of the doll in chapter 1, and to Jo Ann McNamara for help with the title. Warm thanks to Dorothy Helly for encouraging me to write a biography of a woman whose history has been suppressed and for viewing this book as an example to future biographers of such women—who might otherwise think the obstacles insurmountable.

It is a pleasure to thank Georgia Tsouvala for her ongoing assistance with this project. Ms. Tsouvala spent a year at the American School of Classical Studies in Athens while I was writing this book, and this coincidence enabled her to help in countless ways with on-site research and with obtaining photographs. I am also grateful to the Andrew W. Mellon Foundation for a Mellon Emeritus Professorship that supported my work on this project and Ms. Tsouvala's participation in it.

Thanks are due to Archer Martin and the Photo Archive at the American Academy in Rome for assistance in obtaining photos of Regilla's estate on the Via Appia, and to Dr. Gianni Ponti for discussing the archaeological evidence with me at successive site visits. I am grateful to Lorenzo Quilici for personally inspecting the female figures in the medallions on the ceiling of the temple of Faustina (San Urbano alla Caffarella) in response to my query (personal correspondence addressed to Larissa Bonfante, May 3, 2006). I wish to thank the American Academy at Rome for hospitality when I began writing this book. I am also grateful to Maria Pilali of the American School of Classical Studies in Athens for obtaining official permissions to take professional photographs in Greece; to Jennifer Tobin for permission to use two of her photographs; and to Ioulia Tzonou-Herbst, Curator of Corinth Excavations at the American School of Classical Studies, for supplying two photographs and a drawing from Corinth.

Thanks to my son Jeremy Pomeroy for legal counsel with leavening, to Bernard Kho for computer advice with grace, and to Angela Blackburn for her thoughtful and respectful work on the manuscript. And last, but certainly not least, I wish to express my gratitude to Joyce Seltzer, my editor, who provided invaluable and intelligent advice, and helped me to turn this study into an evocation of an appalling and riveting story.

ART CREDITS

Genealogical Chart. Adapted from Marie-Thérèse Raepsaet-Charlier, *Prosopographie des femmes de l'ordre sénatorial (Ier–IIe s.)* (Louvain, 1987), stemma xxvii.

Fig. 1.1. Doll. End second–beginning third century A.D., Palazzo Massimo alle Terme (National Museums, Rome). Photo: courtesy of Barbara McManus.

Fig. 2.1. Portrait bust of Polydeucion. Second century A.D., found in Cephisia. Athens, National Museum, 4811. Photo: DAI, 1972/423, by G. Hellner.

Fig. 2.2. Portrait bust of Herodes. Second century A.D., found in Cephisia. Athens, National Museum, 4810. Photo: DAI, 1972/418, by G. Hellner.

Figure 2.3. Achilles. Youth from Cephisia. Marble, early Antonine period. Piraeus Museum. Photo: courtesy of Marie Mauzy.

Fig. 2.4. Memnon. Thyreatis, Pentelic marble, ca. A.D. 160. Berlin, Staatliche Museen, SK 1503. Photo: Bildarchiv Preussischer Kulturbesitz/Art Resource.

Fig. 2.5. Ground plan of the estate at Marathon. Drawing reproduced from Jennifer Tobin, *Herodes Attikos and the City of*

Athens (Amsterdam, 1997), fig. 75. Reproduced with permission of Jennifer Tobin.

Fig. 2.6. Wall on Regilla's estate at Marathon. From Tobin, *Herodes Attikos,* fig. 80. Photo: Jennifer Tobin. Reproduced with permission of Jennifer Tobin.

Fig. 2.7. Inscription from the Gate of Eternal Harmony, Marathon, *IG* II² 5189. Photo: Craig and Marie Mauzy.

Fig. 2.8. Seated female figure dressed in a thin chiton from the Gate of Eternal Harmony. Photo: Craig and Marie Mauzy.

Fig. 3.1. Altar of Demeter Chamyne at Olympia. Photo: Craig and Marie Mauzy.

Fig. 3.2. Statue of bull with inscription. Olympia Museum, 610. Photo: Craig and Marie Mauzy.

Fig. 3.3. Head of Regilla from her statue at her nymphaeum. Olympia Museum, L 163a. DAI–ATH 1979/454. Photo: G. Hellner.

Fig. 3.4. Statue of Regilla from her nymphaeum. Olympia Museum, L156. DAI–ATH, 1972/432. Photo: G. Hellner.

Fig. 3.5. Statue of Elpinice from Regilla's nymphaeum. Olympia Museum, L165. DAI–ATH 1979/436. Photo: G. Hellner.

Fig. 3.6. Statue of Athenais from Regilla's nymphaeum. Olympia Museum, L162. DAI–ATH 1979/400. Photo: G. Hellner.

Fig. 3.7. Statue of Faustina the Elder from Regilla's nymphaeum. Olympia Museum, L155. DAI–ATH 1979/416. Photo: G. Hellner.

Fig. 3.8. Statue of Atilia Caucidia Tertulla from Regilla's nymphaeum. Olympia Museum, L156. DAI–ATH 1979/396. Photo: G. Hellner.

Fig. 3.9. Statue of Vibullia Alcia from Regilla's nymphaeum. Olympia Museum, L157. DAI–ATH 1979/409. Photo: G. Hellner.

Fig. 3.10. Panathenaic stadium, Ardettos Hill, and temple of Tyche. Photo: Craig and Marie Mauzy.

Fig. 3.11. Peirene fountain at Corinth. Photo: Craig and Marie Mauzy.

Fig. 3.12. Female figure from Corinth: Regilla's portrait? Corinth excavations, American School of Classical Studies archives. Photo: courtesy of Ioulia Tzonou-Herbst.

Fig. 3.13. Musical instruments from the base of a statue of Regilla. Corinth Excavations. a. Statue base. b. Drawing reproduced from B. H. Hill, *The Springs—Peirene, Sacred Spring, Glauke: Corinth,* 1.6 (1964), 102. Photos: American School of Classical Studies, courtesy of Ioulia Tzonou-Herbst.

Fig. 3.14a. Base for a statue of Regilla at Delphi from the temple of Apollo. b. Base for a statue of Regilla at Delphi from the temple of Apollo. Photos: Craig and Marie Mauzy.

Fig. 5.1. Sarcophagus at Kephisia showing Leda and the swan. Church of Panagia tes Marmariotissas in Halandri. Photo: Craig and Marie Mauzy.

Fig. 5.2. Odeion auditorium, Acropolis in background. Photo: Craig and Marie Mauzy.

Fig. 5.3. Cryptoporticus at Regilla's estate. Photo: Andrea Ceccaroni.

Fig. 5.4. Tomb of Caecilia Metella. Photo: Antonio Pietro Ortolan.

Fig. 5.5. Cenotaph of Regilla at Deus Rediculus. Photo: Antonio Pietro Ortolan.

Fig. 5.6. Temple of Faustina: exterior. Photo: Antonio Pietro Ortolan.

Fig. 5.7. Temple of Faustina: interior fresco. Photo: Antonio Pietro Ortolan.

INDEX

Achilles (epic hero), 54–55, 60, 63, 66–67, 200n78, 201n93, 224n31

Achilles (foster son of Herodes), 53–55, 60, *61*, 63–67, 139–140, 155, 202n97

Adams, J. N., 206n5

Aelius Antoninus, T., 100

Aeneas, 13, 31, 32, 170, 171

Alcia, 33, 48, 55, 68, 100, *102*, 197n45; relationship with Polydeucion, 56, 59, 66; relationship with Regilla, 52–53

Alcimedon, 53, 119–120, 123, 125–127, 129–133

Alcock, Susan E., 182n18

Alexander I, 208n19

Alexander the Great, 8, 17, 87, 200n71

Alexander Troas: aqueducts at, 150, 154

Ameling, Walter: *Herodes Atticus,* 183n30, 189n60, 193nn99,105, 197n35, 198n58, 199n65,

202n97, 207n17, 212n58, 213n64, 217n23, 228n85

Amenhotep, 83, 206n11

Anchises, 13

Annia Faustina, 25, 100

Annii Regilli, the, 14, 15, 39, 40, 121, 124, 149, 150

Antinous and Hadrian, 9, 59, 60, 66, 199n69

Antiochus IV, 211n42

Antoninus Pius, 1, 14, 27, 49, 100, 158, 168, 190n64; and Athens, 71, 84–85; and Bradua (son of Herodes and Regilla), 49, 157, 171; relationship with Herodes, 29, 30, 120–121

Antony, Mark, 82, 191n78

Apatouria, 139

Apollo, 145

Appian Way. *See* Via Appia

Appius Annius Gallus, 14, 23, 27, 39, 100, 160, 184n5

Appius Claudius Caecus, 14

Apuleius, 108

Aqua Claudia, 150
Aqua Marcia, 150
Aristotle, 133; on first pregnancy, 36; on household and state, 134; on moderation, 64
Arsinoë II, 3, 67
Asclepius, 98
Aspasia, 3
Athena, 48, 173; as Minerva, 162, 169; statue of Athena Parthenos, 105–106; temple of Athena Nike, 106
Athenais, 47–48, 51, 52, 68, 95, *97*, 100, 104, 138–139, 143, 148
Athens, 9, 68, 81–87, 115; Acropolis, 105–106, 136, 141, 145, *146*, 164; Arch of Hadrian, 76; attitudes toward Herodes in, 41, 49, 51–52, 71, 130, 134, 154–155; Erechtheion, 141, 164; Hadrian's Library, 43; imperial policies regarding, 43, 71, 84–85, 127–128, 134; Marousi, 137, 143, 158, 220n2; monument of Philopappus, 95, 98, 210n36; odeion of Herodes Atticus, 95, 113, 122, 145, *146*, 147, 150, 222n23; Panathenaic stadium, 47, 103, 104, *105*, 133, 143, *146*, 158, 212n55; statue of Athena Parthenos, 105–106; temple of Athena Nike, 106; Temple of Olympian Zeus, 43, 76; Temple of Peace, 43; temple of Tyche, 103–106, 143, 158, 162,

212n51, 213nn60,61; theater of Dionysus, *146*; and will of Claudius Atticus, 26, 130, 134
Atilia Caucidia Tertulla, 15, 100, *101*, 184n8
Atilii, the, 14
Atticus, Claudius, 33, 48–49, 100, 193n105; as suffect consul, 23–24; wealth of, 25, 26, 27, 130, 134
Augustine, St., 121
Augustus, 82; marriage policy of, 23, 25; policies regarding religion, 85; policy on athletic competitions, 208n26
Avotins, I., 197n41, 210n33

Balbilla, Julia, 21, 83–84, 94–95, 210n36
Barnes, T. D., 196n30
Bei, 76
Berman, L. M., 206n11
Bernand, A. and É., 198n54
Birley, Anthony R., 217n27, 218, 227n73
Blake, Marion Elizabeth, 224n33
Boethius, Flavius, 191n86
Bol, Renate, 209n33, 210n39, 211nn43,44,46
Bonfante, Larissa, 184n5, 211n47
Bousquet, J., 213n64
Bowersock, G. W., 206n11
Bowie, Ewan, 9–10, 182n24, 198n53, 199n65, 201n96

Bradley, Keith R., 185n13

Bradua, Appius Annius Artilius, 21, 48, 162, 184n5, 186n26; Herodes accused of murder by, 26, 34, 49, 119, 123–129, 135–136, 138, 148–149, 151–152, 166, 217n16; patrician status of, 49, 157, 171; and Regilla's estate on Via Appia, 147, 148–149

Bradua, M. Appius, 100

Bradua, M. Atilius Metilius, 23

Bradua Atticus, 47, 48–50, 86, 100, 149, 157, 196nn30,31, 197n35, 223n28; character traits, 52, 197n41; relationship with Herodes, 46, 48–49, 51–52, 66, 68, 122, 130, 132–133, 148, 152, 155, 158, 162, 171, 196n27, 219n43, 223n27; relationship with Regilla, 49–51, 148

Brundisium, 39

Caecilia Metella, 82; tomb of, 154, *155*, 224n36

Caesar, Julius, 13, 43, 108, 168, 200n71

Callimachus, 169

Calvisius, Publius, 124

Calza, R., 224n32, 226n56

Cambridge Ancient History, The, 182n18, 183n29

Canusium/Canosa, 39, 40–41, 75, 149; aqueduct at, 94, 150, 193n102

Castelli Romani, 151

Castor and Polydeuces/Pollux, 56, 141

Caudicia Tertulla, 15

cenotaph for Regilla in Rome, 140, 144, 156–158, 161, 169

Cephisia: Herodes' estate in, *57, 58,* 59, *61,* 66, 70, 72–73, 76, 143, 167; sarcophagi at, 138–142, *142, 164*

Ceres, 111, 144–145, 158–159, 164, 169, 222n17, 225n50

Champlin, Edward, 217n23

childbirth, 15, 35–36, 45–46

child rearing: Greek customs regarding, 12, 49; Roman customs regarding, 12, 16–18, 20–21, 37, 46, 49, 181n15, 183n2, 192n94, 194n7

Cimon, 27, 29–30, 33, 47

Clarke, John R., 181n11, 224n30

class vs. gender, 2, 3

Claudia Alcia, 207n17

Cleopatra VII, 3, 191n78

Clinton, Kevin, 207n17

Colosseum, 88, 106

Colossus of Memnon, 83, 84

Condianus, Sextus, 155

consuls: *ordinarii,* 23–24, 49; *suffecti,* 23–24

Corinth, 87, 107–9; cult of Tyche at, 107, *109,* 111, 213n65; Peirene fountain at, 108–109,

Corinth *(continued)*
    109, 111, 113, 214n69; Periander,
    122; statues of Regilla at, 5,
    109, *110*, *112*, 113
Crassus, M. Licinius, 154
Critias, 35
Cupid/Eros, 31, 64, 141
Cynouria, 76

Damo Synamate, Claudia, 21,
    83–84
Darnton, Robert: on incident
    analysis, 7
daughters, value of, 15–16, 23, 48
Delphi, 113, *114*, *115*
Demeter, 122–123, 166–167, 170,
    173; and Ceres, 111, 144–145,
    158–159, 164, 169; Eleusinian
    Mysteries, 86, *91*; and Isis, 145,
    163; Regilla as priestess of, 35,
    73, 79, 87–88, 89, 90–91, *91*,
    92, *93*, 94–95, *96*, *97*, 98, *99*,
    100, *101*, 103, 111, 116, 161,
    209n29, 212n58; temple of
    Demeter/Faustina, 158–161,
    159, *160*, 162, 225n50
Demetrius of Phalerum, 133
Demosthenes, 163
Deus Rediculus, 156, *157*, 169
Dickey, Eleanor, 206n5
Dionysus, 145, *146*
dolls, 18, *19*, 25
Domitia Faustina, 100
Domitia Lucilla, 17, 22, 24, 35,
    173
Domitian, 27

education: Greek customs re-
    garding, 29, 81–82, 189n60;
    Musonius Rufus on, 135; Ro-
    man customs regarding, 20,
    21–22, 69–70, 82, 180n8,
    186n27
Edwards, M., 214nn72,73
Eleusis: Herodes' dedication of
    Regilla's clothing at, 86, 122–
    123, 140, 144–145, 161–162;
    Mysteries of Demeter and
    Kore at, 86, *91*
Elis, 87, 88
Elpinice, 40, 51, 86, *96*, 100, 115,
    116, 139, 148; birth of, 38–39,
    46–47; sarcophagus of, 140–
    142, 221nn11,12
Elpinike. *See* Elpinice
Epictetus, 90
Epicurus, 64, 163
Erinna, 95
ethnicity, 7–8, 12, 136; imperial
    assimilation policies, 24, 25;
    relationship to gender, 2, 50–
    51, 71; relationship to Regilla's
    murder, 8. *See also* Greek cus-
    toms; Roman customs

Farnell, L., 208n24
Farnese sarcophagus, 226n56
fashion, 18
Faustina, Annia Galeria (the El-
    der), 2, 14, *99*, 100, 164, 170,
    172, 173; temple of Demeter/
    Faustina, 158–161, *159*, *160*, 162,
    225n50

Faustina, Annia Galeria (the Younger), 14, 21, 31, 36, 100, 121, 158, 164–165, 211n45, 218n35, 227n73
Finley, M. I., 181n8, 208n19
Fortuna, 104
foster sons. *See* Trophimoi
Frazer, J. G., 205n127
freedmen. *See* Alcimedon; slaves
Fronto, Marcus Cornelius, 4; children with Gratia, 36; relationship with Domitia Lucilla, 22, 24; relationship with Herodes, 24, 29, 35, 37, 38, 120, 124–125, 187n39; relationship with Marcus Aurelius, 29, 30, 37, 38, 120, 124, 217n23; relationship with Regilla, 35
Fundanus, Minicius, 37

Galen, 36, 191n86
Galli, Marco, 213n65
Gardiner, E. Norman, 210n33
Gardner, Jane F., 197n46, 198n49
Gasparri, Carlo, 213n61
Gazda, E., 198n56
Gellius, Aulus, 4, 59, 70, 72–73, 204n120
gender, 12; vs. class, 2, 3; and Greek Renaissance, 9–10; relationship to ethnicity, 2, 50–51, 71; separation of the sexes, 81–82, 88, 89, 104, 133–134. *See also* marriage; women
Gibbon, Edward: on Rome in 2nd century, 1–2, 8

Goette, Hans Rupprecht, 199n64, 204n124, 205n129
Gordian I, 4
Graindor, Paul, 6, 190n65, 202n98, 213n60
Greece: Horace on Rome and, 20, 152; as Roman province of Achaea, 8–10, 108
Greek customs: regarding childbirth, 35–36, 45–46; regarding child rearing, 12, 49; regarding civic status, 53–54, 56, 59; regarding death, 37–38; regarding education, 29, 81–82, 189n60; endogamy, 12, 33–34, 52; regarding homes, 71–72; regarding homosexuality, 9, 10, 30, 56, 59–60, 63–67, 70, 122, 200n78, 201n81; regarding marriage, 2, 12, 32–34, 36, 41, 44–46, 52, 66, 68–72, 75–76, 133–135, 136, 164–165, 191n78; naming conventions, 50–51, 55, 196n33; Olympic games, 87, 88, 89, 90, 116, 208nn19,25, 27; Panathenaea, 103, 104, *105*, 133; vs. Roman customs, 2, 8, 10, 11, 12, 17, 21–22, 28, 32–38, 41, 44–46, 49, 52, 53–54, 60, 64, 65, 66, 68–72, 81–82, 88, 111, 133–134, 140; regarding separation of the sexes, 81–82, 88, 89, 104, 133–134; regarding slaves, 45; tracing of lineages, 46

Greek language, 11, 17, 18, 24,
    191n83; Aeolic dialect, 84;
    Herodes' use of, 29, 124, 152,
    164, 217n20; spoken by
    Regilla, 20, 21, 34–35, 82, 166;
    use in inscriptions, *77, 91, 112,
    114, 116,* 152, 165–167, 168–174,
    204, 227nn76,78
Greek Renaissance, 9–10
Griffin, Miriam, 187n41
Gros, P., 225n50

Habicht, Christian, 212n55
Hadrian, 1, 40, 108, 168, 189n63,
    190n64, 191n85; and Athens,
    43, 71, 84; policies on religion,
    85; policy toward Eleusis, 144;
    relationship with Antinous, 9,
    59, 60, 66, 199n69; and
    Sabina, 21, 83, 84, 100
Haines, C. R., 217n23
Hammond, M., 189n64
Hanson, Ann Ellis, 191n85, 218n33
Harmon, D. P., 190n74
Harris, William V., 217n16
Hedea, 104
Helen, 141
Hellenistic period, 133
Hemelrijk, Emily A., 180n8,
    186n24, 187n32, 203n108
Herculanus, 95
Herodes Atticus, 90, 100, 116;
    Athenian attitudes toward, 41,
    49, 51–52, 71, 130, 134, 154–155;
    betrothal to Regilla, 22–23,
    24–27; and Canusium, 40–41;

character traits of, 3, 4, 29–31,
    37, 38, 40–41, 49, 55, 59, 64–
    65, 72, 120–122, 123–124, 131,
    134–135, 152, 154–155, 190n65,
    218n31; death of first baby, 35–
    38; displays of grief at
    Polydeucion's death, 59, 60,
    64–65, 66; displays of grief at
    Regilla's death, 2, 30, 65, 66,
    86, 120, 122–123, 125, 129, 136,
    139, 140, 143–145, *146,* 147, 151,
    156, 165, 167–174; early life,
    23–24; erotic life, 9, 10, 30, 56,
    59–60, 63–67, 70, 122, 133; ex-
    periences in Rome, 7–8, 29,
    41; family of, 23–24, 50,
    188n51, 207n17; as governor of
    free cities in Asia, 29, 154, 162,
    168, 189n61; and hunting, 59,
    63, 72, 76, 155, 165, 202n99,
    224n31; lineage claimed by,
    27–28, 29–30, 33, 47, 50–51, 55,
    67, 73, 144, 171, 228n91; mon-
    uments and architectural proj-
    ects commissioned by, 9, 10,
    41, 47, 65, 66, 67, 84–85, 86,
    87, 94, 103–104, *105,* 105–106,
    107–108, 122, 136, 137, 140–
    142, 143–144, 145, *146,* 147,
    150–152, 154, 156–161, 162–174,
    212n51, 213n61, 222nn19,23,
    226n66; Philostratus on, 4, 27,
    30–31, 38, 40, 49, 60, 94, 119,
    120–121, 122, 124, 127, 131,
    196n27, 212n51, 219n43; rela-
    tionships with foster children,

8, 53–56, 57, 59–60, 63–68, 71, 72, 76, 77, 79, 129–130, 139–140, 155, 165, 199n69, 201n93, 202n100; relationship with Achilles, 53–55, 60, 63–67, 71, 139–140, 155; relationship with Alcimedon, 53, 119–120, 125–127, 129–133; relationship with Antoninus Pius, 29, 30, 120–121; relationship with Bradua (son), 46, 48–49, 51–52, 66, 68, 122, 130, 132–133, 148, 152, 155, 158, 162, 171, 196n27, 219n43, 223n27; relationship with Fronto, 24, 29, 35, 37, 38, 120, 124–125, 187n39; relationship with Lucius Verus, 24, 28; relationship with Lucius Vibullius, 48, 55, 68; relationship with Marcus Aurelius, 24, 29, 30, 31, 34, 35, 37, 38, 119, 121, 124–125, 126–128, 134, 144, 147, 155, 161, 171, 217n23; relationship with Memnon, 53–55, 60, 63–67, 139–140, 155; relationship with Polydeucion, 53–54, 55–56, 57, 59–60, 64–68, 139–140, 155, 199n69, 201n93, 202n100; relationship with Quintilii brothers, 29, 64, 154–156; relationship with Regilla, 2, 10, 30–31, 34–35, 38, 44–46, 49, 52, 65, 67–71, 72–73, 75, 79, 84, 85, 87, 95, 106, 115, 119–120, 121–123, 125–126, 131–132, 133–135, 138, 142–143,

154, 164–165; as Sophist, 4, 9–10, 11–12, 24, 26–27, 35, 54–55, 58, 60, 64–65, 85, 122, 133, 163; sources of information regarding, 3–6; and Sparta, 29, 47, 48–49, 54, 56, 141, 189n60; trial for murder, 2, 4, 13, 26, 31, 34, 49, 119, 123–129, 130, 132, 136, 138, 150, 151–152, 166, 217n16; use of Greek language, 29, 124, 152, 164, 217n20; wealth of, 25, 26, 27, 34, 75, 86–87, 94, 123, 130, 134, 136, 147, 150–151

Herodotus, 6, 75
Hipparchos, 134
Holford-Strevens, Leofranc, 194n7, 199n65, 204n120
Homer, 169; Achilles, 54–55, 60, 61, 63, 66–67, 200n78, 201n93, 224n31; Patroclus, 55, 63, 67, 200n78, 201n93
Horace: on Canusium, 193n101; on Greece and Rome, 20, 152
hunting, 59, 63, 72, 76, 155, 165, 201n81, 202n99, 224n31
Hygieia, 98, 209n33

infant mortality, 35–37
Isis, 145, 163
Isthmian festival, 104

Johnson, Franklin P., 214n74
Julia (daughter of Augustus), 3, 83
Julia Domna, 3, 4, 19

Julia (granddaughter of Augustus), 83
Jupiter, 48
Juvenal: *Sat.* 6.146–149, 120; *Sat.* 6.149–150, 204n125; *Sat.* 6.185–196, 191n83; *Sat.* 6.385, 184n4

Kaimio, Jorma, 227n76
karyatids, 141, 163–164
Kennell, Nigel M., 218nn31,32
Kent, J. H., 213n64
Kephisia. *See* Cephesia
King, Helen, 218n34
Klytemestra, 221n11
Kore, 122–123, 166–167; Eleusinian Mysteries, 86, *91*
Kronos, 169

Lamberton, Robert, 190n65, 199n69
Latin language, 11, 18, 20, 34–35, 81, 165–166, 206n4, 217n20; use in inscriptions, 227nn76,78
Laudatio Turiae, 168
Law of Three Children, 147
Leda and the Swan, 141, *142*
Lefkowitz, Mary, 180n2
Leiwo, Martti, 227n78
Lenormant, F., 220n3
Levick, Barbara, 187n40, 190n65, 198n59
Lex Cincia, 75
Lex Julia et Papia, 184n4
Livia Drusilla, 3, 82

Loukou: Herodes' estate in, *62*, 72, 76, 141, 222n19; nymphaeum at, 94
Lucian, 217n20; dialogue between Herodes and Demonax, 65; *Peregrinus,* 94
Lucilla, 25, 100, 218n35
Lucius Verus, 24, 28, 100, 108

Mallwitz, A., 210n33, 211n43
manumission, 17, 45, 127, 185n13
Marathon: battle of, 27–28, *73, 75, 77*; estates of Herodes and Regilla at, 28, 55, *57, 72, 73, 74,* 75–77, 78, 79–80, 95, 129, 135, 137, 145, 147, 149, 150, 151, 162, 164, 205nn127,129; Gate of Eternal Harmony, 76, *77, 78,* 79, 95, 129, 135, 147, 151, 164, 205n127
Marcellus of Side, 161, 165, 167–174
Marcus Aurelius, 1, 4, 14, 17, 22, 36, 100, 187n40, 190n64, 194n7; and Athens, 43, 84–85; and Canusium, 40; as divine, 158; policy toward Eleusis, 144; policy toward non-Italians, 25, 27, 125; relationship with Faustina, 164–165; relationship with Fronto, 29, 30, 37, 38, 120, 124, 217n23; relationship with Herodes, 24, 29, 30, 31, 34, 35, 37, 38, 119, 121, 124–125, 126–128, 134, 144, 147, 155, 161, 171, 217n23; as Stoic, 64, 135;

and trial of Herodes, 119, 124–125, 126, 127, 130, 132
marriage: Augustan policy regarding, 23, 25; Greek customs regarding, 2, 12, 32–34, 36, 41, 44–46, 52, 66, 68–72, 75–76, 133–135, 136, 164–165, 191n78; relationship to rape, 141–142, *142;* Roman customs regarding, 2, 6, 8, 12, 22–23, 25–26, 31–34, 36, 41, 44–46, 52, 66, 68–72, 75–76, 142–143, 144–145, 147, 191n78; *sine manu,* 52, 121, 143, 147; wife abuse, 12, 33, 121–123, 144, 158–159, 222n17. *See also* women
Masi, 76
Maxentius, 6, 163
Mayer, R., 216n11
Memnon (epic hero), 54, 66
Memnon (foster son of Herodes), 53–55, 60, *62,* 63–67, 139–140, 155, 202n97
Meyers, Rachel L., 210n34, 212n48
Mielsch, H., 225n50
Miller, Stephen G., 206n10
Miltiades, 27–28, 73, 188n57
Moretti, L., 228nn84,90
motherhood, 15–17, 45–46
Musonius Rufus, C., 22, 135, 186n27, 201n85, 220n51

naming conventions: Greek customs regarding, 50–51, 55, 196n33; Roman customs regarding, 13–15, 46–48, 50–52, 54, 184n5, 195n19, 196n33, 197n35
Nani, T. G., 198n48
Nemean festival, 104
Nemesis: cult at Rhamnous, 111, 162, 173
Nero, Tiberius Claudius, 82, 87; and Agrippina, 132, 216n11; Golden House, 151; and Poppaea, 122, 216n11
Nerva, 1, 154
Nevett, Lisa, 203n114
Ninoi, 76
nurses. *See* child rearing; wet nurse
Nussbaum, Martha C., 220n51
nyphaeum. *See* Olympia

Octavia, 82
odeion. *See* Athens
Oliver, James H., 218nn27,31,32, 224n41
Olympia, 11, 115; aqueduct of Herodes at, 94, 95, 150; cult of Demeter Chamyne at, 209n27; games at, 87, 88, 89, 90, 116, 208nn19,25,27; nymphaeum of Regilla at, 50, 90–91, *91,92, 93,* 94–95, *96, 97,* 98, *99,* 100, *101, 102,* 103, 107, 108–109, 117, 161, 209n33, 211nn43,45, 212n50; Regilla as priestess of Demeter at, 35, 73, 79, 87–88, 89, 90–91, *91, 92, 93,* 94–95, *96, 97,* 98, *99,* 100,

Olympia *(continued)*
101, 103, 111, 116; statues of
Demeter and Kore at, 152
Opper, Thorsten, 211n45
Ovid, 83

Palace of Maxentius, 6, 163
Pallis, Georgios N., 220n2
Panathenaea. *See* Athens
Panathenaic stadium. *See* Athens
Panathenais. *See* Athenais
Panhellenion, 84, 103
Parkin, T. G., 192n87
Parthians, 28
Patroclus, 55, 63, 67, 200n78,
201n93
Pausanias, 4, 43, 87, 88, 90, 94,
145, 208nn25,27
Pax Romana, 20
Peachin, Michael, 185n8
Peek, W., 228n90
Periander and Melissa, 122,
216n11
Pericles, 9, 134; relationship with
Aspasia, 3
Perry, Ellen E., 207n17,
221nn8,10
Persephone, 162
Perusine Wars, 82
Peterson, Scott and Laci, 129
Petronius: Trimalchio in *Sat.* 71,
221n4
Phidias, 106
Phila, 67
Phile, 94
Philip II: and Olympias, 47; and
Olympic games, 87, 208n19

Philopappus, 95, 98, 210n36,
211n42
Philostratus, Flavius: on
Alcimedon, 119; on Bradua
(son of Herodes), 52, 196n27,
219n43; on Colossus of
Memnon, 84; on foster sons of
Herodes, 53, 56, 127; on
Herodes, 4, 27, 30–31, 38, 40,
49, 60, 94, 119, 120–121, 122,
124, 127, 131, 196n27, 212n51,
219n43; on Panathenais/
Athenais, 47, 51; on Regilla's
death, 119, 120–121, 122, 124,
128, 131; relationship with
Gordian, 196n27; on
Scopelianus, 132–133; on
women, 180n6
Plato, 22; on self-control, 17;
Symposium, 60
Pleket, H., 208n19
Pliny the Younger, 50, 69,
185n14, 223n27; and
Calpurnia, 25, 33–34; on grief
of Fundanus, 37
Plutarch, 4, 81, 90, 108, 164; *Advice to the Bride and Groom,*
69, 70, 186n29; on Alexander
and Caesar, 200n71; on
Cimon, 29–30; on community
of property in marriage, 75–
76; on conjugal love, 201n85;
Consolation to His Wife, 11,
185n16, 194n7; on dancing, 22,
186n29; death of daughter, 37–
38; on education of wives, 69;
Eroticus, 60; on exogamy and

endogamy, 33–34; on Greek vs. Roman customs, 12, 33–34; on hunting, 201n81; on husbands and wives dining together, 70; on Marathon, 28; *Moralia*, 12; on mothers favoring sons, 51, 52, 197n40; *On the Education of Children*, 49, 195n26; *Parallel Lives*, 12; on persuasion in marriage, 134–135; on Philopappus, 211n42; on presence of wives at gatherings, 70; on teaching women mathematics, 22; on wife abuse, 12, 33, 121, 123; on wives and moods of husbands, 44–45; on women and marriage in Sparta, 36

Polydeucion, 190n65, 198n59, 202n99; character traits, 68, 202n101; death of, 59–60, 64–65, 66, 199n65, 199n69, 201n93, 202n97; relationship with Alcia, 56, 59, 66; relationship with Herodes, 53–54, 55–56, 57, 59–60, 64–68, 139–140, 155, 199n69, 201n93, 202n100

Ponti, Gianni, 181nn11,14

Poppaea, 122

Priene, 94

Puech, Bernadette, 183n30, 202n97

Pythian festival, 104

Quilici, L., 181n11, 224n33, 224n36, 225n50

Quintilian, 20

Quintilii brothers (Sextus Quintilianus Condianus/ Sextus Quintilianus Valerius Maximus), 8, 29, 64, 154–156, 163

Raepsaet-Charliet, Marie Thérèse, 207n17

Ratte, Christopher, 211n47

Rawson, Beryl, 186nn23,30, 190n65, 199n62

Regilla: as benefactor at Corinth, 106–9, *110*, 111, *112*, 113, 117; betrothal to Herodes, 22–23, 24–27; death of, 2, 4, 8, 12, 13, 30, 34, 46, 49, 66, 76, 79, 119–136, 137–138, 142–145, 158, 162, 164, 166, 228n88; death of first baby, 35–38; early life in Rome, 13–18, 20–22, 183n2; family estates of, 6, 8, 26, 39, 40–41, 49, 64, 75, 94, 126, 141, 145, 147–152, *153*, 154–174, 181n11, 223n28, 224n30; fertility of, 46, 48; Greek and Latin spoken by, 20, 34–35, 82, 166; inscriptions in honor of, 3, 4–5, 11, 17, 107–108, 113, *115*, 115–117, 129, 131, 137, 145, 147, 151, 156–158, 161, 164–174, 215n80, 227nn73,76,78, 228n84; monuments and architectural projects commissioned by, 5, 10, 11, 50, 85, 87, 90–91, *91*, *92*, *93*, 94–95, *96*, *97*, 98, *99*, 100, *101*, *102*, 103, 107–109, *109*, 117; and

Regilla *(continued)*
  musical arts, *112*, 113, 151,
    215n79, 222n20; names of, 13–
    15; personality of, 3, 17; as
    priestess of Demeter at Olym-
    pia, 35, *73*, 79, 87–88, *89*, 90–
    91, *91*, *92*, *93*, 94–95, *96*, *97*, 98,
    99, 100, *101*, 103, 111, 116, 161,
    209n29, 212n58; as priestess of
    Tyche at Athens, 35, 103–107,
    116, 143, 158, 162, 212n51,
    213n65; public life in Athens,
    35, 81–87; relationship to im-
    perial family, 2, 3, 14, 18, 20–
    21, 25, 94, 98, 100, 103, 108–
    109, 111, 121, 158–161; relation-
    ship with Alcia, 52–53; rela-
    tionship with Bradua Atticus,
    49, 51, 148, 158; relationship
    with Fronto, 35; relationship
    with Herodes, 2, 10, 30–31,
    34–35, 38, 44–46, 49, 52, 65,
    67–71, 72–73, 75, 79, 84, 85,
    87, 95, 106, *115*, 119–120, 121–
    123, 125–126, 131–132, 133–135,
    142–143, 164–165; self-control
    (*sophrosyne*) of, 107, 113, *115*,
    115–116, 131, 157–158; sources of
    information regarding, 3–7;
    wealth of, 86–87, 94, 106, 108,
    117
Regillus, 46, 50–51, 139, 197n35
Reydams-Schils, Gretchen,
    201n85
Richlin, Amy, 190n68
Ridgway, B. S., 214n72

Robert, Louis, 198n59, 201n93
Robinson, Betsey Ann, 108,
    209n33, 214n69
Roman customs: regarding adop-
    tion, 53, 68; regarding child-
    birth, 15–16, 35–36, 45–46,
    191n85; regarding child rear-
    ing, 12, 16–18, 20–21, 37, 46,
    49, 181n15, 183n2, 192n94,
    194n7; regarding civic status,
    53–54, 68, 139, 184n4; regard-
    ing death, 36–37, 137–142,
    167–168, 192n98; regarding ed-
    ucation, 20, 21–22, 69–70, 82,
    180n8, 186n27; exogamy, 8, 12,
    33–34; regarding gifts between
    spouses, 8, 75; vs. Greek cus-
    toms, 2, 8, 10, 11, 12, 17, 21–22,
    28, 32–38, 41, 44–46, 49, 52,
    53–54, 60, 64, 65, 66, 68–72,
    81–82, 88, 111, 133–134, 140; re-
    garding Greek language, 17,
    18, 20, 21, 24, 34–35; regarding
    homes, 71–72; regarding ho-
    mosexuality, 65–66; Lares and
    Penates, 32; regarding mar-
    riage, 2, 6, 8, 12, 22–23, 25–26,
    31–34, 36, 41, 44–46, 52, 66,
    68–72, 75–76, 142–143, 144–
    145, 147, 191n78; naming con-
    ventions, 13–15, 47–48, 50–52,
    54, 184n5, 195n19, 196n33,
    197n35; *patria potestas*, 52, 120,
    129, 131, 143, 148, 223n27; re-
    garding slaves, 16–18, 20–21,
    45, 132; tracing of lineages, 13–

15, 31; wax portrait masks (*imagines*), 14, 28, 46, 71; regarding women, 10, 21–22, 25–26, 31–34, 41, 44–46

Sabina, 21, 83, 84, 100
Saller, Richard P., 186n31, 195n21
Sappho, 3, 63, 84, 180n2
sarcophagi, 137–142, *142*
sarcophagus of Caecilia Metella, 226n56
Sartorio, G. Pisani, 224n32
Saturn, 169
Schaps, David M., 183n2
Second Sophistic, 11–12, 67, 85, 106, 182n24; and Herodes, 9–10, 26–27, 35, 54–55, 60, 122
self-control (*sophrosyne*), 16–17, 22, 107, 113, *115*, 115–116, 131, 135, 157–158. *See also* Plato; Regilla; Xenophon
Senatus Consultum Orfitianum, 148
Seneca, 83, 192n98; and Helvia, 25
Septimius Severus, *19*, 206n4
Settis, S., 211n43
Simpson, O. J., 220n54
Sinn, Ulrich, 208n27, 209nn29,33
slaves, 48, 54, 59, 66, 141; vs. freedmen, 119–120, 130–131, 132; manumission of, 17, 45, 127, 185n13; Roman customs regarding, 16–18, 20–21, 45,

132; as wet nurses, 16–17, 18, 20, 37, 38–39, 46, 194n7
Snowden, Frank M., Jr., 200n74
Social Wars, 40
Socrates, 11, 60, 135
Solin, H., 196n33
Sophists. *See* Herodes Atticus; Second Sophistic; Socrates
Sophocles: *Tereus,* 44, 194n4
Sophrosyne. *See* self-control
Soranus: on first pregnancy, 36; on wet nurses, 16; on women, 25, 218n35
Souli, 76
Sparta, 12, 63, 82, 95, 116, 133, 207n16; education in, 29, 189n60; helots, 54, 198n50; and Herodes, 29, 47, 48–49, 54, 56, 141, 189n60; marriage in, 33, 36
Spartacus, 154
Spawforth, A. J. S., 189n60, 190n75, 210n37, 223n27
Stephanidou-Tiveriou, Th., 202n99
Stern, Daniel, 182n15
Stoicism, 21–22, 75; *apatheia* in, 64–65, 120, 135; and Marcus Aurelius, 64, 135
Sulla, 82

Talbert, Richard J. A., 217n24
temple of Demeter/Faustina, 158–161, *159, 160,* 162, 225n50
Theocritus, 67
Thucydides, 6

Tiberius, 82–83

Tisamenis, 29

Tobin, Jennifer, 200n75, 202n97, 203n101, 204nn118,124, 209n33, 213n64, 220n2

Tomlinson, R. A., 209n33

Tracy, Stephen V., 212n55

Tragounera, 76

Trajan, 1, 40

Triopeion, 161, 162, 166–167, 169–174

Trojan War, 54–55

Trophimoi. *See* Achilles; Herodes Atticus; Memnon; Polydeucion

Tsouvala, Georgia, 187n41, 222n23

Twelve Tables, 12

Tyche, *109*, 111, 214n73; Regilla as priestess of, 35, 103–107, 116, 143, 158, 162, 212n51, 213n65; temple of, 103, 105–106, *105*, 143, 158, 162, 212n51, 213nn60,61. *See also* Corinth

Tzonou-Herbst, Ioulia, 215n78

Valerius Maximus, 121

Varnava, 76

Venus, 13, 25, 31

Vestal Virgins, 23

Via Appia, 14, 39, 136; estate of Quintilii brothers on, 8, 64; Regilla's and Herodes' estate on, 6, 8, 26, 49, 64, 75, 94, 126, 141, 144, 145, 147–152, *153*, 154–174, 181n11

Via Latina, 158

Via Traiana, 39

Vibia Aurelia Sabina, 218n35

Vibius Varus, T. Clodius, 124

Vibulli, the, 55–56, 68

Vibullia Alcia Agrippina. *See* Alcia

Vibullius Claudius Herodes, Lucius, 48, 55, 68

Vibullius Hipparchus, Lucius, 48, 56, 95, 100

Vibullius Rufus, Lucius, 48, 68

Walker, S., 209n33

Wallace, Rex, 184n5

Weber, Thomas Maria, 199n64, 204n124, 205n129

Wenskus, Otta, 206n5

Westbrook, H. T., 202n101

wet nurses, 16–17, 18, 20, 37, 38–39, 46, 194n7

Wilamowitz-Moellendorff, U. v., 228n85

wills, 147

wives, 41, 44–46. *See also* marriage; women

Woloch, Michael, 191n79

women: as athletes, 104; attitudes toward, 3, 4, 10, 16–17, 21–22, 25–26, 30–31, 32–34, 37–38, 44–46, 65, 68–71, 120, 141–143, 180n6, 184n4, 191n83, 208n27, 218n35; cults oriented toward, 85–87; *materfamilias* status, 26, 33, 44, 45, 52; separation from men, 81–82, 88,

89, 104, 133–134; virtues of, 16–17, 22, 107, 113, *115*, 115–116, 121, 131, 135, 157–158; wife abuse, 12, 33, 121–123, 144, 158–159, 222n17. *See also* education; marriage

Xenophon, 22, 198n50; *Oeconomicus*, 69; on self-control, 17

Zeus, 90, *91*, 100, 141, *142*, 170, 171

CPSIA information can be obtained
at www.ICGtesting.com
Printed in the USA
LVHW110923041122
R17565200001B/R175652PG731991LVX00007B/1